EDITED BY STEVE ZEITLIN

A TOUCHSTONE BOOK

Published by Simon & Schuster

BECAUSE GOD LOVES STORIES

AN ANTHOLOGY
OF JEWISH STORYTELLING

For my great uncle Adolph Platt, my great aunt Reva Davidson Platt,
Moishe Sacks, Henry Sapoznik, Barbara Myerhoff, Abe Lass, and
Marc Kaminsky who brought about a *tikkun olam*, a repair in
the fabric of creation, so that I might reclaim a heritage of
Yiddish culture and Jewish stories.

刀к

TOUCHSTONE
Rockefeller Center
1230 Avenue of the Americas
New York, NY 10020

Manufactured in the United States of America

5   7   9   10   8   6

Library of Congress Cataloging-in-Publication Data
Because God loves stories: an anthology of Jewish storytelling /
edited by Steve Zeitlin.
p.   cm.
"A Touchstone book."
Includes bibliographical references.
1. Legends, Jewish.   2. Short Stories, Jewish.   3. Jewish Folk
Literature.   4. Jews—United States—Anecdotes.   5. Holocaust,
Jewish (1939–1945)—Personal narratives.   I. Zeitlin, Steven J.
BM530.B317   1997
808.8'08924—dc21   96-49806
CIP
ISBN 0-684-81175-8

TABLE OF CONTENTS

CONTENTS

CONTENTS

CONTENTS

Why were human beings created?
Because God loves stories.
Traditional Jewish Saying
adapted from Elie Wiesel

ACKNOWLEDGMENTS

Writing this book, I've often thought of myself as a character in a Jewish folk story, traveling on a donkey from village to village, stopping at an inn or a cottage. At each stop I met a storyteller. I traveled that route so many times, these storytellers became good friends, and the memories of writing this book are not of sitting at my computer, but of sharing meals and stories with people who have become lifelong friends—sharing a Chinese dinner of kosher vegetarian "pork" with Ilana Harlow; listening to Ruth Rubin tell her "Grandma" story in her apartment above Gramercy Park; talking stories with Cherie Karo Schwartz (who was visiting from Denver) at Katz's Delicatessen; shlepping Roz Perry to elementary schools to tell her stories about coming to America; trading tales with Nina Jaffe at Tom's Restaurant (made famous in the sitcom Seinfeld); hearing Canadian-born Michael Wex expound on how to talk dirty in Yiddish at KlezKamp, the Yiddish folk arts retreat in the Catskills; having Abe Lass regale me with dirty Yiddish jokes at his home in Fresh Meadows, Queens; laughing hysterically with the late former vaudevillian Charlene Victor while I interviewed her in her bedroom in Brooklyn, where she was attached to an oxygen machine; meeting Zypora Spaisman in the lobby of Manhattan's Central Synagogue, where the Folksbiene Theatre has its headquarters; visiting folk painter Ray Faust, who wouldn't talk to me on the telephone or answer her door if I said my name was Steve Zeitlin—only if I pronounced it Steve Tseitlin, in honor of the famous poet Aaron Zeitlin and other Yiddish scholars by that name to whom she was convinced I am related; I look forward to taking those journeys many times again, even without a book to write.

I would like to extend my deepest thanks to the board and staff of City Lore, the folklore and oral history center I direct in New York. The board of directors—Fran Mandel, Wendy Wolf, Bill Pearson, Marissa Wesely, and all of the others—and the staff—Marci Reaven, Roberta

Singer, Yusef Jones, Ben Salazar, Lois Wilcken—were supportive of this "extra project" in a million ways.

I want to thank the people who read the manuscript or portions of the manuscript for me, offering their comments: Marci Reaven, Henry Sapoznik, Marc Kaminsky, Barbara Kirshenblatt-Gimblett, Ilana Harlow, Amanda Dargan, and Peninnah Schram. Peninnah and I both found ourselves working on books of Jewish stories at the same time, though mine took a few years longer to complete. Her generosity of spirit reminded me of the prophet Elijah stories she has told and written about so well— Peninnah showed up in the most unusual places and was always there when I needed to call for stories or advice. I also want to thank Michael Schlesinger for putting me in touch with a number of storytellers and advising me to check out Sam Levenson.

I would like to thank my thoughtful editors, Sheila Curry and Penny Kaganoff at Simon & Schuster, and my agent and good pal, Carla Glasser, who believed in this project when it was nothing more than a handful of family stories. I also want to thank the American Jewish Committee for compiling their unparalleled Oral History Library, now deposited in the New York Public Library. In particular, I would like to thank Hilary Ziff Bosch, their transcriber, whose suggestions proved extremely useful, as well as Dr. Leonard Gold at the New York Public Library. I also want to thank Yaffa Eliach for allowing me to reprint some of the tales in her marvelous book, *Hasidic Tales of the Holocaust*.

My beautiful wife, Amanda, who read draft after draft of these stories (as long as I brought her cups of tea and let her read them in bed), remains my toughest and yet most understanding critic. I'd also like to thank my children, Benjamin and Eliza, for offering their totally truthful opinion on many of these stories during our unconventional Sabbath celebrations.

And to my dear aunt Elaine, who wanted so much to be in this book: Hi Elaine!

A Note on Yiddish and Ladino in the Manuscript

"Words," Henry Sapoznik told me, "are road maps to where Jews have lived. You express your Jewish identity, for instance, according to whether you say 'Good Shabbes' or 'Shabbat shalom.' They represent two parallel Jewish identities, one Eastern European and Yiddish, the other Hebrew and Israeli. If you hear someone who is a Yiddish speaker say 'Shabbat shalom,' you're hearing someone who is reconstituting his cultural identity."

In this work, my editors and I needed to decide how to spell Yiddish words in English—how to express the book's "cultural identity." On the one hand, we wanted to respect the YIVO Institute for Jewish Research's standard Yiddish orthography, and I thank Henry Sapoznik and Sheva Zucker for their assistance. On the other hand, we needed to respect our English readers who have grown accustomed to seeing words spelled in certain ways. The end result is that words that we felt have a common usage in English and can be found in English dictionaries were rendered that way, while other Yiddish phrases and sentences adhere to YIVO spellings in an uneasy compromise. I would also like to thank Professor David Altabe for his assistance with Ladino, the Spanish-derived language spoken by Sephardic Jews.

About the Cover

The cover painting, "Blessing the New Moon in the Wintertime," is by the late folk artist Rachel Ray Lehrer Faust. The painting was inspired by the Astronauts landing on the moon in 1969. She wrote a poem relating the moon landing to her girlhood memories of Kiddush Levonnah, the monthly blessing of the new moon, in her Eastern European shtetl. These are some lines from her poem:

When the astronauts
Made their first steps on the moon

A scene of my childhood came to mind:
Blessing the new moon on a winter night:
A very cold night,
The roofs with snow are white,
The frost is freezing,
A circle of Jews stand
With their prayerbooks in their hands
Their eyes are looking to the moon . . .

In that circle of Jews,
I see my father.
The Jews are
The oldest astronauts.

INTRODUCTION

My father, an enlightened spirit, believed in man. My grandfather, a fervent Hasid, believed in God. The one taught me to speak, the other to sing. Both loved stories.

ELIE WIESEL

"It was family life," Marc Kaminsky's grandmother told him, "it was *simkhes*, joyous occasions, and not such *simkhes*, but it was always a *tish mit menschen*. A table with people. Everything I remember, the events of my life, holidays and times of grief, news from the family, all the gatherings took place here at the kitchen table."

And what did they do at that table but talk. As Michael Gold writes, "Talk has ever been the joy of the Jewish race, great torrents of boundless, exalted talk. Talk does not exhaust Jews as it does other people, nor give them brain fatigue; it refreshes them. Talk is the baseball, the golf, the poker, the love, and the war of the Jewish race." The Jews are a loquacious people, their conversations overflowing with talk. "Even old Mrs. Fingerman's parrot," Gold continues, "talked more than other parrots. Mr. Fingerman's last distraction before he died was to teach the parrot to curse in Yiddish."

This book, too, is a table with people. At her home in West Philadelphia, my grandmother Bella Stein housed the family's snapshots beneath a pane of glass that covered her kitchen table. That was where I counted out the change from my ice-cream route when I was in college, where my grandfather spritzed his seltzer from a bottle, and where my great-uncles all played pinochle on Saturday nights. In this book I am inviting storytellers to a mythic version of my grandmother's kitchen table.

The tales of these tellers come together to form a larger story. For Passover, my grandmother's table was pressed into service, joined to the dining room table along with a few card tables, all covered with a white tablecloth, to accommodate all the relatives for the *seder*. Similarly, the *tish mit menschen* becomes, in this book, a figurative Passover table at which a group of storytellers gathers to retell not the traditional Passover story of the Exodus from Egypt, but many stories of another exodus and another promised land; stories of *shtetlakh* (East European small towns), *pogroms* (organized anti-Jewish violence), and the Holocaust; coming to America from Eastern Europe as well as from Turkey and the Middle East; settling on the Lower East Side. They recount the Jewish American experience in story.

Present at this "storytelling *seder*" are a few who consider themselves professional storytellers and who refashion traditional tales from the Jewish experience for appreciative audiences at synagogues, libraries, schools, Hadassah and B'nai B'rith meetings. They also include well-known comic raconteurs such as Sam Levenson and Joey Adams, whose stories made them famous, as well as storytellers like Rita Fecher, whose only stage is the dining room table. They include a prominent Hasidic *rebbe*, the grand rabbi of Bluzhov, Rabbi Israel Spira, who tells an astonishing array of miracle tales about the Holocaust; and Rabbi Edward Schecter from a suburban temple, who retells and reinterprets the classic Hasidic tales for a Reform suburban congregation.

"Eloquence is highly valued in East European Jewish culture. A storytelling tradition has been part of the Jewish religion from earliest times. It took place in the synagogue and temple during public worship, on feast days, on the Sabbath, and on ordinary weekdays...Ultimately," writes Barbara Kirshenblatt-Gimblett, "oral tradition is an institution in Jewish religious learning as sacred as the written word."

But today, a cherished Jewish sensibility is expressed in the most everyday forms, in the anecdotes and family tales. Jewish culture is rendered palpable in what I am fond of calling the rags or remnants, the *shmattes* of culture—not the finery of opera and ballet, but the hand-me-downs, the well-worn traditional forms, the songs, stories, customs, holiday foods, and proverbs that are part of everyday life. Present this evening are not only our "culture heroes," but also our culture bearers, ordinary people who don't see themselves as either storytellers or comedians, but who pass on the culture through stories.

I've also invited those who talk and think and ponder stories (they might be considered the other side of the family). Why? Partly because the commentators are storytellers in their own right; the stories they tell in their lectures and essays are deep and as touching as any. Their commentaries are often stories about stories, and I have identified them as "Stories about Stories" where they appear in this book. Part of what makes this gathering so unique is that it brings together for the first time professional storytellers telling traditional tales, everyday Jewish people telling family stories, comedians delivering monologues, rabbis narrating sermons, and commentators thinking about stories as they talk about them —their disparate stories deserve to be brought to the table together, for all are part of the Jewish storytelling tradition.

For this book, I have gathered my material from oral tradition, much of it from personal interviews and tapes of storytelling performances. I have tried to remain faithful to the spoken word, retaining the informal, oral quality of performance in the tales. At the same time, I recognize that people speak in rough drafts. The stories in the book are lightly edited to present the most coherent tales possible. I have also drawn on material that had its origin in interviews but has been rewritten in what anthropologist Barbara Myerhoff called "the third voice," which brings together the voice of the teller and that of the folklorist or writer. But even in the commentaries, most of which are from lectures or talks, I am trying to capture the oral flavor of a garrulous "storytelling *seder.*"

One of my tasks in putting together this conversation was deciding how many storytellers and commentators to invite. I needed a way to limit the occasion. At first, I thought of relying on Jewish numerology. In the *Gematria*, which assigns numerical value to certain letters, the letters of the word *"chai,"* which means "life," equal 18. Double *chai* is 36, a number that can also be rendered by the letters *Lamed Vov*, referring to the thirty-six *Lamed Vovniks*, as they are called in America, the thirty-six righteous and unknown men (and we, of course, would add women) in each generation whose good deeds, according to Jewish tradition, make it possible to sustain the world. Other magical numbers were also suggested: why not forty storytellers? It rained for forty days and forty nights on Noah's ark, and Moses spent forty days on Mount Sinai and forty years in the desert.

In the end, I decided to forgo numerology and, since it is an imaginary table, to simply continue adding places. For as the evening proceeds, there are, in addition to the main storytellers, visitors who stop in for ten minutes, to *kibitz* for a moment and *shmooze*. Their comments, too, had to be fitted in edgewise, and they are found in sidebars. In this way I have sought to add different perspectives on the material, often providing an ironic counterpoint or offering tales that make the opposite or a complementary point, or simply different versions of the same story. I've sought to capture the cacophony and the grandeur of Jewish storytelling as a dialogue, with storytellers borrowing from storytellers, with scholars retelling stories as they comment upon them and everyone trying to have the last word. Presenting material in the style of Rashi commenting on the Talmud, I hope to suggest the Talmudic quality to Jewish storytelling, with the essential tales being enhanced and continually reinterpreted by the commentaries running along with them on the page.

In her poem "Poetry," Marianne Moore compares her work to "an imaginary garden with real toads"; storyteller Arthur Strimling recontextualized Moore's line by calling his own Jewish stories "an imaginary pushcart with real vegetables in it." These are apt descriptions for the stories retold here, for these tales are imagined creations containing within them real episodes, facts, and oral histories.

I have organized the book into eras, from ancient times through the *shtetl* (which still figures in the living memory of many American Jews), through immigration, the Holocaust, tenement, and contemporary life. Although the stories could not stand alone as a full history of the Jewish-American experience, they enhance our understanding of each era, offering valuable corroborating details and quintessential experiences that are at the heart of history.

People often speak of folklore and myth as synonyms for falsehood, as the equivalent of *bubbe mayses*, old wives' tales. Although *bubbe mayses* literally means "grandmother tales," the term emphasizes the falsity of the stories. Many of the stories in this book are grandmother and grandfather tales—not *bubbe mayses*, but oral histories from the Jewish American experience.

Yet despite the real toads, the stories are still set in imaginary gardens. They have a foot in two worlds, the world that unfolds in the tale and the contemporary world of the storyteller. Recounting stories, each of these tellers holds out two hands; with one he or she clasps the characters in the story, sometimes his or her ancestors, his *zayde* (grandfather), his *bubbe* (grandmother); with the other, the teller reaches out to take your hand. As the tale pushes through the air, it seems so real that you can almost reach out and touch a lost world, pull on the rabbi's garment. You can almost touch—picture, feel, smell, and understand—the characters and their world. It's easy to forget that the hand you are holding is the storyteller's.

In this book, the storytellers are as important as the stories. The stories are not just about what is being told but also about who is doing the telling. The tales are not only about the wonder-working rabbis of ancient times or the Lower East Side tailors, but about the storytellers who have refashioned that experience in story. Even when the tales are told about ancient times, or about the *shtetl*, these are still Jewish American tales, reflecting the experiences of Jewish American storytellers.

In the introduction to each storyteller, I have tried to convey something of what it is like to be in their presence as they tell a story—to be gathered into the arena of their giftedness. Writing about Yiddish singer and storyteller Ruth Rubin (whose story about her grandmother is told on page 134), Marc Kaminsky comments, "Folk arts as a source of great nurturance is palpable in her presence." In the words of these great storytellers, Jewish tradition is reborn and reinvigorated, rendered relevant and palpable in today's world.

Some of the storytellers in this book are part of what's been called a Jewish revival. Henry Sapoznik, one of our featured tellers, helped initiate the revival of *klezmer* music, Peninnah Schram to rekindle the Jewish storytelling tradition. But all of the tellers in this book are engaged in their own revivals; whether it's Shelley Brenner applying the parable of Ezekiel's wheel to her own family, or Melvin Katz reviving his memories of the concentration camp for me, all of the tellers are reworking and reimagining their personal and collective past. Many of the storytellers in this book know one another and are part of a loosely connected community of cultural activists committed to propagating Jewish culture by studying about and telling stories. Their tales hold secrets—about the past, of course, but also about what these storytellers choose to remember, about the dreams they project backward onto their ancestors, about what they would have liked them to be, and about what is needed from them now.

There is no way to do justice to the variety of Jewish American stories. In this book, I have included a vast array of Jewish experiences, including those of Hasidim, Sephardim, southern Jews, and a recent Russian immigrant. But Jews have lived all over the country and have been part of every era in American history, from the Revolutionary War to the Wild West. In this book, the approach I have taken is that, though Jews have lived all over the United States, and been engaged in a multitude of endeavors, there is a core Jewish American experience. Lenny Bruce got to the heart of that core experience in his famous monologue:

> Dig: I'm Jewish. Count Basie's Jewish. Ray Charles is Jewish. Eddie Cantor's goyish. B'nai B'rith is goyish; Hadassah, Jewish. If you live in New York or any other big city, you are Jewish. It doesn't matter even if you're Catholic; if you live in New York, you're Jewish. If you live in Butte, Montana, you're going to be goyish even if you're Jewish.

Rather than trying to capture the endless varieties of Jewish experiences, I am after a particular quality, a certain sensibility that emerges from some of the settings where Jews have lived together in close enough proximity and in great enough numbers to develop and maintain distinct cultural forms—there is a certain critical mass that is necessary for the folklore of any group to reach its full expression. Although my family, living as Jewish Americans in Brazil, and the Jews who were among the earliest settlers of New Amsterdam during the Colonial era do tell a part of the Jewish story, it is not the story I am telling here.

Many of us look at Jewish American lore as if it were a diminished thing, a devolution from a richer corpus that existed in Eastern Europe, that exists today in Israel, or that existed in biblical times. This book makes the case that the contemporary Jewish American storytelling tradition is immensely distinctive and rich. In the work of the new professional storytellers, brief fragmentary tales of Chelm and the rebbes become fully fleshed narratives; many of the classics of Yiddish literature, such as the story of the Golem (the Jewish Frankenstein) or Peretz's "Bontshe the Silent," are retold and reinvented by a new generation of storytellers. Although they are thought to have evolved from the Eastern European *badkhn* (the Jewish jester or master of ceremonies at Old World weddings), as well as the circuit-riding preacher, or *maggid*, this century's unprecedented gaggle of Jewish comedians has added stand-up comedy to the age-old forms of Jewish tale telling. The tales are also enriched by the central role of women in contemporary Jewish American storytelling. The early pioneers of the storytelling revival, including Peninnah Schram, Diane Wolkstein, and Laura Simms, were women, and women outnumber the men in the world of professional Jewish storytellers.

But what makes these stories, told by contemporary Americans, Jewish? Is it that the tellers themselves are Jewish? Some scholars suggest that any story told by a Jew is a Jewish story. On the other hand, Dov Noy, the founder of the Israel Folktale Archive in Haifa, suggests that there are four major qualities of Jewish stories. The first is Jewish time; does the story takes place on the holiday of *Sukkos*, at the *bris* (circumcision) of a boy, or during the blessing of the new moon? The second is Jewish place; does the story take place in the synagogue or around the *Shabbes* table? The third element is Jewish characters; is the story about King Solomon or the Baal Shem Tov, the founder of Hasidism? Finally, does the story have a Jewish message or moral?

The stories in this book have all of these qualities, but, in them, I am searching for even deeper strands. I would like to be able to take out the references to Jewish places and personages, take out the Jewish holidays and calendar, even take out the patently Jewish moral, and still know they are Jewish stories. I am looking for the ineffable in these tales; I am after what is Jewish to die for (or at least to *kvell*, or revel, over).

In Jewish folklore, the prophet Elijah is the most beloved of all folktale characters. Although he was a stern, zealot preacher in the kingdom of Israel in the ninth century B.C.E., he has been transformed into a folklore hero who specializes in miracles. In Jewish folklore, he is a figure who returns in every generation to knock on the cottage door. He visits in order to discover how he is treated, rewarding the poor husband and wife who share their loaf of bread with him with wishes, testing and retesting our values. Elijah is also the prophet of the Messiah, and legend has it he will judge when mankind has achieved the necessary goodness to call the Messiah down. It is said that when that happens Elijah will also solve all the unsolved intellectual riddles that confound mankind. We still open the door for him during the Passover *seder* in a moment pregnant with the possibility of his portentous arrival.

But perhaps there is another reason he returns in each generation to knock three times on the cottage door. Perhaps it is because he knows that this is the way so many good stories begin, and he returns in every generation to make sure those stories still unfold and are still told and handed down. Perhaps he knows that to herald the Messiah is to bring on a world of absolute goodness. But a world with no ethical conflicts, poor choices, and villains is a world without stories. Perhaps he suspects that it is best to hold off for a little while—because God loves stories.

ANCIENT TIMES

IN

CONTEMPORARY

TALES

The Jewish Talmud is divided in two sections, the *Halacha* and the *Aggadah*; the *Halacha* lays down and interprets religious law, the *Aggadah* employs storytelling and folkways to interpret the scripture. The sages of long ago described the relationship between the two: "Bread—that is *Halacha*; wine—that is *Aggadah*. By bread alone we cannot live."

Each generation of Jews has poured old wine in new bottles and told stories. The Torah (the five original books of the Bible given to Moses on Mount Sinai), the Talmud, and the *midrash* still represent the core stories for the Jewish faith. A portion of the Torah is read on the Sabbath each week of the year; Jews gather to retell the story of Moses and the Exodus each Passover and to read the Megillah, the Book of Esther, on Purim. These early Jewish stories continue to provide inspiration not only to rabbis and their congregations, but also to the new generation of professional storytellers.

When these stories are recast by contemporary storytellers, what emerges is, at least partially, a reconstruction. The storytellers are careful to cite their sources; that, too, is mandated by tradition. But the tales are continually *re-membered* from the echo of an echo, ricocheting off the centuries, and retold according to the storyteller's talent and whim.

When Peninnah Schram first began telling stories, she recalled a line from her childhood. "It was the phrase 'And Elijah gave a whistle.' And I could hear my father's voice in Yiddish saying that phrase, and you know, a voice of somebody, especially if you don't have a tape, is the first thing that evaporates of all the senses. But I heard this voice very clearly, and I realized there was a story there, and I began to search for that story and I couldn't find it, so I reconstructed the story based on the structure. Elijah, always in disguise, is walking down the street and he comes to a little cottage. And the cottage is broken down, needs paint, the roof has holes in it. He approaches the cottage as a beggar and receives warm hospitality. In return he grants three wishes to the hospitable couple, and each time 'Elijah gives a whistle. . . .' "

NINA JAFFE

Nina Jaffe's connection to storytelling goes all the way back to Genesis, to a time when, according to the Torah, all people spoke the same language. A decision is made to build a tower "with its top in heaven." As His builders got closer and closer, God confounded their tongues, so they could no longer understand one another. The Tower of Babel never reached heaven. But it inspired Nina to become a storyteller.

In the early 1970s she studied in Israel and New York City with Katya Delakova, a choreographer who pioneered new forms of Jewish dance in Israel and the United States. Katya used ancient stories, particularly Bible stories, to teach the art of improvised movement. During one of her residencies, she asked each dancer to pick a role in the Tower of Babel story—builder, architect, king. "It was that moment," Nina told me, "that I realized I would be the storyteller—the word 'storyteller' came to me. I opened the piece by telling the story through the eyes of

Nimrod, the king, who in a midrashic legend is the one who orders his people to build the tower. And I always had the dream of telling stories in many languages, because stories are a language everyone can understand."

"The Most Precious Thing" is a Talmudic tale dating back to the second century and was first chronicled in the Midrash Rabbah, a collection of midrashim about the Song of Songs. For this story, Nina, an accomplished storyteller, musician, and children's book author, takes a brief passage from the Talmud and spins a lyrical tale about love, marriage, and divorce that resonates for our times. In the Talmud, the historical figure Rabbi Simeon Bar Yochai is a character in the tale.

THE MOST PRECIOUS THING

The city of Sidon, on the coast of Lebanon, was said to be the jewel of the Mediterranean. Sea breezes blew gently through the city's fragrant gardens and cobbled streets. Sidon's ships sailed far and wide, and with their constant trading, the merchants of the city brought spices, cloth, and riches of all kinds back to their home port. The tall cedars of Lebanon gave cool shade to all who traveled there. Fine craftsmen and artists carved marvelous designs on the doorposts and gateways of its busy streets, which glistened in the light of the radiant sun.

In this fabled city, there once lived a couple who had been happily married for many years. They lived and worked side by side and cared for each other dearly. But as the years went by and no children were born to bless their home, a great sadness fell upon them. By law, they had a right to a divorce. Every year they thought about it. And every year they put off their decision. But finally the husband said to his wife, "We have waited many years, but since fate has not granted us children, I have decided that it is best for us to separate, for I truly want a child. You must go back to your father's house, as the law requires." And the wife, knowing she could not change her husband's mind, agreed to his decision.

The next day, under a cloudy morning sky, they set off to seek the advice of Rabbi Simeon Bar Yochai, who had come to live in Sidon from the holy city of Jerusalem. Simeon Bar Yochai had traveled to many places, sometimes to study with the great teachers of the region, sometimes to teach at the centers of learning and law. And sometimes he found himself in flight from the Romans, who resented his harsh criticisms of their emperor and imperial governors. In Sidon he enjoyed the warm air and sea breezes, and he was pleased to answer all who came to him for help and advice.

As the couple arrived at his door, Bar Yochai set out two chairs for them in the small inner courtyard of his home and waited to hear what they had to say.

"Rabbi," began the husband, "my wife and I have been happily married for more than ten years. But we have not been fortunate enough to have children. Now, as the law permits, I have decided that she should return to her father's house. Please grant us a divorce so that we can separate with honor and dignity."

Rabbi Bar Yochai looked at the couple for a long time. Then he said to them, "My children, I do not like to see you separate, but as the law requires, I give you my permission. I ask only one thing of you both. Before your wife takes her leave of you, have a feast and celebrate together. For just as you rejoiced at your marriage, so should you do the same at the hour of parting." The couple agreed to his terms and set off back to their home sadly, preparing to take their leave of one another.

As they walked through the cobbled streets, the husband turned to his wife and said, "My dear wife, you have been faithful and loyal to me always. Do not go empty-handed to your father's house. When you leave you must take a gift. Look over all that we own, and choose whatever in your eyes is the most precious thing in our household." With that final word, they opened the door of their house and stepped inside to do as Rabbi Bar Yochai had bidden them. . . .

That afternoon the wife went to the marketplace and filled her basket with dates and almonds, pomegranates and spices, and the finest of delicacies. From their wine cellar she carried out many jugs of their best wine, made from the sweetest grapes in the vineyards of Sidon. As evening fell, she set the table as beautifully as if it were the Sabbath. Her husband ate and drank his fill. Whenever his glass grew empty, she filled it to the brim.

"This is the last meal we shall ever eat together," she said to him. "Let us enjoy it to the last crumb of bread and the last drop of wine." Her husband continued to eat and drink, but she herself tasted just a little of everything. By the time the sun had set and the moon had begun to rise, her husband, drunk with wine and sated with the food, fell snoring into a deep sleep.

As soon as she saw this, the wife called one of her servants, who helped put her husband into a wagon. As he lay there on the straw, she rode with him to her father's house, where once again the servant helped her place him on a wooden bed. As dawn broke, the husband woke up from his sleep and looked around him. Nothing looked familiar to him until he saw his wife standing by the bedside.

"Where am I?" he asked. "What am I doing here?"

"Don't you remember your promise to me?" she replied. "You told me before we parted that I could take with me the most precious thing I could find to my father's house. That is where you are now, under his roof. I looked over all that we owned, but I could find nothing as precious as you."

When he heard these words, the husband smiled and said, "You have done wisely, and I have been a fool. Let us return home and continue on as we have always done, happy and content with one another."

And so they did for many years, living and working together under the sunny skies of Sidon. The *midrash* says that when Simeon Bar Yochai heard the news, he went and prayed for them, and some time after, the child they had been hoping for was born. . . .

STORYTELLER: CHERIE KARO SCHWARTZ

This lovely tale is one of my favorite Jewish stories and I frequently retell it during my performances. In my version, the couple doesn't miraculously give birth to a child. Instead they realize that they are happy in their love for one another. Larry and I don't have children of our own, and in that way, I think the story was meant for me.

FROM THE TALMUD, MIDRASH RABBAH, THE SONG OF SONGS

They again went to Rabbi Simeon b. Yochai, and he went and prayed for them and they became fertile. This shows that just as God makes barren woman fertile, so the righteous can make barren women fertile. And is not the lesson clear: If a woman on saying to a mere mortal . . . , "There is nothing I care for more in the world than you," was visited, does it not stand to reason that Israel, who waits for the salvation of God every day and says, "We care for nothing in the world but Thee," will certainly be visited?

SYD LIEBERMAN

Syd Lieberman is not from an observant Jewish family. He was inspired to become a storyteller in the early 1970s not by hearing traditional Jewish tales, but by telling personal anecdotes to a classroom of high school students in Evanston, Illinois, where he is still a teacher. But when Syd discovered Jewish stories, there was instant recognition. "Jewish stories," he told me, "are in my voice, and in my bones. You know, you don't have to think about how you move — the stories are just in my body. And it's a testament to the power of Jewish stories that they put me in touch with a part of me that I didn't pay much attention to until I got older."

"Challas in the Ark" is a story Syd reworked from Howard Schwartz's Gates to the New City. *Schwartz learned the story from Rabbi Zalman M. Schachter Shalomi, affectionately known as Reb Zalman, one of the central figures in the Alliance for Jewish Renewal. The original story was about a butcher who brings a heart to God, but Reb Zalman transmogrified the butcher into a bread baker. "When I first wrote to Reb Zalman to ask permission to retell the story," Syd told me, "I received a call. The voice on other end said simply, 'This is Zalman. Wonderful, wonderful, wonderful.' Then he hung up."*

CHALLAHS IN THE ARK

At the beginning of the sixteenth century, when the Jews were expelled from Spain, they went all over—France, Germany, Salonica in Greece. Some went to the holy land. Among them was Jacobi. He was a shoemaker by trade, a round man, with a round face, a round body. He was even a little bow-legged. A kind man. But the thing that everybody said about Jacobi was that he was so devout.

He would go to the synagogue every Sabbath and listen intently to what the rabbi was saying, and that was odd because Jacobi spoke Spanish and the rabbi spoke Hebrew. But still he'd screw up his face and listen and listen, trying to catch every word.

On one Sabbath the rabbi gave a sermon, and in it he mentioned how twelve loaves of bread were offered to God when the Holy Temple was still in Jerusalem. Jacobi understood the word "bread," and he understood "God." He got so excited he ran home to his wife. "Esperanza," he said, "guess what I found out? God eats bread! You are the best baker in the whole country. Make this week a *pan de Dios* and I'll bring it to God."

That week Esperanza kneaded in the best ingredients, put in her best intentions, and braided the bread with love. The next week Jacobi proudly carried his loaves to the synagogue. "Señor Dios," he said when he entered, "I've got your bread. You'll see, you'll love it. My wife, Esperanza, she's a wonderful baker. You'll eat every loaf, every crumb!" And with that he took the bread and put it into the holy ark.

No sooner did he leave than in came the *shammes*, the synagogue's caretaker. "Lord, you know I love to be here in this holy place. That's all I want. But seven weeks now I've been working and I haven't been paid. I need you to do something—a miracle! You should make for me a miracle. I believe you're going to. Maybe you've even done it already. Maybe I'll open the holy ark, and there will be a miracle there." The *shammes* walked to the ark and opened it, and there indeed was his miracle —twelve loaves of bread. Two for the first Sabbath meal, two for the second, two for the third, and one loaf for every day of the week.

The next day, when Jacobi and Esperanza opened the ark and saw that there was no bread there, you should have seen the look of love that passed between them. The next week it was the same, and the week after it was the same. The *shammes* learned to have faith in God. But if he hung around the synagogue too much or came to work too early, there was no miracle.

And so, thirty years went by.

Thirty years later, Jacobi came to the synagogue with his load of bread. "Señor Dios, I know your bread's been lumpy lately. Esperanza's arthritis. Maybe you could do something? You'd eat better." Jacobi put the bread in the ark and started to leave, when suddenly the rabbi grabbed him.

"What are you doing?" the rabbi demanded.

"I'm bringing God his bread," Jacobi replied.

"God doesn't eat bread!"

"Well, he's been eating Esperanza's bread for thirty years!"

The rabbi and Jacobi hid to see if they could figure out what was going on. No sooner did they hide than in came the *shammes*. He began to mutter, "I hate to bring it up, but you know your bread's been lumpy lately. Maybe you could talk with an angel." And he reached in to grab the bread, when suddenly the rabbi jumped out and grabbed him. The rabbi began to yell at the two men, telling them how sinful they were. He ranted on and on until all three men began to cry. Jacobi began to cry because he wanted only to do good. The rabbi began to cry because all of this had happened as a result of his sermon. The *shammes* began to cry because suddenly he realized there was going to be no more bread.

Over the sound of their weeping, the three men suddenly heard laughter in the corner. They turned. It was the great mystic of Safed, Isaac Luria. He was shaking his head and laughing. He said, "Oh, rabbi, these men, these men are not sinful. These men are devout. You should know that God has never had more fun than watching what goes on in your synagogue on the Sabbath. He sits with his angels and they laugh. I mean, this man brings the bread and that man takes the bread, and He gets all the credit.

"You must beg forgiveness of these men, Rabbi." Then he looked at Jacobi, and he said, "Jacobi, you must do something even more difficult. You must bring your bread directly to the *shammes*. And you must believe with perfect faith that God will be just as pleased and have just as much fun."

And so it was, and so it is.

Visitor: Rabbi Zalman Schacter Shalomi

I first saw this story, which I named *"Challahs in the Ark,"* in a Yiddish newsprint penny booklet. Instead of comic books, we had pious stories about *tzaddikim* (righteous men), printed for those who could not read Hebrew.

When a storyteller first tells a story he sees, feels, and lives the story. Later he finds the words to tell it to others with all the embellishments of a lived event. The tale takes place in the synagogue of Safed in Israel. I've been to the synagogue and even performed the story there for a group of pilgrims.

The story helps us to understand the ways in which human beings in all their cupidity and their misunderstanding serve the larger purposes of God. Jacobi's misunderstanding of a rabbi's sermon, and his kindhearted yet "blasphemous" actions based on that, points both to simple faith and divine providence and captures the idea that God enjoys to be entertained.

CHERIE KARO SCHWARTZ

In the 1500s Rav Josef Karo, Cabalist, mystic, and author of the Shulkhan Arukh, believed that his teacher, his maggid, perched on his shoulder and whispered stories in his ear. Five hundred years later, Cherie Karo Schwartz, who carries the Karo name, firmly believes she is related to the famous rebbe on her father's side and that he now sits on her shoulder and whispers stories into her ear. She imagines that her London-born bubbe on her mother's side, Rae Olesh, the storyteller in her more immediate family, whispers family tales into her other ear. The world comes through "in stereo. I feel both sides of the family coming through me as guides, as friends," she said, "and there is an imperative to tell."

Cherie comes from a wonderfully storied family. For her kin, the miracle of the oil that lasted for eight days during Hanukkah is retold as the miracle of the oil in her mother's frying pan. During World War II, her mother brought soldiers home from the USO for potato latkes. The oil held out for an entire year. But the stories that interest Cherie most are the older tales, handed down not from one or two generations, but for hundreds of years. Based in Denver, she has been telling the stories since the early 1970s and is an "elder" among the contemporary Jewish American storytellers. When she mentors storytellers, she tells them, "There have been some moments in which something will come out of my mouth when I tell that has never been there before, that will never happen again. It's a secret that's coming through the story; it's coming through the five thousand years."

ELIJAH AND THE POOR MAN'S WISH

Once in a long ago faraway place, there lived a man who was old, blind, penniless, and childless. Even though there were so many troubles in his life, he was able to get by with joy in his heart, for he had the love of a sweet and kind wife. They had so little, but they were rich in the love they shared for each other. And whatever little they had, they would gladly share with others.

One day the man just needed the time and space to think about things. He had never complained, but now he needed to go somewhere and reflect on his life. He made his way down to the riverbank and began to think of all that had happened to him and how things could have been different. He was lost in thought when suddenly he heard something in the distance. It was the tap, tap, tapping of a cane coming closer and closer. There was the rustling of a long satin cloak. He smelled an aroma that reminded him of scents so sweet, they might have been in the Garden of Eden. And someone came and sat beside him, saying, "Do you know who I am?"

The old man thought of the sounds and the scent. "Are you . . . you must be Elijah the Prophet!"

"Yes, you are right. I am Elijah, and I have been sent here for a very special reason. God has looked here and has seen your suffering. Yet you do not complain; you are still grateful for life, and you and your dear wife share much joy. And, too, you are always ready to share with those less fortunate than yourselves. So I have been sent here to bring you a message. You will be granted a wish! What shall it be? What is it that you want?"

The old man did not move. He stayed very still, very quiet, thinking. What wish could he make? What did he really want? Should he wish for his sight? his youth? money?... Dared he wish for a child? Try as he might, he just couldn't make up his mind.

Finally Elijah spoke again. "I can see that this is a difficult decision, one not easily made. So why not think about it for a while? Go home and consider what you will do. And then I will meet you here tomorrow, same time and same place. You can tell me then what you will wish."

Then the old man heard the rustling of the long satin cloak as Elijah rose to go. He heard the tap, tap, tapping of the cane going off into the distance. But the smell, like all of the scents in the Garden of Eden ... that scent lingered long after. The old man stayed by the river, listening to the water gently flowing by. After a while the old man slowly made his way back home.

"Wife! Beloved wife! Come and hear of my adventure!" called the old man as he entered their house. And he told his wife the whole story. When he got to the end of his tale, he asked, "So please help me. What one wish can I make?"

"Do not worry, my wonderful husband. All will be for the best. For now, it is time for dinner. Sit down, have some nice soup and good bread. After dinner, we can rest and tell each other stories. Go to sleep tonight and have sweet dreams, and tomorrow we will decide what you should say."

And that is exactly what the loving couple did. The man had the most beautiful dreams all night long; and in the morning, after breakfast, his wife whispered something in his ear.

"Oh, my sweet wife! What a treasure I have in you! That is exactly the right wish. Now, if only I can remember!" Repeating the wish to himself, the old man left his house and made his way slowly back to his place by the river and began to wait. And he waited and waited, listening for the sounds he had heard the day before.

Soon enough, the old man heard it: the tap, tap, tapping of a cane coming closer and closer. There was the rustling of a long satin cloak; and then, finally, there was the smell like every scent in all of the Garden of Eden. And Elijah the Prophet came and sat down next to the old man.

"*Shalom aleichem!*"

"*Aleichem shalom!*"

"Well, so now it is time. I can grant only one wish for you. What will it be?"

What should he wish for? A child? money? his sight? his youth? his health?

The old man hesitated for a moment. He took a deep breath, and he began:

"May I live . . . to see the day . . . when my child . . . will eat . . . from a golden plate!"

Elijah threw back his head and began to laugh and laugh. "I can see that you have managed to get all of your wishes into one wish! I'll bet that God is enjoying this just as much as I am. And I am certain that God will see to it that every part of your beautiful wish is granted."

For a moment, all was still and silent. Then the old man heard the rustling of the long satin cloak and the tap, tap, tapping of the cane going off into the distance. But the smell, like every scent in the Garden of Eden, that sweet smell lingered long into the afternoon. . . .

And it has been told that the old man and his sweet wife and their lovely child lived a peaceful and joy-filled life together for many, many years. So may it be for us all. Amen.

Visitor: Lenny Bruce
Djinni in the Bottle

In this scene the djinni is back in the bottle. The East Side of New York, Hester Street, the back of an old Jewish candy store. The old man is cleaning up the store. And he sings, "*Shayne vit te le vuner, luch vech vit esh . . . lamed tuner, as te may sheyges shet*—I never saw dis bottle before. It's dirty as a cockroach in dat ting. . . . Well, I'll just open the bottle—*Psheew!*

"Who are you?"

"I'm the djinni!"

"Ya come from dis neighborhood?"

"No, old man, you've let me out of my glass prison. Oh, wondrous old man, a wondrous wish is yours, quickly give me a wish, old man."

"I wish I had some income property."

"It's yours, *psheew!*"

And the room filled up with fifteen beautiful girls.

"Old man, another wish."

"Well, I'd like to go Atlantic City."

"Go! "

"Who'll take care of de store?"

"I will!"

"You can take care of a candy store?"

"I'm the djinni, I can do anything. . . ."

He goes. The djinni takes wonderful care of the store. He brings in the milk and the rolls and the bananas and the guess whats and the Mary Janes, and the whole bit. And the little people start to file in in the morning, and they look up. "Vere's Saul?"

"He went to Atlantic City."

"You're taking care of the store?"

"Yes."

"You can take care of a candy store?"

"I'm the djinni, I can do anything!"

"All right, all right, make me a malted."

"You're a malted!"

MERIT OF THE SABBATH

Once, in the south of Yemen near the Gulf of Aden, there was a man who was a jeweler by trade, who repaired everything from necklaces and watches to fine gold rings. All respected his work and his integrity; he was a true artist and a good man. He helped those who were in need, and he always did his best, in his community as in his work.

For six days each week, the man did beautiful work with metal and precious stones, but on *Shabbat* his store was always closed. And he carried the beauty of the Sabbath with him all week. If someone asked him to do a job, he would respond, "By the merit of the Sabbath, I shall do it." The man loved his day of rest and prayer so much that his friends began to call him by that very name; his name became "Merit of the Sabbath." Each week from sundown Friday to evening on Saturday, he would pray, he would read, he would walk through the park, he would study Torah, and he would enjoy the peaceful time with his family.

Merit of the Sabbath had a small shop in the marketplace for his jewelry business. In the booth next to him, there was a leather merchant, someone with no faith. He was an unfriendly sort of man: never happy, sullen with the customers, always looking at the dark side of life. Every day he would look across the way and see Merit of the Sabbath, so cheerful about his work and always talking with people, even if they were just passing by. Day by day the leather merchant grew more and more jealous. He would grumble to himself:

"Merit of the Sabbath, Merit of the Sabbath! Who does he think he is, anyway?" Oh, the merchant was a bitter, jealous man. "Where will all of his faith get him? Let's just see what can happen. . . ." He thought about it all evening, and by nightfall he had a plan.

The next morning, Wednesday, the leather merchant came to the marketplace early and went to the shop next door. He had a special item in his pocket and a peculiar smile on his face. "Merit of the Sabbath! Merit of the Sabbath! I have seen the good work that you do with people's jewelry, the care that you take with their precious items. Now perhaps you can do a very important job for me." At this, the merchant reached deep into his pocket and brought out a lovely old gold filigree ring set with a huge and beautiful diamond, and as he pulled it from his pocket, he twisted and broke the band.

"This ring has been in my family for generations and generations. But now, as you can clearly see, it is broken. Are you really that good at repairs? Do you think you can fix it without destroying the filigree?"

Merit of the Sabbath examined the ring carefully and held it up to the light. He loved the way the light danced around the diamond, and he admired the delicate filigree work. Much skill and love had gone into the creation of this ring. Hmmm . . . it certainly looks like a recent break, he thought. Then he answered, "This is a beautiful family heirloom. The band is quite fragile, but I think that it can certainly be fixed. Yes, by the merit of the Sabbath, the ring can be repaired. If you leave it with me, I will get to it later, after I finish with this necklace I'm working on."

"But of course. I understand entirely. Here is the ring. Please make sure that you take very good care of it. Remember that it is a priceless antique and could never be replaced."

Merit of the Sabbath took the ring, opened the top drawer in his workbench, and placed the ring inside. The leather merchant watched him, then turned and walked out of the store without even a farewell. Merit of the Sabbath turned his attention to the delicate gold-and-ruby necklace he had been working on, and soon it was lunchtime. So he withdrew to the back of his shop to eat and rest.

That was exactly what the greedy leather merchant had been waiting for. He crept over to the jeweler's shop, opened the top drawer, removed the ring, and then stole back to his own shop. He closed his shop early and left, chuckling and muttering to himself, "Merit of the Sabbath, Merit of the Sabbath . . . what will the Sabbath do for you now?" He went down to the pier at the edge of the Gulf of Aden, and there he threw the ring as far as he could out into the sea.

"Ha-ha, ha-ha! Let's just see what poor Merit of the Sabbath will do now! Where will all of his faith get him this time? Hmmm?"

Early on Thursday morning, the evil merchant went to see the jeweler. "Merit of the Sabbath. Merit of the Sabbath! Is my ring fixed yet? Can I have it back? Can I see it yet?"

"I have not fixed it, nor have I touched it," answered Merit of the

Sabbath, which was true enough. He was just then polishing the gold-and-ruby necklace.

"Very well . . . but get to my ring soon! I want to have it back! Remember it is priceless!" With that, the leather merchant left the jeweler's store.

Merit of the Sabbath finished the last of the polishing and then went over to his worktable. He opened the top drawer and looked inside. The ring was gone! Quickly he looked through the entire drawer. Then he opened all of the other drawers. There was no sign of the ring! Where could it have gone?

Merit of the Sabbath tried to concentrate on his other work for the rest of the day. Maybe he had accidentally put the ring in the pocket of his jacket the day before. It must be at home. No need to worry without cause. He would look when he went home.

That night, Merit of the Sabbath searched through his clothes, his room, his house. No ring! Then he called his family together and told them the sad story. "Listen. The ring could not have walked off by itself! It must be somewhere in my shop. If you will come with me to the market tomorrow and help me look around, I am sure, by the merit of the Sabbath, that we will find this priceless ring."

On Friday morning, the whole family went to the jeweler's shop. They searched in all of the drawers, on the floor, on the shelves, and everywhere else, but the ring was nowhere to be found. What were they to do? In the middle of the day, just before the shop was closed for *Shabbat*, in came none other than the leather merchant.

"Where is my ring? Where is my antique, priceless gold-and-diamond ring? Give it back to me now!"

"As I told you yesterday, I have not fixed it, nor have I touched it yet. Now, I am closing my shop for *Shabbat*. But, if you will come back on Sunday morning, I promise you, by the merit of the Sabbath, that you will have your ring back."

The merchant spun around and left the shop with this warning: "If you do not give my ring back on Sunday morning, then you shall certainly pay the penalty!"

Merit of the Sabbath quietly shut the doors of his shop and left for home. When he got there, he sent his young daughter to the fish market to buy something for *Shabbat*. As her father explained, "*Shabbat* is our greatest delight and blessing, and nothing should take away from our joy and make us sad on that day. Have faith. All will turn out as it should, by the merit of the *Sabbath*."

Well, time passed, and soon enough it was Sunday morning, the beginning of a new week. Shortly after the shops opened, the leather merchant came running into the shop of the jeweler, demanding, "Hah! It is Sunday, and where is my ring? I demand that you give me back—"

Merit of the Sabbath opened the top drawer of his worktable. "Here, here. No need to be impatient. I promised that you would receive your ring back today, and so you shall." With that, Merit of the Sabbath reached down and brought out the beautiful gold-and-diamond ring and set it on the counter.

"But, but . . . Wait a minute! This is my ring?"

"Well, of course it is. What did you expect?"

"But it . . . it cannot be! This is a trick!"

"Whatever are you talking about? You gave me your ring to fix, and so fix it I did."

"No! It cannot be. No!! I . . . I happen to know that . . . that the ring was . . . stolen!"

"Stolen? Now how would you possibly know something like that?"

"Well . . . I overheard in the tavern that someone, some terrible person, came in here, stole the ring, and then threw it into the sea!"

"And do you know how you happened to know all of that? Because you were the one who did it! Why? Why did you do this?"

The leather merchant was as pale as a ghost. "But how did you know? And how did you get the ring back? Tell me . . . tell me everything that you did after you left here on Friday. Please!" he begged.

"Remember when I closed my shop and headed home? I sent my daughter to the fish market to buy something special to honor the *Sabbath*. She brought a fish home, some small thing to brighten our celebration of *Shabbat*. My wife placed the fish on the kitchen counter to clean it. She took her big knife and scaled the fish, and then turned it on its side to cut it open. Carefully she slit it in half, and then she looked inside. And do you know what she found? There, inside of the fish, gleaming in the light, was this beautiful golden filigree and diamond ring! So, here it is, safe and sound and repaired, by the merit of the Sabbath."

"Merit of the Sabbath. My word! There must really be merit to the Sabbath. I . . . I can see now what your faith has brought you. I wish to know more of this faith and Sabbath."

And the two shopkeepers were seen talking together in the market-place, side by side in the lazy late afternoons, for many, many years, by the merit of the Sabbath.

STORYTELLER: CHERIE KARO SCHWARTZ

I have always been attracted to this story, to the magical twist of circumstance that brings return and reward. Like most people, I knew it first in its Eastern European version, "Joseph Who Loved the Sabbath." I was delighted to find a version from a more exotic culture, Yemen. That's one of the treasures of the Israel Folktale Archives; with director Dov Noy's extensive research, we have access to multiple versions of the same Jewish story from different countries.

Although I connected with this version, I was disturbed by the ending. In the original, the evil shopkeeper sees his wrong and eventually converts to Judaism. I thought that as a folktale coming from an area where Jews lived in a hostile environment, this is wish fulfillment. It just didn't ring true. So I have chosen to end it with the shopkeeper wanting to know more about Judaism. This leaves open the possibility for understanding and *shalom*.

VISITOR: ILANA HARLOW; NEW YORK CITY

I can remember reading this story in second grade at Ramaz, the Jewish day school I attended. It was the story "Joseph Who Loved the Sabbath." Reading it again, I was reminded of a quote by Ahad Ha-am: "More than the Jews have kept the Sabbath, the Sabbath has kept the Jews." The real meaning of this, for me, is that it's a cycle —you keep the Sabbath, and the Sabbath keeps you tied into the tradition.

JOSEPH ELIAS

Like the kzatshka (a Cossack dance), borscht (beet soup), the mambo (known in the Catskills as the Jewish waltz), and the Chinese game of mah-jongg, the folktale character Joha is a cultural creation that Jews borrowed, adapted, and made their own in their travels through the Diaspora. In the years that led up to the Spanish Inquisition, many Jews fled Spain, often settling in the Ottoman republic, which became Turkey. Joha was originally a character in Turkish and Arabic folktales, but the Sephardim made him their own.

Joe Elias, born on the Lower East Side in 1933, heard the stories from his father, who fled the Balkan wars prior to World War I. Joe became an English teacher and later a prominent school administrator, but he never lost his passionate interest in Sephardic music, language, and culture. At P.S. 225 in Brighton Beach, he would ask his Sephardic students to bring in their Ladino-speaking grandparents so he could record their old songs. He visited the Sephardic Home for the Aged on Cropsey Avenue and sang old melodies back and forth with the elderly. As a singer of older Sephardic songs, he was invited to the Smithsonian's Festival of American Folklife and was inspired to start an ensemble that has traveled throughout the world, performing in Ladino.

Joe never forgot the Joha stories he heard as a boy. His father wouldn't formally tell Joha stories. "It's not like he sat us down and said, 'Now I am going to tell a story.' It's like when somebody breaks an egg, for example, that's a time to tell a broken egg story. With seven kids in the house, opportunities to drop an egg are many."

There happen to be a good many stories about Joha and eggs. Once, Joha was dancing with eggs on his head when the basket dropped. Rather than admit he'd dropped the eggs, Joha took a stick, mixed them into the dirt, and claimed he had concocted a potion to chase away the chinchas, or bedbugs; on another occasion he became a busy egg merchant, buying eggs for ten groshes and selling them for nine. Sales skyrocketed. According to Joe, Sephardic businessmen, whether they're selling cars or clothes, have a saying for doing business at a loss: "Like Joha, you buy eggs for ten and sell them for nine."

THE SOUND OF WORK

So you want some tales of Joha? Joha was looking for work, and there was a man who had a job for someone to split wood with an ax. A heavy-duty job. But Joha really didn't have his heart set on doing such manual, heavy labor. Just then a *casalino* (a peasant) comes along who wants the job. The problem is that the *casalino* is mute. So the foreman motions to him what they need him to do.

That gives Joha an idea. He tells the boss, "The two of us will make a pair. Because he's mute, I will help him out." So the *casalino* takes the ax and begins to chop. And with every blow, Joha goes, "Uhh!" He grunts. And the mute man swings the ax and Joha grunts, "Uhh." And he swings the ax and he: "Uhh!" So all day long the *casalino* is chopping wood and Joha is grunting, "Uhh!"

At the end of the day, the boss arrives with the money to pay for splitting the wood. He gives the money to the *casalino*. Joha says, "Wait a second, this is a two-man job. He does the swinging and I do the 'Uhh!'" The boss man is not at all sure about this line of reasoning.

So the boss takes them to a judge, and the judge says, "Tell me what happened." So the mute man stands there, and Joha says, "*Este aquí no puede hablar.* [This man doesn't speak.] He was swinging the ax, and I was going, 'Uhh!' With every blow, every blow, he swung and I went 'Uhh!'"

So the judge says, "Bring me the sack of money. Bring it over here now, in front of me." And the judge pours the coins from the sack into a bowl, slowly. And Joha reaches for the money. The judge says, "No, no, no, you don't touch the money. You already got paid."

Joha says, "What do you mean?"

The judge says, "For the sound of work, you hear the sound of money. But money you don't get."

Joha gets outsmarted a lot in these stories . . .

VISITOR: JULIUS LUCIUS ECHELES

Julius Lucius Echeles, a lawyer in Chicago, frequently uses a version of this story in his courtroom to show that "the punishment should fit the crime." As a boy, he heard the story from his mother, who had been a *dinst*, or housemaid, in the *shtetl*. In this frequently told Ashkenazic version, children from a poor family are accused by a wealthy man of standing outside his window and "stealing" the aromas of his sumptuous meals. Perhaps with a premonition of what was to become the American penchant for suing, the wealthy man takes the children to court. As in the Joha tale, the judge jingles the coins by the man's ear, saying, "You heard the money and they smelled the food. That's justice."

THE TALKING MULE

Joha was hired by the rabbi to teach the rabbi's son how to read. And he hired Joha because the rabbi's son was *um pouco atrazado*, backward. In fact, the rabbi's son was very backward, very slow. And as hard as Joha would try to stuff this information down the kid's throat, nothing seemed to penetrate, *no entrava nada*.

So Joha says to the boy, "You know, you're really trying my patience. You must try harder." And pretty soon Joha is screaming and yelling, "Hay *asno, hijo de un asno!* [You're a donkey! A son of a donkey!] But you are going to learn how to read, you are going to learn to read!"

As luck would happen, one of the sultan's viziers (advisers) was passing by. The vizier doesn't see the situation, but he hears Joha yelling at the child, calling him a donkey and saying, "You donkey! You are going to learn how to read!"

And the vizier believes exactly what he hears. He really thinks that Joha is teaching a donkey with four legs and long ears how to read.

So that day, back at the sultan's court, the vizier tells the sultan about how he overheard this man named Joha teaching a donkey how to read. The sultan is impressed. He says, "If we really can teach donkeys how to read, all the world will have to pay obeisance to us. They will have to say that we are a special breed of people who can teach donkeys how to read. Bring this man Joha to me now."

The next day, the vizier knocks on the door, and Joha says, "Oh, Señor Vizier, what can I do for you?"

"For me, nothing, I don't need you. It's the sultan himself who is calling you."

Joha starts shaking in his boots. Oh, my God, he thinks, what does the sultan want? The man has absolute life and death authority over all of his subjects. He literally and capriciously could order somebody's head cut off.

So Joha goes in front of the sultan and grovels on the ground on all fours and kisses his toes. And he says, "What can I do for you? I'm here to do your bidding, what can I do?"

The sultan says, "Please, stand up, stop groveling. I heard that you know how to teach a donkey to read. And that's something I want to see for myself. So I have brought this donkey over here and I want you to take this donkey and teach him how to read. Now, right away."

So Joha, he figures out that somebody must have overheard him yelling at the rabbi's son, calling him a donkey. But he can't tell the sultan it was the rabbi's son. So he says, "Of course, I'll do my best. But I need time, it takes a long time."

The sultan says, "How much time do you need?"

"Give me a month."

So the sultan says, "Okay, take the donkey, take a month, and here's a bag of gold for your troubles. You shouldn't do this for nothing."

So he goes home, puts on his oldest clothes, bathes himself in ashes (the traditional Jewish style of mourning), and starts to cry.

And his wife says, "What's the matter?"

He says, "I'm in big trouble. I've accepted this bag of gold from the sultan, who expects me to teach this donkey how to read. Of course, there's no way I can make the donkey read. The sultan is going to disembowel me! What can I do?"

So his wife says, "Well, if you give me the bag of gold, I'll show you how to make the donkey read."

He couldn't think of any other solution, so he gives her the bag of gold. She says, "Okay, you take this donkey, and you tie him in the stable, and don't let him eat anything for two days, nothing, just water. Then you bring him over here. And you see this dry corn? I'm going to put a few kernels of dry corn between the pages of this book, so you turn over the next page and there's more corn, turn over the next page, there's more corn, turn over the next page, and pretty soon the donkey's going to figure out that by turning pages, he's going to get more corn."

So he doesn't feed the donkey for two days, and on the third day he brings the donkey in, and sure enough, the donkey looks at the book and sees the corn, and he goes, "Eeah-ahh," and he takes and he eats the corn and he turns the page, and he goes, "Eeah-ahh," and he takes the book, and he turns the page and he eats the corn and he goes, "Eeah-ahh."

And by the time the month is past, this becomes the regular routine. The donkey knows how to turn the pages, he does it with such finesse and alacrity and such care not even to tear the book, he does it very carefully, and he goes, "Eeah-ahh."

So the month goes by and Joha is summoned by the sultan.

The sultan says, "So, you taught him how to read?"

Joha says, "Yes, yes."

"Well, let me see."

So he sets up the book with the corn in between, and the donkey turns the page and he goes, "Eeah-ahh!" Eats the corn, carefully turns the page with his nose and his tongue. Then he does it again: "Eeah-ahh."

"See, he's reading."

The sultan says, "What do you mean, he's reading?"

"Can't you see he's reading?" Joha turns the page and the donkey goes, "Eeah-ahh."

The sultan says, "How come I don't understand what he's saying?"

"Aha!" says Joha. "Now that's a different story. I didn't say I was going to teach the sultan to understand what donkeys say. After all, that's another skill altogether. For that you have to find someone else."

The sultan understood that he had been taken. But, like any sultan, he did not wish publicly to acknowledge that fact. So he said, "Ah, yes, very good." And he gave Joha another bag of gold and told him to go away and never come back again.

STORYTELLER: PENINNAH SCHRAM

I love telling stories about the trickster Joha. He's found in the folklore of Turkey, Greece, and Morocco and is a character in Arab folklore whom Jews have adopted. Joha is the more Sephardic pronunciation, while Juha is more Arabic and Moroccan. When I tell these stories, I see Sephardim in the audience suddenly break into huge smiles at the sparked memory of hearing about Joha when they were children. One man remembered that as a child, whenever he did something foolish his mother would raise up her hand with a wave and say, "Joha!" That was all he needed to realize the foolishness of his actions.

RABBI EDWARD SCHECTER

"Religion," says Rabbi Edward Schecter, "should comfort the afflicted and afflict the comforted." At Temple Beth Shalom in Hastings-on-Hudson, about twenty-five miles north of the old immigrant neighborhood on the

Lower East Side, Rabbi Schecter uses stories to do both. In his conversations and his readings, he listens for stories with a "third ear."

On Yom Kippur "Rabbi Eddie," as he is affectionately known to the congregation, appears before the children's group as Jonah, carrying an umbrella. He places a goldfish in a bowl in the front of the room to symbolize the whale and proceeds to tell the Jonah story traditionally told on Yom Kippur.

At Bar and Bat Mitzvahs he tells youngsters about a Talmudic discussion among a group of rabbis arguing over when there is enough sunlight at dawn to say the morning *shma*, or prayer. One rabbi says it's when there's enough light to distinguish a blue thread from a purple; the second says it's when you can distinguish a purple from a black. The third says that it's when you can discern the faces of your fellow women and men; the Bar or Bat Mitzvah is the time when youngsters can first distinguish faces, understand and empathize with their fellow human beings.

Rabbi Schecter "afflicts the comforted" in his Reform temple with provocative Hasidic stories and new interpretations of scripture. On Rosh Hashanah, 1987, he refashioned biblical history to challenge his congregation.

STORIES ABOUT STORIES

ISAAC'S BAR MITZVAH

In the *midrash*, the legends of the rabbis, time and place take on different meanings. Personalities crisscross centuries in the blink of an eye to talk with people who lived centuries before them or centuries after them. In this world of *midrash*, man and God are in constant debate and anything can happen.

A story. In one *midrash*, Isaac goes back in time to talk with God at the moment God is creating the world. Isaac watches silently as God goes through each day, creating the earth and sky, the animals, and, finally, man and woman. As God finishes, Isaac speaks up: "I don't understand. After each thing you created you said 'It was good'—but after you created man and woman, you didn't say that they were good. Why?"

And God said, "Isaac, everything I just created I made complete and perfect. Nature can function on its own. But human beings I created incomplete and imperfect; when human beings perfect themselves, when they create goodness in their world, I will call them good. Go back to the future, Isaac. Go back and create the goodness that only you can create in your world; then I will call you good."

So in Jewish tradition there is an interplay of personalities across the centuries. This will help you appreciate what happened to me sometime ago.

I was sitting in my study when a husband and wife walked in with their two sons and a young woman. "Rabbi," the man said, "my name is Abraham. This is my wife, Sarah, our two sons, Isaac and Ishmael, and our mother's helper, Hagar. We were wandering through the Hastings area —I didn't know there were Jews here—and we're thinking of joining your synagogue. We want the boys to get a Jewish education. We're not very religious, Rabbi. My wife's family comes from Babylonia; my father wasn't Jewish; we don't know anything about my mother; I myself am a convert. I did it to make my mother-in-law happy—she always wanted a Jewish son-in-law. She's still not happy."

By this time, the two boys were fighting with each other. Sarah said to Abraham: "Would you tell Hagar to take Ishmael out. He is driving my Isaac crazy!"

Abraham looked up as though he heard a voice and reluctantly sent Hagar and Ishmael out.

Abraham continued: "To be honest, I don't know if Ishmael wants a Bar Mitzvah, but for Isaac it's important to me. You see, Rabbi, we had a bit of a mishap a couple of years ago. We went on a three-day hiking trip together and ... er ... well, Rabbi, you wouldn't believe it."

Now Isaac looked at me as though he had something to say—but he decided to wait.

I handed Abraham the membership form and dues information. "Building fund?" he said. "When I was growing up, all we had was a tent."

Sarah interrupted: "Abraham, remember to tell the rabbi that Isaac has soccer on Sundays at twelve—he has to leave Hebrew school early. Oh yes, and by the way, Rabbi, when do we choose a Bar Mitzvah date?"

Now I finally said something: "But he is only eight years old."

"Yes, Rabbi, but we hear it is hard to find a place."

It is five years later, just prior to Isaac's Bar Mitzvah. I have come to know Isaac as much as he will allow himself to be known. He is quiet, secretive, doesn't want to share very much with anyone; but after all, he has grown up alone. He has never quite understood why Ishmael was completely ousted from the family—Isaac misses Ishmael. He remembers their fighting with a certain fondness.

Isaac has written a Bar Mitzvah talk, but he refuses to read it to me or his parents. We come to the big day—for him and for me. How many rabbis get to officiate at Abraham's son's Bar Mitzvah? The service goes smoothly and we come to the Torah reading. Isaac has chosen a special portion from the Torah for his Bar Mitzvah—the portion about his name-sake, the portion our congregation just read this morning, the binding of Isaac. Isaac gets up to speak to the congregation. He announces that the title of his talk is "Isaac's Version."

"I have a confession to make," Isaac says. "It hasn't been easy growing up in my family. My mother was overprotective of me and had little use for my brother, Ishmael. My father was a religious fanatic. He thought he heard God call to him to leave Babylon. It was nice there—we had a big house, and I had lots of friends. After we settled in Israel, things were okay—but then one night, God called to my father again, commanding him to sacrifice me. You think you know the story, but you don't. I overheard their conversation, and I want to share it with you. I want to tell you my version.

"My father had no questions about the command. For Sodom and Gomorra, he argued with God for hours. But for me—silence. I couldn't believe he would go through with it—how could a father take a knife and plunge it into the heart of his son? But I saw the look in his eyes—he was going to do it—he was a madman. When God finished talking to him I realized the future depended on me—not on God, not on Abraham, but on me—Isaac. So I changed the text without telling God or my father. I added a messenger to intercede...because after God commanded my father, God looked away—as He always does—assuming no other human being could hear His voice. I changed the text, I added life to the story instead of death. There was my father, the knife in the air, his eyes overflowing with tears, about to fulfill the command.

"You thought I was so passive? All those years you wondered: 'How could Isaac have allowed it? Why didn't he do something? He was such a passive victim!' Well, I wasn't. I might have looked that way, bound on the altar, but I had changed the text, the command, and now I am telling you the story.

"You should have seen the look on God's face when it was over. You should have seen the look on my father's face. They didn't know where it came from—well, it came from me. My father and I have never spoken about that day. But if I had not acted, it would have been both the beginning and the end of Jewish life. And if you ask: How could I rebel like this? Why do I tell this story on the day of my Bar Mitzvah? Why don't I follow in the footsteps of my honored father? I respond to you by saying: But I do—for my father *also* did not follow in *his* father's footsteps." Isaac sits down.

Not exactly your typical Bar Mitzvah talk, I say to myself. ("I'd like to thank my parents, grandparents, the rabbi. . . .") Isaac has just told us what we always wondered—what was it like to be Abraham's son? What really happened in the midst of the silences on Mount Moriah? But now he deserved a response, or maybe we needed to give him one, because if he was the beginning and not the end, we are the continuation of his story. And I feel for Abraham as well, looking at Isaac with a certain pride mixed with remorse, wanting to explain himself, but no more capable than any father of trying to explain himself to his son. I don't know what I am going to say, but I have to say something. Just as I am about to stand, Sarah gets up from her chair and approaches the pulpit.

"Isaac, we're proud of you, we really are. And we realize now how difficult it has been for you growing up in our family. But perhaps it takes a mother to explain to a son some of what a father is all about. Your father didn't understand those voices, either—he spoke to me about them. He told me how he destroyed his father's religion as a child, how he heard a call as a young man to leave Babylonia, and the same voice that made so many promises for the future suddenly asked him to sacrifice you . . . you, Isaac, the son whom he loves so much.

"Your father was devastated, beyond words, so much so that he left with you early one morning without telling me. But I knew that the day would come. He told me he had to trust the Voice he heard to be the Voice of life. And your father was right, Isaac, but not for the reasons he thought. He was right because the God who commanded him was the same God who gave you the mind and heart and courage to fill your role in the story, to make the call of God your own.

"How fortunate you were, Isaac. Your ears were attentive, you acted quickly, and no blood was shed. But, Isaac, there is something you should know. Your father and I have spanned the centuries as well—God never let us die. He gave us a task to wander the earth through eternity and bear witness to Jewish life, and yes, to Jewish suffering.

"We were there when our great-great-grandchildren were enslaved in Egypt, and we stood with them as they walked through the parted waters; we were there when Jerusalem burned the first time and the second time and when our progeny were expelled from Spain; we were there to hear the poetry of Yehuda Halevi, to study at the Academy of Maimonides, and to sing a Hasidic melody in Lublin. . . . But we also saw, Isaac, we saw that a million Jewish children could not change the text of the Holocaust, could not add a messenger to cry, 'Stay thy hand—do not harm the child. . . .' You see, Isaac, Jewish life is a mystery to us as well.

"Isaac, we could not finish what we began, but we know it is a sacred task, a holy task, to unite the peoples of the world under one God. This task was ours, it became yours, and you must hand it to generations to come who won't understand you any more than you understand us. Remember this: 'It is not yours to complete the task, but neither are you free to desist from it.' "

It is two decades later. Isaac is now a father to two sons, twins, named Jacob and Esau. He is speaking to them at their Bar Mitzvah—I myself am a very old rabbi. Isaac's brother, Ishmael, has been reunited with the family. Isaac speaks to his extended family, and we are all invited to listen to it. Isaac begins:

"I was there at the moment of creation, and I asked God questions. He commanded me to go back to the future, to create goodness in my own world. I did this as best I could. . . .

"Now I speak to you—my children, Jacob and Esau; my brother,

Ishmael. I charge you, out of your loins will come three major religions of the world. From you, Jacob—the continuity of Israel. From you, Esau—the religion of Christianity. From you, Ishmael—the Arab peoples and the birth of Islam. Generations of your children to come will look at the same text—the Bible—and claim it as their own. They will see within it, hear within it, the call of God to kill each other in God's name, to persecute each other, to throw each other off the lands of the earth. Christians will kill Muslims, and Muslims will kill Christians, and both will kill Jews. The children of Esau and Ishmael will devour Jacob, and Jacob will never trust Esau or Ishmael again. And the day may come when Jacob himself will become the aggressor.

"I charge you, you must change the text, reinterpret the text. You must go back to the future and tell your children and your children's children. . . . God cannot call you good unless you create goodness in your world. The knife is in the air, and your generations to come will be sacrificed unless you, Jacob; you, Esau; and you, Ishmael become the messengers, the messengers of peace.

"I leave you now, my children and my brother: the Torah is in your hands . . . the call of God is in your hands."

That's the way it happened some time ago in my study. I am the rabbi of a small congregation, but with Jewish history you never know who might walk in off the street one day.

My friends Abraham, Isaac, and Jacob are here with us; the patriarchs and matriarchs of ancient Israel are with us; Elijah beckons at our doors in the footsteps of the Messiah—if we from this place will go back to the future and create goodness in our world.

VISITOR: BOB DYLAN

FROM "HIGHWAY 61 REVISITED"

God said to Abraham, "Kill me a son"
Abe say, "Man, you must be puttin' me on"
God say, "No." Abe say "What?"
God say, "You can do what you want, Abe, but
The next time you see me comin' you better run"
Well, Abe say, "Where do you want this killin' done?"
God say, "Out on Highway 61."

THE *SHTETL*

[The shtetl was] a jumble of wooden houses clustered higgledy-piggledy about a marketplace. . . . The streets . . . as tortuous as a Talmudic argument . . . bent into question marks and folded into parentheses.

— MAURICE SAMUEL

The Holocaust obliterated the Jewish *shtetl* and enshrined it in memory. The musical and film *Fiddler on the Roof* (based on Shalom Aleichem's *Tevye the Dairyman* stories), Marc Chagall's paintings, and some influential books about the *shtetl*—*Life Is with People* (1952) and its predecessors, Maurice Samuel's *The World of Shalom Aleichem* (1943) and Bella Chagall's *Burning Lights* (1945)—imbued the Jewish towns of Eastern Europe with a nostalgic glow. Rabbi Edward Schecter talks about the meaning of the *shtetl* to his Reform congregation. Real or imagined, the *shtetl* Jews "were the real Jews, and we are a poor facsimile, ashamed that we don't know what they know, don't observe what they observe, don't spend as much time being Jewish as they do. But psychologically, we define our own Jewishness by the radiance of the *shtetl*."

Contemporary scholars have studied how the *shtetl* has come to play so important a role in the popular imagination. As an icon of Jewishness, the image of the *shtetl* has clouded the variety of Jewish life and its complex history in Eastern Europe (most of the Jews killed in the Holocaust, for instance, lived in cities). Barbara Kirshenblatt-Gimblett notes that the term *"shtetl"* in English tends to conjure up an imagined Jewish community, whereas in Yiddish, *shtetl*, is often just a word for town, as distinguished from city or village. Her introduction to *Life Is with People*, a popular work of anthropology by Mark Zborowsky and Elizabeth Herzog, shows how their work depicts primarily the imagined community of the *shtetl*. Their book made the term *"shtetl"* part of the vocabulary of American anthropology. It was also consulted by the producers of *Fiddler on the Roof*. Margaret Mead supervised the project and saw affinities between the *shtetl* of *Life Is with People* and the kinds of communities—small, insulated if not isolated, and traditional—that she had studied in the South Pacific.

In this book, our concern is for the *shtetl* as a locus of stories. Regardless of the historical accuracy of the popular image, the fascination and nostalgia of Jewish Americans for the partially imagined community they call the *shtetl*, still within the living memory of many older Jews, have assured it a firm place in Jewish American folklore. In a world forever changed by the Holocaust, stories about the *shtetl* are a way of saying Kaddish (the mourner's prayer) for an obliterated way of life.

A.
THE *SHTETL* IN FOLKTALE

EVE PENNER ILSEN

When Eve Penner Ilsen first heard this story, she burst into tears. In the tale, the well-known rebbe of Chernobl puts his spiritual life above the material well-being of his wife and family; they are barely able to eke out a living, but he still steadfastly refuses to part with his most valuable asset—a beautiful set of tefillin (phylacteries, or prayer devices consisting of leather boxes containing Torah scrolls worn by observant Jews during prayer). The traditional ending for the story justifies the rabbi's actions. Hearing it, Eve Ilsen was dismayed. She believed that the story called for a new ending, a tikkun, a repair.

Yet Eve Ilsen was enough of a traditionalist to know that repairs are not always so easy with stories. She wanted to remain true to the rhythms and beauty of the traditional tale. She also realized that the notion of a respected rebbe "embracing poverty" and seeking a life of material simplicity and spiritual satisfaction was an important message for our times. Finally, the story pertained to a real personage, the rabbi of Chernobl, and she didn't want to tamper with the historical record.

Her solution was to speak with the rabbi's descendants for their permission and not to change the way the story turns out, but to create an alternate ending, a tikkun. The concept is wonderful; it evokes the tikkun olam, the repair or continuation of the work of creation that, according to Jewish tradition, occurs in stories and our lives. It suggests, too, the kind of psychological repair or healing that can happen through self-conscious intervention in our lives. And it illustrates how contemporary Jews both preserve and transform or, more exactly, preserve through transformation, their ancient tales.

A TALE OF REB NAKHUM
CHERNOBLER — AND A TIKKUN

Reb Nakhum of Chernobl and his family lived in the direst poverty. While he was intensely engaged in the holy life of prayer and learning, ministering to the needs of his community, it fell to his wife, the *rebbetzin* Sarah, to do everything else. She cared for the house, the cleaning and shopping and cooking, the washing and mending. She bore and raised the children, keeping them safe and as healthy as she could and teaching them the ways of *menschlechkeit*, of becoming good human beings. And what meager living sustained them, she made. Often, the pillows, candlesticks, and other household items had to be pawned just to put food on the table for *Shabbes*. Often, these items stayed at the pawnshop longer than expected. Sometimes they never came back home at all.

Reb Nakhum's poverty was voluntary. When his Hasidim would offer gifts to make his life easier and more comfortable, the *rebbe* would refuse. He did not want to be distracted from essentials and become attached to the material things of this world; and he had a positive dislike for owning money. He preferred to attach himself to things he considered of permanent value: Torah and *mitzvas*; and for these he was willing to make sacrifices. For instance, the joy he felt in fulfilling the *mitzva* of putting on *tefillin* in the morning was enhanced by a very special pair of *tefillin* that he owned. They were the only items of any real monetary value in the whole house. The small scrolls had been written by a very holy scribe, each letter fashioned with intense *kavannah* (inner purpose) in a unique script. Reb Nakhum treasured these *tefillin* and held them in high regard. When he bound them to himself he felt he could fly in his prayers far above his physical surroundings.

Other pious Jews knew about the *tefillin* as well, and several of the better-off householders had asked to buy them. In fact, one man had offered Reb Nakhum *four hundred rubles!* That was enough to marry off a daughter, from the expense of a matchmaker and a respectable dowry through the wedding celebration with musicians, new clothes for the bride and groom, and enough to feed all the poor of the town plus the honored guests, with even a little left over. This was an enormous sum.

And all this while, Rebbetzin Sarah continued struggling to make ends meet. When times were so hard that she did not know where the next meal would come from, when the children were hungry and there was nothing left to pawn, she would approach her husband and plead with him to sell the *tefillin*. "My husband," she would say, "if you sell your *tefillin* and replace them with a more ordinary pair—no small expense— still, what would remain, if I managed carefully, could free us from worry for a long time. After all, isn't the *meaning* of the verses written in the *tefillin* what is really important? And isn't that the same in every pair of *tefillin*? And isn't the *kavannah*, the intent, what counts most when you *daven* [pray] on your own?"

But Reb Nakhum wouldn't hear of it. "Don't worry," he told her. "The Holy One will help us." And somehow they continued to squeak by from day to day, from *Shabbes* to *Shabbes*, from season to season, from festival to festival.

One autumn, it was almost the eve of Sukkos and Reb Nakhum had still not found an *esrog* (citron) to make the blessing in the *sukkah*. *Esrogim* were always imported with cost and difficulty from the warm countries to the east, since they would not grow in the colder climates of Russia. This year there was scarcely an *esrog* to be found in all of Chernobl. As the last afternoon leading to Sukkos deepened, Reb Nakhum was beginning to wonder seriously how he would be able to fulfill the *mitzva* of blessing the *lulav* and the *esrog* as commanded for the festival, when he had a stroke of extraordinary good luck. He came upon a traveler rushing through Chernobl on his way home for Sukkos; and among his other possessions, he was carrying—an *esrog*! At first the traveler was unwilling to part with it at any price. But, when faced with Reb Nakhum's entreaties, the traveler told himself that if the *esrog* was so important to the *rebbe*, the money was equally important to his family, and he owed it to them to consider selling the *esrog*—but only for a stiff price: four hundred rubles. It was exactly the sum that Reb Nakhum had been offered for his *tefillin*.

Reb Nakhum stood in thought: on the one hand, he wouldn't need his *tefillin* for the next eight days, since on Sukkos one isn't obligated to wear them. And on the other hand, this was the only time in the whole year that he could fulfill the *mitzva* of blessing the *esrog*. So he quickly came to a decision. He asked the traveler to wait a short time while he ran to complete a business transaction and return with the money. He ran home, took his *tefillin,* and rushed to the house of the buyer who had offered him four hundred rubles before and who now happily paid the high price and considered himself lucky. Reb Nakhum took possession of the rare *esrog,* and he sent the traveler off with the four hundred rubles and a blessing. He wrapped the *esrog* in its protective coverings and put it carefully in its box. Once home, he put it in a special place so that nothing would damage the delicate fruit and spoil it, for the fruit had to be whole and perfect in order to be used for the blessing in the *sukkah.*

As Rebbetzin Sarah was making the last preparations for greeting the holiday—making the food and the house and the *sukkah* as neat and festive as possible on next to no money—she caught a faint whiff of the sweet scent of *esrog.* She knew it wasn't possible; even if an *esrog* were to be found in Chernobl, *they* hadn't the money to buy it. So she smiled to herself, thinking that the very thought of Sukkos was strong enough to draw down the vivid memory of the fragrance. Then she caught sight of the box, unmistakable in its safe place. Such a box, such a fragrance—it had to be an *esrog.* She didn't believe her eyes.

Just then, Reb Nakhum entered the room.

"My husband, that couldn't be—an *esrog?*"

"Yes!" Seeing her look of disbelief, he took down the box, opened it, and unwrapped the fruit to show her.

"How wonderful! But—how did you ever manage to buy it?" she asked.

And he told her what he had done.

ONE TRADITIONAL ENDING

Something in her snapped, after all those years of hardship and privation.

"The *tefillin?*" she gasped. "Your precious *tefillin,* which could have supported the whole family for so long, which I have been begging you for years to sell and you refused—you *sold* them today, to buy from a passing traveler an *esrog* that we will use for only seven days?"

The *rebbetzin* was beside herself with fury.

She seized the *esrog* and bit off the *pitom* end. Now the *esrog* could not be used for the festival.

Reb Nakhum was silent for a long moment. Then he said: "My precious *tefillin* are gone. And now, the *esrog* is lost to me. Satan would now like me to lose one last thing to make his victory complete: my temper. *And that I will not do.*" And Reb Nakhum left the room.

ONE POSSIBLE TIKKUN

Something in her snapped, after all those years of hardship and privation.

The *rebbetzin* was beside herself with fury.

She seized the *esrog*, bit off the *pitom* end, and burst into a high, keening wail.

Reb Nakhum stood frozen in shock. He had, by a near miracle, managed to acquire an *esrog* in time for Sukkos, the only time in the whole year that he would have the opportunity to perform this *mitzva*. Now they couldn't use it. And his wife was crying as if her heart would break.

"Sarah, Sarah, what is it? Why did you do this? Please, talk to me!" He stood by helplessly while she rocked herself to and fro, convulsed by sobs, almost retching. He had never seen her so distraught. A long time passed before she could breathe easily again, and it was longer before she could speak.

"My husband," she whispered, "for years you have been *davening*, learning, teaching, and caring for the needs of the community." He looked at her, head to one side, puzzled. "For those same years," she said, "I have barely been able to snatch a moment to pray at length, not on the run, let alone to learn a little. Because I have spent every waking moment of every hour keeping worry from you, making it possible for you to do what you do, and eking a life out for ourselves and our children." She was trembling.

"And it's barely a life. Sometimes our sons can hardly keep their minds on their learning because of the rumblings of their empty bellies. We shiver and our noses run for over half the year because we can't afford more wood for heat." Her voice, soft and intense, began to gain strength. "Our daughter is almost of an age to marry, and all of her few rags of clothing are threadbare. When it comes time for her wedding, will she even have a dowry?"

She continued: "When I asked you to sell your *tefillin*, it was not for the sake of luxuries, but in order to buy bare necessities. Did you think that I would ask you to part with your treasured *tefillin* for the sake of a frivolity? Each time I asked, and you told me G-d would provide, G-d *did* provide—something. Then you would tell me not to worry: didn't I see, G-d had provided? But I *live* in worry: in what form will G-d's help come? Of course our sustenance comes from Him; but every evening, it is *me* that you and the children ask for dinner. It is *my* task to see that it gets from G-d to the table. I use all my heart and all my strength trying to patch it together so we can survive. It is my job to persuade the shopkeepers to wait just a little longer until we can pay our bills. Whatever comes, I am the one who counts each *kopeck* and makes it stretch to last."

Rebbetzin Sarah's voice lowered to just above a whisper. "My husband, do you really think it is right that we all pay such a high price for your attachment to poverty?"

Reb Nakhum sat in shocked silence. His eyes filled with tears.

For the first time, Rebbetzin Sarah had found her voice.

And now, for the first time, Reb Nakhum found his ears: he heard her deeply.

He moved closer to her, and they looked deep into each other's eyes.

Cradling the ruined *esrog* between them, the couple stood and cried together, the salt of their tears sweetened by the fragrance of the fruit.

And we are told that the joy of Sukkos had never been sweeter in their house than in that year.

STORYTELLER: EVE PENNER ILSEN

It happened that my partner was recently talking to a descendant of the Chernobler and the subject of the *tefillin* came up. (Reb Nakhum's Hasidim bought the *tefillin* back for him, and they are in his family to this day.) Did my partner know the story of the Chernobler's *tefillin* and the *esrog?* Yes, my partner said, he did; and he had also heard a new alternative ending (this one), which he then recounted.

The Chernobler's descendant smiled and said: "And if it didn't happen that way—it should have."

RABBI EDWARD SCHECTER

"*A story. The congregation expects me to start every sermon with the words 'A story.' And I always do, on the holidays,*" *Rabbi Schecter told me.* "*I got it from Wiesel. That's the way he begins so many of his lectures at the 92 Street Y. Wiesel got it from the* midrash, *where it says 'davar akheyr,' which really means 'another thing,' or 'story,' or 'another word'—davar is a 'word' or a 'thing,' akheyr is 'another.' And the* midrash *runs 'another word, another word, another thing, another thing.'*"

When Rabbi Schecter asks his congregation to picture in their mind the image of a Jew, most envision Chagall's Hasidic rebbes. Schecter admonishes his congregation, "*You could have pictured yourself! How come the real Jew is always someone else? I'm the fake Jew, I'm the Jew who's not religious enough. Why isn't your story a Jewish story?*"

"The Teller of Tales," *told by Rabbi Schecter in a sermon on Rosh Hashanah morning in 1981, helps answer that question.* "Levi Yitzak Burns the Evidence" *is a retelling of a classic Peretz story about the fiery Jewish preacher, the eighteenth-century Hasidic tzaddik (righteous person) who again and again had the gall to stand up to God.*

THE TELLER OF TALES

A story. There was once a Jew who made his living telling Jewish tales. He would travel the countryside of Poland, sharing his stories with whoever might listen, hoping in return to be invited for a meal or, even better, given a kopeck for his efforts.

One day the teller of tales met Israel Baal Shem Tov (*Besht*), the founder of Hasidism. The *Besht* was already known throughout Eastern Europe for his marvelous stories and for his ability to bring inner peace and joy to his fellows. Moments spent with him, a mere glance from his radiant eyes, would relieve even the worst suffering. Poland and Russia were on fire with his religious power.

The *Besht* invited the man to spend six months with him. "Live with me," he said. "Watch very closely what I do and who comes to see me. Then you will have enough tales to tell for the rest of your life. And who knows, you too might one day through your stories relieve a man of his suffering and pain."

The teller of tales accepted the invitation. Who could turn down the *Besht*? And after six months of observing and listening, he left, overflowing with tales and experiences to share. But again, to his dismay, few wanted to listen. Sometimes at an inn, some fellow who had imbibed too much would listen to a story and offer him a vodka, but times were tough.

Now he is traveling through the outermost parts of Poland in search of someone to listen. On a cold winter's night, he arrives at an inn on the Polish border. He goes around trying to tell his tales: but tonight no one, not one soul, is interested. Finally the innkeeper calls him over.

"Listen," he says, "no one here is interested in you or your tales. But a few miles from here there lives a Polish nobleman who not only loves to hear stories, but will pay you handsomely for each tale he has never heard before."

The teller of tales leaves the inn, trudges through the snow on this dark wintry night, until he sees a flame in the distance. He walks toward the light, which turns out to be one of the many torches that light up the nobleman's castle so brightly that it appears to be on fire. Here there are guards and sentries, magnificent hallways covered with huge paintings and red velvet curtains. The doorkeeper asks the purpose of his visit.

"I have a story to tell," he says.

The doorkeeper leads him through the castle until they arrive at two huge doors, which he flings open. There, at the end of a long table, sits the nobleman, stone-faced, disinterested, with two high stacks of kopecks at his side.

The teller of tales sits down and starts telling stories. The nobleman sits unimpressed, unmoved. Every so often, after a tale he had not heard, he pushes over one kopeck. The teller of tales reaches for every story he has ever heard, every experience he has ever had. The face of the nobleman doesn't budge, doesn't show the slightest emotion.

Finally, the teller of tales has told everything; he knows nothing more. He rises to take leave. Now the nobleman says, "Is that all?" Their eyes meet for the first time.

"Well, there is one more, just one more. While I was staying with the Baal Shem Tov, a man once came to him, very upset. 'Master of the Good Name,' he said, 'I was once a Jew, but the outside world beckoned me— its knowledge, its material possessions, its culture. I felt constrained by the Jewish tradition, and in order to partake of it all, I converted and became a Christian. Now I am successful and rich, but also forlorn. I feel I did the wrong thing. What shall I do?' The *Besht* responded, 'Don't worry, my son. Just use your good fortune and knowledge to help the poor and the needy.'

" 'But,' the man continued, 'when will I know I have been forgiven?'

"And the *Besht* said, 'You will know you are forgiven when one day you hear this story told.' "

Now the teller of tales looked up, and a radiance illumined the nobleman's face. Tears flowed down his cheeks as he embraced the man who had set him free.

This tale contains so much that is dear to the Jewish tradition: the importance of words, the telling of stories to set mankind free, the waiting, the wandering, the longing for redemption, the concept of a miracle for man by man. The belief that somewhere a human being waits, and another human being pursues him. They don't even know each other, but when they meet, history will never be the same....

STORYTELLER: RABBI EDWARD SCHECTER

I get the chills over that story.... How uplifting for all these people in my congregation who feel that they've left the fold, they left their people, when will they know they're forgiven? When you hear your story told—to me that's moving beyond words. It's as if when they hear the story that the teller of tales relates about the nobleman, they are hearing their own story, and they too are forgiven.

LEVI YITCHAK BURNS THE EVIDENCE

A story by the master Yiddish writer Israel Loeb Peretz:

In a vision, there was the heavenly court, totally empty, except for the table upon which stood the great scales of justice. Beyond the courtroom were two gates: one led to Paradise, where the righteous were studying Torah in the radiance of the Holy One; the other gate led to the fire of *Gehenna*. To the left of the courtroom was a door with the sign "Kategon —Prosecuting Attorney." To the right was a door with the sign "Sanegon —Defense Attorney."

Sanegon's door opened and he entered the courtroom with a small, thin case containing the records of the good deeds of mankind over the previous year. At the same moment two assistants from Kategon's office entered, carrying heavy boxes overflowing with the evil deeds of mankind. As the two assistants left to get more evidence for the prosecution, the defense attorney held his head in his hands and let out a great sigh of anguish.

That sigh was so loud, it reached through the gates of Paradise and interrrupted the study of the great rabbi Levi Yitchak of Berdichev—the compassionate one and defender of Israel—who was always ready to hear the cry of the children of Israel.

Without a second thought, Levi Yitchak left his place in Paradise, entered the courtroom, and, without hesitation, took hold of the box of evil deeds and threw them into the fire of *Gehenna*. And he continued to do so with all the evidence the assistants brought in, until Kategon, the DA himself, entered the courtroom. When Kategon saw the last bit of evidence burning, Levi Yitchak tried to sneak back to Paradise. But Kategon grabbed the coat of Levi Yitchak and cried out in a voice so loud that it could be heard throughout the seven heavens: "Stop, thief!"

The righteous of Paradise entered the courtroom in surprise, and after them the judges, and then Satan, glowing with pride that Levi Yitchak had finally been caught right in the act. Levi Yitchak readily admitted his deed and agreed to submit himself to the law. When Satan was asked what punishment he thought was appropriate, he quoted the verse from the Torah: "The thief shall be bought as a servant for the price of his theft." This was the law, and there was no getting around it. If found guilty, Levi Yitchak would be purchased as a servant in a public auction.

Each group began to bring out their wealth—Satan on one side, the righteous on the other—and place it on the scales. The patriarchs, the matriarchs, the righteous of all generations, lined up one after the other to place the meritorious deeds they had accumulated on the right side of the scales. But then Satan, who possessed unaccountable treasures, placed all his wealth on the left side. When both groups were finished the scales were in exact balance. Satan, in desperation to possess the precious soul of Levi Yitchak, then removed the crown from his head and placed it on the scale. The righteous let out a wail as the scales began to tip to the left. The prosecuting attorney, a smile on his face, grabbed Levi Yitchak and pointed the way to the gate of *Gehenna*.

Then, suddenly, a voice was heard from the Holy Throne of the Master of the Universe. "I give heaven and earth for Levi Yitchak." And as he spoke, the Holy One, praised be He, placed the heavens and earth on the right side of the scale. "For the heavens and the earth are mine, and in my eyes the soul of Levi Yitchak is worth the entire universe."

STORYTELLER: RABBI EDWARD SCHECTER

Levi Yitchak of Berdichev . . . I use some of his stories in my sermons because he's the defender of Israel. He's the one who will stand before God on Yom Kippur and threaten Him with a law suit. He was a real radical, Levi Yitchak, the defender of Israel. He argued with God for the Jewish people all the time. He wanted to show his followers that one may be Jewish with God—or against God—but not without God.

VISITOR: NATHAN AUSUBEL

RABBI LEVI YITCHAK OF BERDICHEV

On the evening of the Day of Atonement Rabbi Levi Yitchak of Berdichev, "the poor man's rabbi," asked an illiterate tailor, "Since you couldn't read the prayers today, what did you say to God?"

"I said to God," replied the tailor, "Dear God, you want me to repent of my sins, but my sins have been so small! I confess: There have been times when I failed to return to the customers the pieces of leftover cloth. When I could not help it, I even ate food that was not kosher. But really—is that so terrible? Now take yourself, God! Just examine your own sins: You have robbed mothers of their babes and have left helpless babes orphans. So you see that your sins are much more serious than mine. I'll tell you what, God! Let's make a deal! You forgive me and I'll forgive you."

"Ah, you foolish man!" cried Rabbi Levi Yitchak. "You let God off too easily! Just think! You were in an excellent position to make him redeem the whole Jewish people!"

THE TALES OF CHELM

SYD LIEBERMAN, STEVE SANFIELD

Throughout Jewish history and folklore, wise rabbis have reasoned their way around difficult religious questions, clever merchants have found ways to survive even when the laws were turned against them, and astute women have found ways to raise their families in tough times. But of all these wise souls, none thought themselves wiser than the fools of Chelm. Chelm is a real town in Poland, but it holds a special place of honor in Jewish folklore as a town of fools.

When God created humans, according to one Chelm story, he wanted to distribute the wise and foolish souls evenly across the planet. He packed the souls into a large sack that looked like a pillow filled with feathers and assigned an angel to distribute them evenly across the earth. While flying over Poland, the bag got caught on a mountain peak, and many of the souls drifted down to Chelm. Many people, in fact, complained that Chelm got more than its share of foolish souls. The truth is, there were plenty of foolish souls to scatter almost everywhere else. For, as we know, there is a little foolishness in every wise person and a little wisdom in every fool.

A number of Jewish American storytellers—among them Syd Lieberman and Steve Sanfield—still recall some of the remarkable fools of Chelm. Steve Sanfield, researching his book of Chelm stories, The Feather Merchants, even visited the real town of Chelm. "It is a lovely place situated, not deep in a valley as is the Chelm of legend, but high in the Lublin uplands, with a sweeping view of the surrounding countryside." Fifty years ago almost half the population was Jewish, fifteen thousand. But Steve found no Jews in the town during his visit. They had all disappeared, most murdered at the killing camp called Sobibor, thirty miles to the northeast. He could find only a few people who remembered the Jews, and none who knew these tales. But the Chelm of story remains replete with tales, "a magical place filled with honest and righteous men and women for whom the idea of defeat passes as quickly as a gaggle of geese flying south."

THE FOUNDING FATHERS

STEVE SANFIELD

The Founding Fathers of Chelm looked out across the broad, flat valley below. A wide river sparkled in the sunshine as it meandered slowly from east to west. Like an immense pair of arms hugging a child in a snug embrace, soft, rolling hills encircled the valley on three sides. Here and there chestnuts and maples mingled with birches and beeches, creating a dozen shades of dancing greenery.

And where the men stood, near the top of the mountain to the north, grew the towering pines and firs with which they planned to build their town.

After the proper prayers and ceremonies of dedication, they began their great work. They selected the largest and strongest trees. Nothing less would do. They carefully felled and limbed the sturdiest ones, but immediately a problem arose.

How were they to get these huge logs down to the valley?

The early Chelmites had no beasts of burden, no carts or wagons. All those would come later. But it is said, "When you must, you can," so the men simply lifted the logs onto their shoulders, a dozen to each, and amid much huffing and puffing, they carried them down the mountain.

While all this activity was going on, a stranger happened to be passing through the valley. He watched in amazement as the men of Chelm struggled and wrestled with their heavy burdens.

"This is ridiculous," he said to himself. "These men are fools," which may have been the first time anyone ever applied that term to the good people of Chelm.

The stranger joined the workers up on the mountain and suggested they try another way. He gave one of the logs a hearty kick, and it rolled down into the valley as if it knew exactly where it was going.

"Remarkable! A genius!" exclaimed the Chelmites. They immediately descended into the valley, hoisted the logs on their shoulders once more, and with muscles straining and eyes popping, carried them back up the mountain. Then, one by one, they *rolled* their logs back down.

A Chelm Medley

SYD LIEBERMAN

In our tradition we have a town of fools, and that town is called Chelm. I can tell you lots of stories that show you what the town was like. But I think I will just tell you a few stories about Mendel the *shammes* (the synagogue caretaker) and you'll see what I'm talking about.

Mendel was the kind of man who when he went to the sweat bath on Friday night was afraid to take his clothes off. You see, he thought if he took his clothes off, he'd forget who he was. So what did he do? He tied a string around his legs so he'd remember. But when he got into the sweat bath, the string fell off. Mendel looked up and there sat another man with a string tied around his leg. He, too, was afraid he'd forget who he was. When Mendel looked at the second man, he said, "Oh, my God, if you're me, who am I?"

Another time, Mendel was walking down the road when a stranger came up to him and said, "Take this, Yankel." Then he punched Mendel. Mendel fell to the ground. As soon as he hit the ground, he began laughing. The stranger said, "What are you laughing about? I just punched you. I knocked you on the ground."

Mendel looked up and said, "The joke's on you. I'm not Yankel!"

Once Mendel was looking out the window of his house, watching his wife wash his underwear. Well, in those days, you dipped your clothes in the river and then you put them on a rock and you beat them and beat them and beat them. His wife took his underwear and put it in the river and then on the rock and beat it and beat it and beat it. Then back it went in the river and back on the rock, where she beat it and beat it and beat it again. Finally, after about the fifth time, Mendel looked up and said, "Blessed be Thou, O Lord, who gave me the wisdom to get out of my underwear—just in time."

Once, Mendel was heading into Warsaw with his arms outstretched and his thumbs pointing up rigidly about nine inches apart. When people saw him walking down the road, they said, "Look at the poor cripple, paralyzed, with his arms straight out. My, what a hard life he must have. "

Now, when he arrived at the wagon, he said to the wagon driver, "Please, could you reach into my pockets and get the money out? You know, for obvious reasons." The wagon driver thought, What a pity, a poor man, paralyzed like this with his thumbs out. So the wagon driver got down, reached into his pocket, and took his money. He even lifted Mendel up onto the wagon. All of the people treated him with respect and dignity. They all thought about his hard life. So when they stopped, they helped him down, and when they started again, they put him back up. When they ate, he opened his mouth and they put food in. All the way to Warsaw it was like this. Finally one woman asked him, just as they were pulling in, "Uncle, how long have you been inflicted with this paralysis?"

"What?" Mendel replied. "What paralysis? I'm not paralyzed. My wife knew I was going to Warsaw. She wanted me to buy her a pair of shoes. This is the size of her foot. You don't know my wife. If I got the wrong size, she would make my life miserable."

Another time, Mendel was heading into Warsaw. This time he used his own wagon and horse because he didn't have to keep his thumbs in the air. On the way he stopped at an inn. A man at the inn realized Mendel was a Chelmite and knew he could trick him and cheat him. The man quickly disappeared with Mendel's horse, rode to a nearby town, and sold the horse to a horse trader.

After the meal, Mendel came out and found the man who sold his horse standing in the horse's harness. Mendel looked at him and said, "What are you doing? What happened to my horse?"

The man said, "My name is Motl, and I am your horse. I've been your horse for ten years. I used to be a man, but I was so sinful, God turned me into a horse. But for the last ten years, I've been praying and I've been repenting, and today, he turned me back into a human."

Mendel said, "Oh, my God, how wonderful! Wonderful! God bless you! Go have a good life. Only Motl, you know you shouldn't sin anymore." Now as soon as the man left, Mendel realized he had a problem: no horse. So what did he do? He went into the horse trader's. And what did he find? His horse.

As soon as he saw his horse, Mendel slapped himself, his eyes opened wide, and he said, "Oy, Motl, not ten minutes and already you're sinning?"

VISITOR: NATHAN AUSUBEL
THE WORRIERS OF CHELM

The people of Chelm were worriers. So they called a meeting to do something about the problem of worry. A motion was duly made and seconded to the effect that Yossel, the cobbler, be retained by the community as a whole to do its worrying and that his fee be one ruble per week.

The motion was about to carry, all speeches having been for the affirmative, when one sage propounded the fatal question: "If Yossel earned a ruble a week, what would he have to worry about?"

MICHAEL WEX

Living in Toronto with a television set and two mezuzahs, Michael Wex is a self-proclaimed member of the renowned (but little known) "international Yiddish avant-garde." He is a monologuist and writer who grew up in an Orthodox Hasidic family, studied in yeshiva, and, ranting and raving against all of it, became a unique voice among Jewish storytellers.

While the professional storytellers whisper and gesticulate earnestly, Michael Wex, dressing like James Dean, wearing all black in ironic counterpart to the Hasidic garb worn by the characters he describes, mutters cynically in a seamless combination of English, Polish, Hebrew, and Polish Yiddish. There is nothing "precious" about his tales. They are filled with sex and rebellion, rather than inspiration and affirmation. Unlike many of the other professional storytellers, he is of the culture; he didn't return to his roots and learn about it from books. He is singing its praises as he curses in its face.

Ironically, "The Kugel" does present a traditional Jewish folktale character, the "wonder-working rabbi," but he's working in the unusual capacity of a sex therapist. The story evokes a kosher version of Kafka; instead of the metamorphosing of a man into a roach, a rabbi becomes a kugel. The story offers an unusual take on East European Jewish life; people are concerned not about "tradition!" but about sex.

VISITOR: HENRY SAPOZNIK
YARMULKE OR TOUPÉE?

One of the funniest moments I ever had the honor of being on the periphery of happened a few years ago at KlezKamp in the Catskills. It was three or four in the morning, and I heard Michael Wex and a few other insomniacs working through a *paskan shayle,* one of those problems about what's kosher in a particular situation. The question they were discussing was, If a religious Jew has a toupée, does he have to wear a *yarmulke* on top of the toupée?

And Michael has this voice that carries a hunched-over rabbinic presence, and he answered: If the toupée looks like a toupée, he doesn't have to wear a *yarmulke.*

Too brilliant.

THE KUGEL

On a Friday afternoon in the winter of 1897, Mrs. Yoshke Furmanovsky, a stout *hausfrau* of Praga-by-Warsaw, opened her oven door and plunged her fork into the *kugel*, the potato pudding baking inside, to see if it was ready. Her husband looked forward to nothing so much as his Friday night *kugel*. Indeed, it was one of the great sorrows of Mrs. Furmanovsky's life that her husband looked forward to the *kugel* with somewhat more enthusiasm than to certain other Friday night activities. He'd rush home from the synagogue, gobble down the whole *kugel*, along with some chicken and fish, and then fall straight to sleep—despite rabbinic injunctions concerning private duties.

Mrs. Furmanovsky, *nebekh*—poor thing—tried everything. She put in fewer potatoes, hoping to make the meal lighter, but her Sabbath frock just wasn't designed to go with a *kugel* tiara. She purchased herbs guaranteed to wake the dead; her husband, *nebekh*, spent the night in the outhouse. She made the tea extra strong, the soup extra weak, the chicken extra lean, but by the time the weekly glimmer stole into Mrs. Furmanovsky's eye, old Yoshke, *nebekh*, would be stretched out on the bed, as level and as useful as a bench in the ritual bath.

So Mrs. Furmanovsky decided to avenge herself on the whole cursed race of *kugelen* in the only way she knew how: whenever she went to test one, she'd thrust her fork murderously into the *kugel's* tender, yielding flesh, twisting it so hard that she could almost hear the hapless concoction screaming for mercy. *"Zuln alle kugelen geyn tsu di alle shvartsyor,"* she would mutter. "Let every *kugel* go to hell. They've ruined my life. . . . I sweat, I toil, I break my back like a slave in Egypt six days a week, and *Shabbes*, instead of a little *nakhes*, a little pleasure, like everybody else, what do I get? A *kugel* bowl to be washed out with my tears. They say that on *shabbes* you're supposed to get a *neshomeh yeseireh*, an extra soul. *Nu*, how can I get when my extra lies there as useful *vi bankes a toytn*, as cups on a corpse? Ay, a plague on every *kugel*, and may the Lord deliver us from them speedily and in our day, amen."

She was otherwise a very nice woman.

And her husband? A purblind tailor with the mind of a goose. Shortly after their marriage, Mrs. Furmanovsky began to suspect him of infidelity, so weak and inconsequential was his desire. But when would he have had the time? He spent all day in the shop, which was the front room of their meager apartment, and he spent all night chomping and *shnorkhing*. She began to think that perhaps he was punishing her; perhaps she'd sinned against him in some way, and he was taking his revenge by denying her. She bought potions and philters, perfumes, negligees like the Polish women wore—but all they produced was snores. Where some men had such powerful evil inclinations as to be veritable mad dogs for the bed regardless of the time of month, Yoshke Furmanovsky wasn't even inclined.

She sought reasons, excuses. A whole week he works from dawn to dusk, shut up in an airless and stifling room—all right, he's too tired. But Friday, Friday, when he stops work at two o'clock, goes to the ritual bath, has a little time to relax and a day of relaxation to look forward to— Friday night stuck in her craw. Many women shared her problems during the week, but Friday night? Why else had God invented it?

And Yoshke, after she finally got up the nerve to ask him, on their eighth anniversary, Yoshke merely replied that he ate so well he could think of nothing but sleep. And that *kugel*—*oy*, so heavy and hearty, it warmed him so, that the vapor shot straight up to his brain, telling it to close his eyes so that Yoshke could savor the taste and aroma—undistracted.

"Ah-*nu*," said Mrs. Furmanovsky. "From now on, no more potato *kugel*. It's coming between us. I have my rights as a wife."

"Wife," replied Yoshke, "if you should fail even one Friday night to fix me my favorite potato *kugel*, you lose all your cherished rights. *Oys*, wife! I'll divorce you forthwith, and then we'll see about your wifely rights."

So Mrs. Furmanovsky, who, when all was said and done, did love her husband, began to hate his *kugel*. Every Friday afternoon was a war between her, the potatoes, and the spices, with Mrs. Furmanovsky always the loser. Loudly she lamented the fate that had kept her from being born in Ireland.

On the Friday afternoon in question, in the winter of 1897, Mrs. Furmanovksy stuck her fork into the *kugel* with her usual vigor, gave it a twist, and removed it gleefully, studying the tines for traces of *kugel* blood.

Disappointed as always, she was about to shut the oven door when the *kugel*, with an alacrity really quite shocking in an inanimate object, leapt from the oven straight to the floor and sank its teeth into Mrs. Furmanovsky's ankle.

Mrs. Furmanovsky was more shocked than pained; the *kugel* is known for its blunt, yielding teeth, and she had no difficulty shaking it loose. Bits of *kugel* clung to her ankle, but no toothmarks were to be seen. Hungry for vengeance, she kicked at the errant pudding, only to see it leap, cackling, onto the table, where it sat smugly, humming "The British Grenadiers."

A woman of valor, this Mrs. Furmanovsky, she grabbed her broom and set after the *kugel* like a hound to the fox. She cursed, she shrieked, the sound of the broom slapping the floor reechoed through the kitchen, but the giggling *kugel* was always one step ahead, baiting her, egging her on, in a *heymishen geshmakehen* Yiddish, a down-home tasty Yiddish: *"Me ret fun Aleksandr, un oykh fun Herkules,"* until Mrs. Furmanovsky, no Hercules, threw down her broom and sank to the floor in despair.

Casting her eyes heavenward, "Why me?" she cried. "What did I ever do to deserve this? The rest of the world lives in peace and quiet, while I, Khayke Furmanovsky, am condemned to do battle with a dancing *kugel*. If potatoes can sing, it's the end of the world. The Messiah must be on his way. Soon all calves will have two heads and a stillborn child will assume the throne. Men will walk on their hands and horses become rabbis, while I . . . while I am murdered to death in my own kitchen by a *kugel* from hell."

"And this is how you say thank you?" asked the *kugel* angrily. It was reclining peacefully in one of the chairs and fixed Mrs. Furmanovsky in its gaze. "I come here to help, and this is the thanks I get? Poked like a pig, chased like a thief, and cursed like a Cossack. I've got a good mind to get up and go right now, except that once I'm finished here, maybe, just maybe, I can get out of this lousy *kugel* and go back to the Garden of Eden where I belong. *Kugel* from hell! A *shvartsyor af dir*, lady, I'll give you a *kugel* from hell!"

Mrs. Furmanovksy's eyelids grazed the ceiling. "Oh, my God, it's possessed yet!"

"Possessed, shmossessed. If you'd shut up and listen for a minute, you'd understand the whole thing." And the *kugel* began its story. "While

I was still on earth, I was a famous man. The *rebbe* of Dlugaszow, maybe you've heard of me?"

The *rebbe* of Dlugaszow? Who hadn't heard of the holy *rebbe* of Dlugaszow! A saint, a wonder worker. He made the dumb to speak, the lame to walk, the barren to give birth. It was said that merely touching his walking stick or the hem of his garment was enough to ensure a man's prosperity all the days of his life. A dwarf who looked upon the *rebbe's* face one Yom Kippur night awoke the next morning a giant.

The *rebbe* of Dlugaszow. Sweet tempered, kindly, modest. He was never known to have lost his temper or to have uttered an angry word. And what people didn't know, didn't hurt. Once, shortly after his marriage, the future *rebbe* made the grave error of trying to explicate certain rather complicated kabbalistic ideas to his wife. She was a simple, pious girl who wanted only to serve her husband, and she rapidly became lost in the chain of emanations he was describing. The young scholar looked at her bewildered countenance and spat in contempt. "The brains of a *kugel*, that's what you got." Her tears so affected him that he vowed never again to insult or speak ill of any living creature.

This vow was never broken, but after a hundred and twenty years, when the *rebbe* came before the heavenly court, the *kategor*, the accusing angel, held this one incident up before the judge as proof that the *rebbe* was not worthy of Paradise. What would scarcely have been noticed on any other record was the sole blemish on this one and, as such, deserved to be treated with appropriate severity.

The judge disagreed. True enough, the *rebbe's* sin had been a grievous one. True enough, his wife had been left with a nervous tic for the rest of her days as a result of the outburst; still, he did not merit *Gehenna* (hell). Rather, the *rebbe's* soul was to be returned to earth in the very form with which he had insulted his wife, *id est*, a *kugel*, and was there to wander about until such time as the *rebbe*, in the form of a *kugel*, was able— *kugel*wise—to repair some breach of domestic harmony and thus counterbalance his own sin on the scales of judgment.

"And so," continued the *kugel*, "*ot bin ikh*, lady. Here I am. Your cries have reached the ear of heaven, and it's been decided that the nature of your problem makes your household particularly well suited to my mission."

"And some kind of help you're gonna be," said Mrs. Furmanovsky. "My husband'll come in, take one look at you, and gobble you up before you can say Rabbi Eliezer ben Horkanos, and I'll be back where I started from. Do me a favor and go somewhere else. Go to St. Petersburg and poison the czar for all I care, just leave me in peace."

"Look, lady, I didn't ask to come here, so let's just try to make the best of it. Remember, if I mess up here—straight to hell. And remember, lady, I was a *tzaddik*, I don't *know* anybody in hell." The *kugel* wept so piteously that Mrs. Furmanovsky finally gave in. What did she have to lose?

The *kugel* paced the floor for an hour or so, racking its brains to come up with a solution. Paced and racked, and racked and paced, until: "Hey, Mrs.! I got it. We'll scare your husband out of ever wanting *kugel* again for the rest of his life. We'll fix him so that the merest mention of the word will set him to trembling and begging for mercy. And I know just how to do it...."

Yoshke Furmanovsky found everything in order when he returned from the synagogue that night. The soup was on the table, and just as he was lifting the last mouthful to his lips, his wife came in with the *kugel*. Yoshke gazed at it affectionately, saliva dripping onto his beard as he prepared to consign it to his belly. He reached over, pulled the bowl toward him, and almost dropped dead of a heart attack when it told him to keep his hands to himself.

"I've had just about enough of you and your gluttony," barked the *kugel*. "Every Friday night, the same story. Wolf down the *kugel* so you can avoid your duty to your wife. Well, we *kugelen* are sick and tired of being made an occasion for sin by the likes of you, and we've decided to take matters into our own hands, so to speak. From this day forth, if you should so much as try to swallow a single morsel of any *kugel* whatsoever, that same morsel will tear your throat to a thousand pieces and scatter them to the four winds. Furthermore, if word should ever reach us that you have been ... remiss ... in your duties as a husband, a group of picked *kugelen* will see to it that you are deprived of your manhood. And remember, Yoshke, there are some things that grow, but don't grow back."

With that, the *kugel* leapt up, smacked him in the face, and strode over to the window. It sprouted wings and flew off, never to be seen again.

When Mrs. Furmanovsky came in with the chicken, she found her husband pale and trembling. So sickly was he feeling, he averred, that he had lost all his appetite for food. And for food alone. He led Mrs. F. from the kitchen, and they lived normally ever after.

Nu. How the *rebbe's* soul came to lodge in a *kugel*, which is not exactly an animate, organic unity, is a mystery that will never be solved. But that it did, and that in so doing saved the married life of Mr. and Mrs. Furmanovsky, this cannot be questioned. I have the story straight from Mrs. Furmanovsky herself, and I can see no reason to doubt it. For Mrs. Furmanovsky, the sainted Mrs. Furmanovsky, the Mrs. Furmanovsky who realized her destiny as woman through the agency of a bunch of crushed potatoes to which the proper heat was at long, long last applied—Mrs. Furmanovsky was my mother.

VISITOR: HENRY SAPOZNIK

Wex works in much the same way as *yeshiva* boys, when they're really deep into Mishna, Talmud, and Gemora—they cease to make distinctions among the languages. Michael was one of those excessively brilliant *yeshiva* boys, poking each other in the ribs and sharing a brilliant cynicism. His stories are filled with hilarious allusions to Yiddish culture, but unless you're cruising at a particular altitude, you're not going to get the references. I went to *yeshiva*, too. The only difference is, he remembered it all.

VISITOR: SYLVIA COLE
A COLD ASS

There is a story about the *shtetl* that I particularly like because I enjoy seeing women getting their own. I also like it because it suggests that women in Eastern Europe may not have been so happy to have been the workhorses, the breadwinners, as their husbands endlessly studied the Talmud. It's a story of two friends, two neighbors, who one night went to the *mikva* (ritual bath) together. It was a very, very cold, wintry night. They were on their way home and were just at the point where two paths diverged, one to Sorele's house and one to her friend's. And to the absolute astonishment of her friend, Sorele lifted up her skirts and sat down in the snow, squished her behind around in the snow. So the other one says, "Sorele, *vos tustu*, [what are you doing], for God's sake?"

Sorele looked up at the lighted room where she knew that her husband was still studying his Talmud, and with a jerk of her head toward the light, she said, "*Ikh zol im nokh aheymbrengen a varemenen tukhes oykh?*" ("I should bring home a warm ass to him yet!")

COREY FISCHER

It's a long way from the shtetlakh of Eastern Europe to the Lower East Side of New York; but it seems even farther—not only in distance, but in cultural space— between the East European shtetl and San Francisco, California. A Traveling Jewish Theatre spans that cultural divide with every performance. As one reviewer put it, in the work of A Traveling Jewish Theatre, "New York is inches away from Romania or Berlin, and the eighteenth century is happening now."

Corey Fischer founded A Traveling Jewish Theatre with Naomi Newman and Albert Greenberg in 1979. Some of Corey's inspiration came from Barbara Myer-hoff (see page 242), the anthropologist who at the time was studying and writing about the Israel Levin Senior Center on the boardwalk in Venice, California. He was taken with Barbara's focus on the hidden power of bubbe mayses and tales of the elderly. A few years before starting the company, he also performed in an experimental revival of Ansky's Dybbuk, the classic play that opened in Vilna in 1919.

Inspired by these experiences, Corey along with his partners concocted a shidakh (an arranged marriage) between the experimental theater of the 1960s and Jewish and Hasidic tales, crafting contemporary theater from ancient legacy. In a series of brilliant stripped-down dramas, with minimal sets, masks, and puppets, the small company explores Jewish culture, framing it always as a kind of quintessential, existential bubbe mayse. For Fischer, storytelling was a way of breaking down the "fourth wall" in theater and talking directly to the audience.

This story about the Jewish cemetery in Prague is based on Corey Fischer's experiences touring with A Traveling Jewish Theatre in Eastern Europe. It combines autobiography with one of the classic Eastern European tales, "The Golem." "The Golem" was originally a legend told about the Maharal, an acronym for the Hebrew words meaning "the Great Rabbi Yehuda Loew." He was a historical figure who lived in sixteenth-century Prague (The Golem was later a play by Yiddish poet and dramatist H. Leivick). Here, the story is revived in a wholly new setting.

"The Golem Haunts the Cemetery in Prague" is about classic Jewish tales being there when we need them, about the reinvention of Jewish tradition with the tales as a resource; it's about stories as a way of experiencing a lost world; and it's about an American Jew trying to come to terms with a past he can no longer touch or even imagine — except through stories.

VISITORS: A TRAVELING JEWISH THEATRE
THE BIRTH OF YIDDISH

A Traveling Jewish Theatre's play *The Last Yiddish Poet* begins with a mythic version of the birth of Yiddish:

Once there was a people who were scattered over the entire earth. Everything was taken from them. Their Queen wandered from land to land, disguised as a beggar. As she wandered and as she traveled, she saw that she would have to find a way for her people to remember themselves. So she gave them Yiddish—a new language, a golden language of the heart—disguised, like her, in rags.

The language was like a golden thread, pulled from the Queen's garment. It bound the people closer together. And they used it. They used it to mend and they used it to weave and they wove it into poems and songs and dreams and they made themselves a home in the language.

FROM A TRAVELING JEWISH THEATRE,
COMING FROM A GREAT DISTANCE

Stories move in circles, they don't move in straight lines. So it helps if you listen in circles because there are stories inside stories and stories between stories, and finding your way through them is as easy and as hard as finding your way home. And part of the finding is the getting lost, because when you're lost, you have to look around and listen.

STORIES ABOUT STORIES

THE GOLEM HAUNTS THE CEMETERY IN PRAGUE

In the fall of 1990, A Traveling Jewish Theatre went on tour in Eastern Europe, performing in Poland and Czechoslovakia. In Prague, we all began to feel that we were performing for ghosts as well as for the living. Aside from the memories of the Holocaust, it had something to do with the theater that we were playing in. It had very black, scarred walls that seemed almost to be breathing. There was a painfully narrow spiral staircase made of steel, which led up to the dressing room, on the street level. The theater itself was underground.

I felt pulled, as if through the earth, to other parts of the city. To the house where Kafka had lived, to the streets where Rilke must have walked. And to the Jewish quarter.

The Jewish quarter of Prague was about a thousand years old by the time it was destroyed by the Nazis. It was not the buildings that were destroyed. They're completely intact. It seems that Hitler planned to preserve the ghetto of Prague as a museum for an extinct race. The oldest existing synagogue in Europe is right there in the Jewish quarter of Prague. There are several other synagogues and houses of study. There's even a magnificent clock with Hebrew characters that runs counterclockwise, in the direction that Hebrew is read. But all the buildings are empty. They're uninhabited. Except for ghosts. And tourists. Prague is full of tourists now that the borders are open. They pour in, busload after busload—Germans, Americans—and the Jewish quarter is one of the main attractions.

In the center of the Jewish quarter is the cemetery.

Even though it was very warm that late autumn in Prague, inside the cemetery, it was cold and damp.

The cemetery was founded in 1493. For hundreds of years, the Jews were not allowed to bury their dead anywhere else. So you can imagine how crowded it is. In some places the graves are stacked twelve high. The gravestones are all leaning. They've been shaped by gravity and weather and time. As I walk among them, I feel a grief that is so huge, I can't see its shape. It's different from the grief I felt in the Jewish museum around the corner, looking at the pictures drawn by the children who died in the concentration camp at Theresienstadt. This grief has something to do with not knowing enough Hebrew to read the names on the stones, so I can't know whose lives these had been. It has to do with how familiar this place feels and, at the same time, how strange.

The gravestones are covered with pebbles and little scraps of paper. People place the pebbles to mark their visits. The scraps of paper are prayers, petitions that visitors leave, asking the dead to intercede in their lives. You can tell which gravestones belonged to famous, miracle-working rabbis. Those are the ones that are covered with pebbles and bristling with scraps of paper.

I notice that one of these gravestones has, next to it, a small plaque with Roman letters that I can read. They say, "Rabbi Yehuda Loew ben Bezalel." I feel a shock of excitement. I know this name. This is Rabbi Yehuda of Prague, known as the *Maharal*, the legendary creator of the Golem. The Golem is a kind of Frankenstein monster that Rabbi Yehuda created to protect the Jews of Prague. I've known this story all my life. I can't remember the first time I heard it.

In the story, the rabbi was so heartsick over the constant attacks against the Jews that he decided to use his magic, his knowledge of Cabala, to create a being that would defend the community. So he gathered great masses of clay and sculpted them into a human form. He inscribed on its forehead the Hebrew word for "truth": *emet*. But the clay remained clay until he wrote the secret, unpronounceable name of God on a scrap of parchment and placed it in the statue's mouth.

At that moment, the Golem began to breathe—imperceptibly at first, then gulping the air as something like blood began to flow in its veins. It soon started to move with footsteps that shook the ground.

In the days that followed, the Golem not only defended the community, it sought out and destroyed all the enemies of the Jews.

But the rabbi realized that the Golem was no longer under his control. It was acting, with a tremendous violence, on its own initiative. He feared that it could turn against its creator and become a threat to the Jews. He had to find a way to return the Golem to its original state of inert clay. He found the creature, spoke an incantation that immobilized it temporarily, climbed a ladder, reached up to its forehead, and erased the first letter of the word *emet*—"truth"—so it became the word *met*, which means "dead." The Golem was clay once again. But there was so much of it that it toppled over and crushed the rabbi to death.

I stand at Rabbi Yehuda's grave, lost somewhere between legend and history. I see a young woman. I think she's part of a busload of German tourists that just arrived at the cemetery. She's browsing through the scraps of paper, the prayers, on the rabbi's gravestone, picking them up, examining them.

Now, I'm not someone who speaks to strangers as a matter of course. Like many performers, I'm a shy person off stage. But I can't let her paw through the prayers. "Excuse me," I say, "I don't think those are meant to be—I mean, you're not supposed to touch— Could you put those down, please?"

But she doesn't hear me or she doesn't understand English, because she just keeps on browsing.

I try again. "I don't think those should be disturbed—" Everything I say feels tentative and overly polite. For a moment I want that blind, unreasoning, indisputable power of the Golem to speak through me. I want to scream at her in a voice that she will never forget:

Put that down!

Go away!

This is not your place!

But I don't do that.

Finally, after glancing at me from the corners of her eyes, she puts down the last scrap of paper and goes on her way. I want to follow her. I'm not angry anymore, but I sense that somewhere between us a language must exist in which I could say:

These are prayers.

They come from people's longing.

They're left here in trust.

This is holy ground.

Not because it's a cemetery,
But because it's almost all we have left here.

But my path is blocked. There's a very large Golem standing between us.

STORYTELLER: RABBI EDWARD SCHECTER
THE GOLEM OF REHOVOTH

The renowned scholar Gershom Scholem was invited to speak at the dedication of the first computer at the Weizman Institute in Rehovoth, Israel. He told his eminent audience the famous legend about the Jews of sixteenth-century Prague and their rabbi, Yehuda Loew.

When Rabbi Loew erased the word *Emet* from the forehead of the Golem, he told the audience, that was the first deprogramming in history. In honor of that deprogramming, Gershom Scholem named the computer of the Weizman Institute "the Golem of Rehovoth." The fact is that technology is neither God nor Golem. It is exactly what we choose it to be; we create it in our own image.

B.

THE *SHTETL* IN
FAMILY STORIES

R I T A F E C H E R

In a charming penthouse apartment on top of the landmark Hotel Chelsea, the chapters of Rita Fecher's life hang on the walls: the politically inspired paintings by her talented art students at Manhattan's Washington Irving High School; her own sexy, whimsical, and farcically humorous renderings of gender-bending actors in Charles Ludlam's Ridiculous Theatrical Company; her oversize silk-screened family portrait from a photograph taken in Zamosc, Poland, in the late twenties; a series of photographs of women mud wrestlers taken during her days as a Harley backseat motorcycle rider; and the poster from her film Flying Cut Sleeves about the street gang presidents in the South Bronx, where she taught twenty years ago. On one of the nights I visited, she stood in her balebatishe (well-stocked) kitchen, the embodiment of all these different selves, chopping an onion with a knife inherited from her father, who had used it in the kosher ritual slaughterhouse where he worked as a shokhet. "I like holding the things of another generation," she told me.

"When we were little," she goes on, "my father was a chicken shokhet, he slaughtered chickens, he was a ritual slaughterer. And on Saturdays, the chicken market opened the minute the Sabbath was over. He had to be there when the market opened, so if he waited to take the bus, he would have delayed the beginning of the ritual slaughter by an hour. And the boss was waiting. So he would have to walk an hour and a half on the Sabbath, so he would arrive at the slaughterhouse as soon as the Sabbath was over—when three stars appeared in the sky. Sometimes he would carry me with him on his shoulders.

"Friday nights, when other kids went out, we stayed in," she told me. "Friday night was the Sabbath, Shabbes. After dinner, we sat around the table telling family stories. That's where I learned about my family's history. That's where the culture was transmitted.

"*They spoke in Yiddish, I answered in English. I lived in two different worlds. I learned how to be American at school and in the movies. And I learned about being a Jew and a moral and socially responsible human being at home. You see, my parents were first generation.*

"*What are you?*" *she asked me.*

"*Third.*"

"*You're almost a goy, for God's sake, a WASP! We had to explain America to our parents. We went to school to learn about America. We'd come home and explain the school holiday: 'Hey, this is Thanksgiving and this is what it means—it's like our holiday of Sukkos, the harvest festival.' We helped our parents learn how to live in this country. We were like equal partners in parenting each other.*" On the lower East Side, there was even an old saying: "*In America, the children raise the parents.*"

THE DAY MY
GREAT-GRANDMOTHER DIED

My great-grandmother had eight children who survived. They had more, but she had six daughters and two sons who survived. One of her children, my paternal grandmother, Chayah Esther Goldfeder, was nine years old when she witnessed her mother's death. So, if my *grandmother* was born in 1864 (as it is written in Yad Vashem, the Holocaust Museum in Jerusalem, by a witness to her death at Majdanek concentration camp in Lublin, Poland, in 1942), we're talking around the year 1873. It's an incredible story that my father passed along to me.

My great-grandmother's husband—my great-grandfather Yitzchak Duvid—was a *shokhet*, the ritual animal slaughterer for the community in Zamosc, Poland, until the Belze *rebbe* arrived in town. You know, Hasidic Jews belonged to particular Hasidic dynasties. And when the Belzer *rebbe* came to Zamosc, he brought with him his followers, his Hasidim. And among his followers was his own *shokhet*. So he said to my great-grandfather, "Yitzchak Duvid, you've been a *shokhet* long enough." Now, he was only fifty-six years old. He figured he could work till he was seventy-five or eighty years old as a *shokhet*.

And my father said his grandfather died from *tsuris* (grief and troubles): "They took away from him his *parnasah*, livelihood." But the Belzer *rebbe* put his guy in—it was like belonging to a labor union! A rabbi arrives in town. He has his followers. They get the jobs. And people say, "Well, I'm eating from the *shkhita*, the slaughter, of the Belzer *rebbe*." "Oh, I don't eat from his slaughter, I eat from this rebbe's slaughter." So my great-grandfather lost his job because he had the wrong *rebbe*. He belonged to the wrong union.

But he still had these six little girls, two sons, and no income to support them. He no longer had work, so the girls baked bread and sold it from house to house. And my father talked about how poor they were. They ate noodles and water all week and couldn't even afford to buy a piece of a foot bone—that's like the cheapest part of the animal—to flavor the *lukshen*, the noodles. But for *Shabbes* they would buy a piece of the head, which was also a cheap part of the animal. And that would give the noodles and water a little taste.

They lived in one tiny little house in Zamosc, and when each daughter got married, they put up a curtain—that was the room that the young couple lived in, with two beds next to each other. And each daughter had her own pot in the kitchen to cook for her husband.

So when my grandmother Chayah Esther got married, she continued to live with all her sisters in the family house in New Zamosc. Her husband's business was in Old Zamosc. You see, there were two towns. There was Old Zamosc and New Zamosc, and New Zamosc was older than Old Zamosc. The original Old Zamosc was burned down. So they built New Zamosc, but that got old—it was a sort of reverse, that Old Zamosc was newer than New Zamosc.

The poor would come around every Monday and Thursday, the days the Torah was read in the synagogue, and my grandmother and her sisters would give them a groschen (a Polish coin). Once, one of the poor women was going over to Old Zamosc, the big city, a kilometer away. So my grandmother said to her, "Surele Yask, bring this pot of *varms* [noodles and beans and water] to my husband, Duvid Fecher [who had a bookstore in Old Zamosc]."

So Surele Yask took it, and she was starving, so she kept tasting it. When she arrived there, she put it down on the window and said, "Duvid

Fecher, your wife sent you this pot of *varms*." But when my grandmother's husband opened it up, there was nothing left—it was an empty pot. It's hard for us in the way we've been raised to comprehend that kind of poverty.

But I wanted to tell you about the day my great-grandmother died. Picture this scene: My great-grandmother is lying on the floor, and the entire burial society, the *Chevra Kaddisha*, is in the room. They've washed her body and they've dressed her in her linen shrouds. She's lying on a stretcher on the floor, which is still, in Israel, how they carry people to their graves. And she says to her husband, "Yitzchak Duvid, I'm going to die, and I know that the *mitzvas* [good deeds] that a woman does belong to the man of the house. But will you give me half of my own *mitzvas* for my *olam haba*, my afterlife?" She's not asking for half of the good deeds that he's done in life, just half of the good deeds that she did in her life of feeding the poor.

She said, "You know, you were a *shokhet*." A *shokhet* is customarily given a part of the animal that he slaughtered—to eat. So in the winter, when geese were slaughtered, he was given the feet. And he would take the feet home, and she cooked it in these huge pots, with potatoes and flour and water, and it was called a *grits*. And then the poor began to come around. Well, there were lots of poor and homeless around Zamosc at that time. On Mondays and Thursdays, the days the Torah was read, the poor went from house to house and would be given a slice of bread. They would save it in their sack tied around their waists, and then, on the day she made the *grits*, they could come to her house and dip the stale bread in the water that had the flavoring of the geese's feet and eat a hot meal in the cold frost.

So, lying in her burial shroud, in the presence of her eight children and the entire burial society, she continued, "Yitzchak Duvid, these people came in the snow and the cold and I cooked for them and I fed them, and I only want half of those *mitzvas*."

And he said, "No!" Can you imagine the terror in his heart that he might not have accumulated enough *mitzvas* to enter the afterlife without hers? He could not give the mother of his eight children half of the *mitzvas* that she herself had done. So my great-grandmother screams, closes her eyes, and dies. And her nine-year-old child, my grandmother Chaya Esther, told this story to her son, who was my father, Moshe Fecher. She said she hated her father till the day he died because he was such a hard man. But she was the storyteller in her family, and she passed the story down to my father, and he to me, and me to you.

STORYTELLER: RITA FECHER
THE GHOST

One night, in about 1910, my father, who was about thirteen years old, was studying in the synagogue by candlelight with a friend. Each month the rabbi held a Talmud competition, where each of the Yeshiva students was questioned in front of the elders of the city. My father and his friend were cramming. And there was almost no light, just the everlasting light, the *ner tamid*, in front of the ark at the end of the dark room, and their candle to read by. And they were exhausted from having studied all night. Suddenly, my father's friend looks up and he faints. My father doesn't know why he's fainted, but he *shleps* him home. It turns out the young man lost his voice for six months.

The next day, my grandmother, Chayah Esther, says to her son that Saul the miller came into the *shul* the night before. He was preparing to say the blessing for the new moon, and he came into the *shul* to wash his hands, and to *daven*, say the evening prayers. He'd been *shlepping* flour sacks all day and was covered with white flour, and he saw the two boys studying.

My father then put it together: His friend had seen a figure all in white and thought it was one of the ghosts of the dead who had come in to pray. He went into shock, and couldn't speak. It's the same story as the one about my great grandfather refusing to allow my great grandmother half of her mitzvahs for her *olam haba* (world to come) — people who are paralyzed by superstition.

PENINNAH SCHRAM

In 1969, four years before the storytelling revival officially got under way with the first National Storytelling Festival, the Jewish Braille Institute asked Peninnah to record some books for the blind, among them a collection of stories by Isaac Bashevis Singer, Zlateh the Goat. Soon after, she evolved a program for her students at Stern College for Women at Yeshiva University called "Kernels of a Pomegranate." (She took the title from Song of Songs Rabbah, which compares children in a row studying Torah to the kernels of a pomegranate.) She founded the Jewish Storytelling Center at the 92nd Street Y, and for twenty-five years she has taught workshops and classes, performed around the world, and helped give birth to a generation of Jewish storytellers.

But Peninnah was not the maggida of Jewish storytelling when she first began listening to tales as a young girl. "I sat on my father's lap and listened to his Elijah the Prophet stories, which I loved," she told me. "I didn't want to listen to my mother's stories because they were very didactic teaching tales. Even if I closed my ears and said, 'I don't want to hear that story, Ma, I've heard it a hundred times,' she'd say, 'You'll hear it one hundred and one times, my child.' So I really was blessed with two parents—Dora Manchester and Cantor Samuel E. Manchester—who were storytellers. They taught me through story. That was a very Jewish way.

"Mother told stories about history, about the pogroms. There was one story that was meant to teach me how to restrain my anger, because I lost my temper a lot. Often, my mother would launch into this story about the czar's army, and I would try to leave the room, and sometimes I did, but she kept telling it to me. One day when I was about to lose my temper at my daughter, suddenly that story came into my head. I'd forgotten it for years, and suddenly there it was when I needed it. . . ."

THE CZAR'S ARMY

This is a story about a young man, a young husband and his wife, and they had a little baby boy. In those years, the men went off to serve in the czar's army for twenty-five years. Often young men would puncture their ear or cut off a finger to stay out of the army. Some paid others to serve in their place or, like my father, bought someone else's papers and fled to America. Many who did go in did not survive, and if they did, they certainly forgot all about their Judaism.

This soldier was lucky. He survived. When he finally returned, years later, wearing his uniform, with his revolver in his holster, he went to the door of his house. He saw it was slightly ajar, and he heard the muffled sounds of his wife talking with a man. His anger and jealousy began to build.

He drew out his revolver and leaned against the door, listening. He could hear the voice clearly now. It was the deep, resonant voice of a man. His anger grew into a jealous rage. He threw open the door, crouched, cocked his gun, and aimed to kill.

Then suddenly he heard the man say, "Mama, Mama."

And the soldier understood that this man who was talking with his wife was his own son, now grown up. And he fell on his knees and pleaded for forgiveness of his wife and his son. And he thanked God that he had not pulled the trigger.

STORYTELLER: PENINNAH SCHRAM

I thought my mother made this story up. But later, I found a version of it in the thirteenth-century *Book of the Pious*, which is filled with didactic kinds of stories. My mother didn't read a book from the twelfth or thirteenth century, of course, but the story circulated through the centuries from Eastern Europe all the way to America, to Harlem, to Connecticut. I'm the third generation that I know of to tell the story. And I will take bets, my daughter will tell that story to her daughter someday—of course, Dorielle is only just two months old, so it's a little early. But maybe not.

STORYTELLER: RITA FECHER

Do you remember in the 1970s when Abbie Hoffman, the radical, was in hiding? There was a rally at the Felt Forum to bring Abbie out of hiding. They played a tape of his old Yiddish grandmother crying, "Abbie, come back. I won't die until you are free." That's when I realized that avoiding military service is part of our tradition! It's not something we dreamed up in America. We knew about it in Russia and Poland a long time ago.

THE CZARINA'S DRESS

Growing up, my mother had a beautiful brocade dress in her closet. It was a blue that is hard to describe, kind of a Mediterranean blue, with a paisley design made of golden threads. She would wear it only to go to *shul* on Rosh Hashanah or Yom Kippur or for some very special occasion. And it was always referred to as "the czarina's dress."

My mother's brother, his name is Irving Markman, was in the army, in the czar's army, the White Russian army. When he was a young man, their family lived in the area of Vitebsk Gabernia in a small little town called Lepl. During the time of the revolution, he was on a train. It was toward the end of the revolution when the czar and the czarina were being thrown out of their palace (of course, they were executed later on).

On this very train, the czar's family was trying to smuggle out many of their possessions. But the passengers discovered this booty and looted all of the czar's and czarina's clothing and belongings. Everybody was grabbing what they could. And my uncle grabbed this dress, this very full gown belonging to the czarina of Russia.

And he brought this dress home to his mother, and there were so many yards of material in that full gown that they had a seamstress make three dresses from that one dress. One of the dresses went to my grandmother, one to my aunt, and one to my mother. And the only one that still survives is the one my mother wears.

When I brought my mother's dress—actually the czarina's dress—to the Israel Museum Ethnography Archives in Jerusalem, and told them about it, they loved the story. But since they couldn't authenticate it, they didn't take the dress. However, I'm thinking that someday some textile curator should test the fabric and carbon date it. I believe without a shadow of a doubt that the material for the dress that my mother wore to *shul* once belonged to the czarina.

VISITOR: ALAN LUDWIG; ALEXANDRIA, VIRGINIA
THE POTS

I had a great-aunt who apparently was arrested by the czar and sentenced to Siberia for holding Jewish Sabbath services in her home. So she disguised herself as a man, so as not to be attacked, bundled up her belongings, which included incredibly heavy copper pots, on her back, and walked across Russia to the Turkish straits, to get a boat to come to this country. We have the pots, which is why the children have the story.

HENRY SAPOZNIK

If humor is a gauge of intelligence—and I would argue that it is—Henry Sapoznik is one of the geniuses of his generation. For proof, call him on the phone. With luck he won't be home, and you will be treated to an episode from "Answering Machine Theater." The most frequent message is a thirty-second "Answering Machine Polka," imploring callers not to "hang up with a big oy vey." But I also remember calling him when his machine played the "lovely strains" of Eastern European Gypsy music. Then Henry's voice came on the line, saying, "Gypsy music, ah, it reminds me . . . ah, it reminds me . . . it reminds me to remind you to leave a message."

In the late seventies and early eighties, Henry was among the first to begin interviewing older klezmer musicians and issuing their recordings. He is correctly regarded as one of the young granddaddies of the klezmer music revival (as well as a fine Bar Mitzvah musician, which he described as "the musical equivalent of Swedish meatballs"). Only a few older musicians were still alive to be interviewed because the communities where the music flourished were destroyed by the Holocaust. Henry wrote the story "Tants! Tants!" consolidating a number of their voices into one character, Mr. Abramovitch, who reminisces about music in the shtetlakh.

Mr. Abramovitch's voice includes that of klezmer drummer Joe Helfenbein. At one point, Henry was giving a talk about klezmer music at a senior center in the Bronx. He was telling the seniors about an old commercial recording of the Joseph Cherniavsky Hasidic American Jazz Band (also known as the Oriental Syncopators). Suddenly an elderly woman in the back of the room piped up, "Oh, yeah, my husband played with them."

Henry was taken aback. "My goodness," he said, "is he alive?"

"Oh, yeah, he's over there playing pinochle."

The voice in "Tants! Tants!" also includes a little of Dave Tarras, the clarinetist who won a National Heritage Award in 1982 and who almost died of a heart attack backstage a few minutes later. Henry remembered Tarras from the days when he sang in the Catskills with his father, a khazan (cantor) who worked at the hotels during Passover and the high holidays. "During the day Tarras would be in shul [synagogue] listening to my father. At night we'd be listening to him in the nightclub, and I'd be hating every minute of it. Round men playing square music. Their idea of contemporary music was a cha-cha."

TANTS! TANTS!
YIDDISH MUSIC IN THE OLD COUNTRY

I went to see Mr. Abramovitch.

"This is my uncle Beresh. He had the finest *kapelye*, the finest band, in eastern Poland."

The old man who holds up the fading photograph is about the same age as the man he points out in the picture. He has white hair and a wrinkled face, and his clear bright eyes reflect the razor-sharp memory he has of his lost youth as a professional *klezmer* (musician) in the old country.

"This band was hired by people who wanted the best music. My uncle's band traveled all over Poland before the First World War, and they played for Jews and *goyim* [non-Jews] alike."

The picture shows eight musicians, the older players with large, flowing white beards and *yarmulkes* seated in front of younger, starry-eyed boys. They all hold their instruments as if caught in midtune: two fiddles, a wooden flute, rotary trumpets, a clarinet, a drum, and a bowed double bass.

"Him," he says, pointing to the drummer, "he wasn't a Jew. I remember him from when I was a small boy: a big, healthy peasant who loved my uncle's fiddle playing. My uncle, you know, was a very religious man. Oh, yes. He would never play on *Shabbes*. Never. Once, the local *graf* [count] called my uncle to his estate. 'My dear Berko,' he said, 'you are the finest musician in the area, and I want you and your band to play for a ball I'm giving on Friday night. For your services I will pay you all one hundred rubles.' Well, at that time one hundred rubles was a lot of money, but Friday night was *Shabbes* and he wouldn't play, and he said so. 'If that's the case,' said the count, taking hold of a large sword, 'I will cut off your hands if you don't agree.' But my uncle Beresh didn't agree. . . . So you know what happened? The count changed the ball to Saturday night after the conclusion of *Shabbes*. I think maybe he secretly admired my uncle's piety.

"Uncle Beresh taught himself to play. He had a God-given ear. He used to mimic everyone and anything in those days. You know, being a Jewish musician was not a respected life. No. You should either be a rabbi or a merchant. If not that, then you had a poor life like a shoemaker or a tailor. A very hard life. But even still below that was a *klezmer*. Oy, was that a hard life. You were seldom home. I ask you, how many weddings do you think that there were in my little town every year? Maybe two or three? Maybe. You had to travel over terrible roads, scared for bandits and always dependent on the charity of strangers.

"But my uncle, whose parents—my grandparents—were not musical, wanted a fiddle. What a *mishegas!* His parents were absolutely against it. So what does he do? He trades his shoes to a Gypsy boy for a fiddle! His father nearly murdered him! But they didn't stop him. Go stop the sun from rising. He had his mind made up. After his Bar Mitzvah my grandfather took him to a fine violinist who lived in a nearby large town. He played for the man, who said that the boy had talent and should be enrolled in the music academy in St. Petersburg. But they didn't take in Jews. So he said that my grandfather should take his son to a priest and he should be converted. Anyway, he never went to the academy.

"My uncle was not at this time a terribly religious child, but one day that changed. As he was walking by the *shul*, he heard the *khazan* [cantor] practicing his songs. His singing was so beautiful that Uncle Beresh stopped still and listened. He then ran home to get his fiddle and stood out in the courtyard, playing along with the *khazan* and trying to match his singing tone. When he stopped playing, he found the courtyard full of people who were attracted by the beautiful music. My uncle went to *shul* every *Shabbes* after that.

"When I was about six years old, my mother, Uncle Beresh's sister, took me to his house, and she begged him, 'Please take the child into the *kapelye* [band] and teach him the fiddle.' By this time my uncle was pretty popular and he really didn't want to do it—but he was her brother, so he couldn't say no. So I came in on second fiddle with my young cousin Monyek.

"We played different kinds of music for the different people who lived around us. Jewish, *goyish*, *khasenes* [Jewish weddings], the light classics. Uncle Beresh wanted us to be able to play everything. But still my favorite music is Yiddish. We used to play all the big *khasenes* around, so I got plenty of experience for tunes. We'd play them all: the fast dances like the *bulgars* [figure dance in two-quarter time] and the *freylekhs* [lively dance], the slower *sherele* [scissors dance]. Where we came from we played what we called a *zhok* [a slow dance in three-eighths time]—you call it a Romanian hora. That was a slow circle dance in three-eighths that went BUM/bum BUM/bum BUM. We also called it a *krimer tants* [crooked dance]. But for *khasenes* we played special dances just for that occasion. Like the *broyges tants* [dance of anger and reconciliation] . . . you know what that is? The mothers of the bridal couple would act out an imaginary fight. . . . They'd dance around in a circle. . . . Then they'd make up. We'd play the tune slow in the fight part and fast at the end. It was supposed to guard them against fighting after the kids were married. Maybe somewhere it did. I don't know.

"And there were other dances. There was the *patsh tants* [handclapping dance], the *mitzva tants* [blessing dance], and the *kosher tants* [ritual purity dance]. But most of all I enjoyed when Uncle Beresh would play a *doina* [a Romanian folksong, usually in the form of a lament]. For this he was famous. The people would all become still when the band played a low, single drone note. Suddenly my uncle would step into the middle of the floor with his fiddle up under his chin and would start to play. Years later, when I got lots of experience playing with jazz musicians, I learned that improvisation was an important thing, but as a kid I always assumed that because Uncle Beresh never played these *doinas* the same way twice . . . who knew? They were beautiful. It was a free-metered rhapsody, his fingers flying over the fingerboard, making the instrument sing. Yes, sing! *Oy*, what a tone! When he'd get to a place where the chord would change, he'd play a few special notes and we'd know where to change. And when he stopped, oh, people would be crying, crying. . . .

"Around 1912 my uncle Beresh packed up and moved to America. He heard the streets were lined with gold and that everyone worked. Seventeen months later he was back. *Oy*, did he complain! 'All the Jews cut off their beards! They go to shows on *Shabbes!*' But most of all I think it was because nobody appreciated his small-town playing. In the old country he was a somebody; in America he was a *greener* [greenhorn]. He tried playing music, and when that didn't work he went into the needle trades. But he was so outraged at the greedy, bloodthirsty bosses that he left and came back. I remember like it was yesterday. When my family was making ready to go to America a few years later, I remember my uncle Beresh coming down to the station to see us off. With tears running down his face he holds my head and says to me, 'My dear child, whatever you do, don't sell your fiddle to the Satan of jazz.' "

"And did you sell your fiddle to the Satan of jazz?"

"No. I never sold it. But I did rent it occasionally."

STORYTELLER: HENRY SAPOZNIK
DISCOVERING KLEZMER

Sir William Hershel, the astronomer who discovered Pluto, did so by a series of mathematical computations that proved by the actions of the planets around it that there was another planet out there. And, of course, once he looked for it, he did, in fact, find it.

Well, in a way, that's how I discovered *klezmer*. I assumed that the fact that there was great traditional Irish music and great traditional Appalachian music, and great traditional Greek music meant that there was great Jewish music out there as well. I said, "Well, it must be out there somewhere."

At the time I realized this, I was studying Appalachian music in North Carolina. I went back to my family and said, "Oh, this will be great, I'll be able to do fieldwork and not have to leave my area code." My late grandfather, who was a very great fan of the YIVO Institute, sent me to the YIVO. And when I contacted the institute, my first call—the fates were with me—landed me with Barbara Kirshenblatt-Gimblett (see page 121), who was my guide. She took me into the institute and exposed me to all of these old Jewish records, cabinets full of Jewish seventy-eight records.

Suddenly I was transported to an old world. Because, unlike every other ethnic group that has engaged in their traditional music revival, we're the only ones who don't have an old country to go back to. What I found was that my old country was those old records.

MATILDA FRIEDMAN

In the early 1990s, Maury Leibowitz, a Jewish philanthropist who was inspired by Barbara Myerhoff's work on the importance of storytelling and reminiscence, initiated the Legacies contest, in which older Americans submitted short stories about their lives. Shirlee Kresh Hecker, whose story appears on page 177, submitted "Ike the Pike" and was selected as one of the prizewinners. Matilda Friedman won no prizes, but her story poignantly captures a turning point in her grandfather's life, a turning point that captures the transition between tradition and modernity in thousands of Jewish lives.

THINK FOR YOURSELF

This is a story my grandfather told me and one that I would like to pass on to my grandchildren. Grandfather Isaac said it was the beginning of how he learned to think for himself.

He lived, at the time of the story, in a thatched-roof house in a *shtetl* in Poland, with his parents and his aunt Fanny. They were poor, naturally, but they had food. For Isaac it was never enough. Growing rapidly from the time he was eleven years old, he was always hungry. During the week the food was very plain, but on Fridays his mother usually managed something extra. On this particular Friday she was preparing a *cholent* (a bean stew) with a good piece of meat. The aroma filled the house, making him restless. He couldn't concentrate on his studies, his chores. He was intoxicated by the cooking smells.

Walking around outside, tossing stones into a bucket, he heard his mother scream. He rushed into the house. His mother was ringing her hands, asking God to forgive her. Aunt Fanny looked stunned. She had been cooking rice and milk. Mother had accidentally taken the milk spoon to stir the *cholent*. Mixing dairy and meat is strictly forbidden according to the laws of *kashrut*.

Isaac was afraid his mother, a pious woman, would throw away the *cholent*. He begged her to sit and be patient. He would go to the rabbi and ask for his advice. Although not agile, he ran the two miles in record time and blurted out the story to the *rebbetzin* (the rabbi's wife). She listened respectfully but said he would have to ask the rabbi, as this was too important for her to handle.

It seemed forever until the rabbi arrived, buttoning his trousers. Isaac retold the story. The rabbi asked him such questions as "In what direction was the spoon facing? What time of day did it happen?" Questions that my grandfather, even at his young age of eleven, decided were foolish and irrelevant. Impatient as he was, he answered to the best of his ability.

Finally, the rabbi asked him how old he was. When he said he was eleven, the rabbi said he was too young, not yet a man, to deal with a matter of such importance. "Go home and tell your mother or father to see me about this," he told Isaac.

Isaac arrived home half-dead from exhaustion and anxiety. His mother asked him, "What did the rabbi say?"

He answered, "The rabbi said, 'Throw away the spoon and eat the stew.'"

He had decided, at that young age, that some rules were impractical and useless and that in this matter he would rely on himself to decide what was appropriate.

MARC KAMINSKY

"In old age," Marc Kaminsky writes, "my grandmother Esther Schwartzman set out on a round-trip to the Bessarabia, whose market days and holy days continued to form the rhythm of her weeks. Starting out early in the morning, she made lightning visits, surprise visits, to the undiminished shtetl that resided nowhere on earth, except in the psyches or souls of herself and a few other old people who journeyed there in memory." In the three years before she died, Marc recorded his grandmother's stories. It took many more years to find the appropriate language in which to tell them.

Marc's book of poetry, A Table with People, was inspired by his grandmother's shtetl tales, and his research on topics ranging from survivor stories to the history of the word "mensch" (the classic and in some ways untranslatable Yiddish term for "good person") are steeped in Yiddishkeit and Jewish socialist politics. A therapist and gerontologist, Marc extends the thinking of gerontologist Robert Butler, who coined the term "life review" in 1963 (suggesting, for the first time, that reminiscence is not, as one social worker put it, "the high road to senility," but instead a constructive and imaginative response to a phase of life). Marc is intrigued by what he calls the "uses of reminiscence," and as he reworks and reinterprets his grandmother's stories and reminiscences, he explores the meaning of memory. "I forget things now," he imagines his grandmother saying to him as he reworks her reminiscences into a piece called "Name Soup," after the way his grandmother cannot remember one child's name without first listing them all.

> I forget Russian, Hebrew, in Rumanian I forget almost everything. And I also forget now in two languages at the same time. Not only in English. Even in Yiddish the words don't come. Don't ask. . . .
>
> It's no use rushing or pushing the memories. They travel slow in an old brain. I call. No answer. So I tell myself, "Sha! Don't make trouble for yourself. Let it go. Give it more time. You're not a spring chicken."
>
> I wouldn't run for a bus anymore, and I can't run after a memory, either.

Fifteen years after his grandmother died, Marc is still running after the memories, trying to make sense of them, to find the story behind the story, and to find the most powerful way to express them.

STORIES ABOUT STORIES

MY GRANDMOTHER'S FAMILY TALES

Between 1976 and 1978 my grandmother Esther Schwartzman and I collaborated on "an oral history of *shtetl* life and emigration to America." Our work together is not yet finished.

It is almost twenty years since we began this—what? It is no longer "an oral history"—this unfinished story, and more than fifteen since she died. Its title and form have continued to change in the years that separate her death and my life.

When we started, I was satisfied to salvage passages. I excised redundancies; collected bits of scattered anecdotal and descriptive material into coherent narrative images; fussed with commas to find a way of precisely notating the cadence of her Yiddish-English, which I found so moving. I treated her utterance as if it were scripture and felt it would have been a sacrilege to tamper with it in any but a self-effacing, editorial way. I considered myself, in short, the embalmer of her living breath, entitled to inject nothing of my own but a fluid punctuation that would preserve the rhythm and hint at the *nigun* (melody) of her spoken speech. I wasn't conscious, of course, that I had assumed (in my pious literalness) the mortician's role. In my inexperience, I believed that it was possible to "finish" the stories of the people we love. The tape recorder and what could be made of its word-hoards were too puny a set of weapons with which to undo so potent an adversary: her death.

It took me many years to see that a new relation to this text, this task, was necessary—and legitimate. Our collaboration had to enter a new phase: it had to become, finally, a dialogue. I had to reenter her reminiscences, question them and relive them in the imagination, break open the shell with which she had covered her guilt, and allow her experience to speak freely, after her death, as it had not been able to speak during her lifetime.

For she had denied, in old age, the accomplishment of her life that— for both of us, equally—had value: in desperation, at the age of nineteen, she had broken out of the suffocating and symbiotic embrace of her parents' home and culture. Poor, anxious, timid, alone, having a small talent for freedom and less by way of resources, she got the one thing she had wagered everything on—a marriage founded upon love, upon the right of free election of her spouse. Not some secondhand, itinerant, elderly fish peddler—the only fate a dowryless oldest daughter could expect—but a man of her choice in the New World: for this she resisted her father for over a year; for this she gave up everything she knew. A marriage open to love was, for *shtetl* girls of her generation, as subversive an idea of freedom as the "career open to talents" was for the young men of the Enlightenment. For this idea she emigrated to America. Of her husband, Alter, and herself she proclaimed time and again, "We were the pioneers. We made the crossing out of the Old World." What she denied was the actual character and cost of the deed she proudly claimed.

The Holocaust turned mere rebellion into betrayal. Like I. B. Singer, she was aware of that astonishing nuance of feeling that is registered in saying that one would speak of these things although she or he has not had the "privilege" of enduring them personally. Suffering from survivor's guilt about the family members left in Europe and killed in Hitler's fire, my grandmother sought to undo her rebellion in early adulthood by emphasizing her lifelong adherence to tradition. This version of herself we took as gospel truth, loved, and, yes, venerated. It served to unify a strife-ridden family. In actual fact, my grandmother secularized everything she touched, all the rituals and customs of her Orthodox parents. Nevertheless, she was able to invest the materials of Orthodoxy—the brass candlesticks, the white tablecloth, the cup of wine—with profound emotional and cultural significance. Without registering or acknowledging the fact that she was embracing contradictions, she would light candles every Friday evening, then profane both the laws of the Sabbath and *kashrut* (Jewish dietary laws) together by lighting the stove to make a cup of tea into which she poured milk (this, after a meat meal).

To tell her life story, not as she reconstructed it as an old woman, but as she had lived it before her guilt bade her erase her rebellion against the *shtetl*—for this I needed a form that realized our collaboration in a profounder way than I had dreamed of—I needed to make Esther's silences speak: to register verbally, in her idiom and accent, what was communicated through gesture, intonation, and a highly inflected language of sighs and expressive sounds, including various kinds of silence—silences of celebratory fullness or guilt-laden grief. For her silences subtlely saturated a limited diction and syntax with a lexicon of sighs, involuntary and extravagantly long, mournful releases of burdened sound. Centuries of Jewish history shaped this nuanced semiology of resignation, endurance, stoicism, and suffering.

The drama of bridging the Old World and the New, of making for herself "a normal life" on a rope bridge she spun and suspended over an abyss of discontinuity, is the subject of the journey that takes place in memory and is told, in part, through silence. Esther returns to the past so that she may begin, once again, the journey of breaking away from the *shtetl*, of breaking, one by one, the traditions in which she was raised. She arrives, again, at the crisis of the story of the two Yom Kippurs. She tells of growing into a new sense of personhood and radiant purity when, at the age of thirteen, she fasted on Yom Kippur for the first time. But she also tells how she consented to go to a basement restaurant in the Bowery, at the insistence of Alter, her betrothed; there they ate a meal together on Yom Kippur. This violation of a sacred custom, a taboo, becomes, on his side, an act of seduction; on hers, a "sexual meal" in which she pledges herself to him and his way.

Without my discovery of the figure of the rebel, I would have gone on accepting the version of herself that she constructed after she married Alter: that she was merely carrying on the old ways, perhaps with a few minor adjustments, here and there. This project seeks to salvage, not the past, but the possibilities for a human future by rescuing the modern adventurer who looks out at us from the fading photographs of the green-horn factory girl.

VISITOR: ESTHER SCHWARTZMAN; BORN KOSTITCHAN, RUSSIA

GO TELL THESE THINGS HOW YOU GREW UP

The *Shabbes*, we couldn't hold on to *Shabbes* long enough. Like a procession for a bride, we used to go walking, a lot of the cousins, and my brothers and sisters, all the kids, we used to go walking through the town, this happened when the sun was going down. In the hot sun I feel like I'm in a trance, pulled along. The light along the main road was like a bridal train, and we followed, we escorted Her to the edge of the forest, where the week was beginning, in darkness.

To me this made such an impression, I can't forget it. So I used to tell *Zayde* [your grandfather], and *Zayde* used to say, "Go tell it to somebody! Go tell these things how you grew up!"

And it was really interesting what *Zayde* had to say about his past, and little things that I remember from my old country, from my family life my relatives, in my home. It really should be interesting to my children and grandchildren where they come from, the roots. Sometimes *Zayde* would remember something, he would say something in passing. But my kids didn't show interest that he should talk more about it.

This is my feeling, and he had a feeling like that. Why shouldn't my kids know where I come from and where *Zayde* comes from and the way we were raised and the customs there and that we also had these things with us and practiced them as much as we could in our life together?

THE IMMIGRANT

EXPERIENCE

Families often tell a migration saga as the first real narrative in the history of a family. As Moses struggled against the pharaoh and escaped across the Red Sea and into the desert, so family members escape from a home riddled with hardship and oppression, making their way across the ocean to establish themselves in a new home. It's just that, for the ordinary family, "the waves were not to part."

The year 1881 was a turning point in the history of the Jews. With the assassination of Czar Alexander II of Russia, an extended calm gave way within weeks to a wave of *pogroms*, or raids, that swept across Eastern Europe. In the years between the assassination and the 1924 restrictions on immigration in the United States, about one-third of East European Jews, almost two and one-half million, emigrated to the United States. This compares with the approximately 265,000 German Jews who immigrated between 1820 and 1880; about 200,000 Jews who came following the Holocaust, between 1945 and 1959; and the less than one-half million recent immigrants who arrived from Russia following the 1964–65 changes in U.S. immigration laws, glasnost, and the fall of communism (the current quota is 40,000 a year).

Jews have played a role in American history since twenty-three Spanish and Portuguese Jews from Brazil landed in the Dutch colony of New Amsterdam. But, inevitably, the large immigrant wave straddling the turn of the century defined the cultural forms and memories that characterized the Jewish American experience.

Jewish immigrant tales often have elements of high drama. In my family, the story is told of my uncles drawing straws to see who would be the one to shoot a dreaded officer of the czar and then flee to America. My uncle Sam drew the short straw.

My grandmother and her sister Rose came out of Russia as small children hidden beneath a pile of straw in an oxcart. And my grandfather's family fled into the snow when a *pogrom* swept through their village, leaving their father to guard their home. They slept in the barren woods for days, and when they returned, bed feathers floated in the air, and my great-grandfather hung from the ceiling on a noose. His housecat lay whining on the floor beneath the corpse. After three days the cat died, and the family began sending its members, two and three at a time, to America.

ROSLYN BRESNICK-PERRY

Roslyn Bresnick-Perry, a retired fashion designer and storyteller, spent several decades of her life running away from a small shtetl in Belarus; she's spent the past two trying to find it again. She was born in the town of Wysokie Litewskie, and came to America with her mother at the age of seven, when her father finally raised enough money to send for his family. She did all she could to rid herself of her Jewish accent, to separate herself from her parents' culture, to become "a real American girl."

But she remembered everything about her old town. Though Roz is dyslexic, she has a prodigious, photographic memory and a storyteller's gift of gab. In her fifties she entered college, earned both bachelor's and master's degrees, and immersed herself in Yiddish studies. Then she began telling stories in earnest. Weaving her memories into tales, Roz Perry shapes a distinctive vision of shtetl life in first-person tales, told through the eyes of a child, with the immediacy of yesterday.

The hero of many of the tales is Zisl, her cousin and playmate in Wysokie-Litewskie. She is the mischievous imp who brought out two strings to use as candles and told Raizele (Roz) that they were going to celebrate Hanukkah together in the barn; inadvertently they burned it down.

Once, when Raizele's mother left her with her aunt Faygl, she saw her aunt hugging and kissing her boyfriend, Srolke. She knew that this was strictly forboten for unmarried couples. She confided this secret to her cousin Zisl, who immediately suggested that Raizele blackmail them into giving the two of them a ride in Srolke's beautiful horse-drawn sleigh. Raizele did demand a ride in the sleigh in exchange for her silence. But when her mother returned home, Srolke and Faygl announced their engagement! The announcement stole some of her thunder, and she forgot all about the ride in the sleigh.

But one night just before their departure for America, her aunt and uncle appeared to take her for that promised ride. She recalls how the sleigh glided weightlessly over the snow, the tingling of the sleighbell, the round moon hanging in the dark blue sky—and her utter panic when she realized that they had forgotten to wake Zisl and take her along with them. She tried in vain to convince her aunt and uncle to return for Zisl. After all, Zisl had conceived the whole plan!

Raizele deeply regretted not returning for her dear friend and cousin, because Zisl was also left behind when they came to America. In the years that led up to the Second World War, her family knew that something awful was happening in their town, but her father could not raise the money to bring his brother's family and Zisl to America. As Raizele fell asleep in the sleigh that night, she remembers dreaming that they were riding to the moon, where Zisl was trapped in a round cage of ice with bars of icicles shutting her in. That dream still haunts Roslyn; her mischievous and ingenious pal—the subject of so many of her stories—was among the six million killed in the Holocaust. Roslyn became a storyteller in America, recalling her dear cousin in her tales.

STORYTELLER: ROSLYN BRESNICK-PERRY
GO FIGURE

A few years ago, I took my mother to a funeral of one of her friends from the old country. There, to my surprise and pleasure, we ran into a neighbor from our little *shtetl*. I told her that my days in our little town were the happiest times of my life. "That's funny," she answered. "You know, I only remember you crying. You cried all the time." Go figure.

LEAVING FOR AMERICA

My mother and I are leaving for America today. It's early in the morning. The sun has not quite risen. There's still dark spots in the shadows. There's a horse and wagon standing in front of my grandparents' house. My mother had decided to move into my grandparents' house two weeks before we were due to leave. We just lived two streets away, but she felt she wanted to be with them the very last days. She had a feeling she would never see them again. Right now it's still so early and yet everyone is up. The horse and wagon wait for my uncle and the porter, who are carrying out a large steamer trunk.

My mother was very hard put to decide what to take with her to America, so she decided to take her underwear, which she had embroidered, because she felt in America you couldn't get underwear like that. Or linens or a *perena*, which is a feather bed, or down pillows. She also took her copper pots and pans, her silver candlesticks, and two wooden rolling pins that she put on either side of the trunk. Now those rolling pins fell out every time the immigration inspectors opened our trunk to see what we were bringing into America. And every time they laughed and asked my mother if she intended using those rolling pins on my father. My mother didn't understand what they were saying or why they were laughing, but when it was explained to her, she didn't think it was so funny. "In America, women hit their husbands with rolling pins?" she asked.

Right now everything's resting very quietly in the trunk. I am running back and forth and back and forth, watching everything. I am so excited. And then I run out, and I see everyone in my family crying. My three aunts, Feygl, Liebe, and Shushka, are all holding each other, crying without restraint. My young uncle, Avrom-Leib, wipes his eyes and his nose every few minutes. My mother and my grandmother are locked in each other's arms. Their individual cries of pain mingle together into one anguished wail. My grandfather, he stands to one side, and his tears roll without a sound into his honey-colored, curly beard.

I love my grandfather. He is a tall, handsome man, who speaks very little and smiles even less. But whenever I am around, he has a twinkle in his eye and a smile on his lips. Seeing my whole world in tears propels me into hysterical sobbing. I cry the loudest—while just a few minutes ago I was running around so happy, so excited. My grandmother, hearing me cry, tears herself out of my mother's arms, runs into the house, and is back in what seems like a minute, carrying a large slice of rye bread heaped high with chopped liver. *Na, mamele,*" she says, *"na, es epes."* ("No, little one, eat a little something, you'll feel better.")

I take the chopped liver and I eat. And I cry, less hysterical. How hysterical can you be eating chopped liver?

My mother finally finds the courage to tear herself out of all these loving arms, and she's sitting on the wagon waiting for me. My grandfather picks me up, as if to hand me to her, and then suddenly stops, holding me in midair. And then he presses me very close to him and whispers into my ear: *"Un du, mayn eynikl. Du vest blaybn an emese Yiddishe tokhter?"* ("And you, my grandchild. Will you remain a true daughter of your people?")

"Avade, Zayde. Of course, Grandfather," I say.

And then I think what a silly question that is. But that question has stayed with me all of my life, and I'm sure it's because of that question that I tell these stories.

STORYTELLER: ROSLYN BRESNICK-PERRY

Once I've written down my stories, it's as if I can't feel their immediacy anymore. I lose the actual sense of memory. I used to be able to hear my grandfather whispering in my ear. I used to be able to feel what it was like to ride in the horse-drawn sleigh over the snow that one night—to sense the smoothness, to hear the bell, and to feel the warmth inside the covers. Now I can only remember the story I tell about them. It's as if I'm telling the stories at the cost of the memories.

A REAL AMERICAN GIRL

My mother and I arrived in America on one of the hottest days of the summer. The day was Friday, the date June 29, 1929, and the temperature was somewhere in the high nineties. It was a sad day for many Americans because on that day the stock market took its first major crash. It was the beginning of the Great Depression.

I was seven years old and very excited about being with my father, whom I hadn't seen since I was a baby. In fact, I was only six months old when he left for America.

For me, crossing the ocean was ten days of complete and total misery. I was seasick from beginning to end. And although everyone assured me that I was not going to die from this, I wasn't so sure. I was sick in spite of all the good advice and remedies offered by the people of our town for seasickness. "Take along some of our good, dark, pumpernickel bread," they told my mother, "and take a generous tin of shmaltz herring." The herring of shmaltz herring fame is a plain little fish that is preserved in salt and oil and eaten raw. It was the main food of poor Jewish people throughout Eastern Europe, good for any kind of occasion and especially when one needed a lift. I must tell you that it is still one of my favorite foods (although nowadays it is hard to find a store that still sells good shmaltz herring). But during the time I was on the ship I couldn't look another herring in the face. Every time I even saw my mother coming toward me with a piece, I started throwing up. If only I was back home playing with my cousin Zisl, I thought. I was sure this trip would never end.

Then one day just before lunch we heard someone shout, "There she is, *Gott tsu danken* [praise be to God], we have arrived in America." I forgot about being sick, I forgot about my nausea, and I joined my mother and all the other shouting, cheering immigrants on the deck of the ship. And there she really was, the much loved lady of the harbor—the Statue of Liberty. People laughed and cried, kissed and hugged each other, and I along with them.

Finally the boat docked and all the people ran off into the arms of welcoming relatives and friends, but not us. We couldn't find my father. We waited and waited until almost all the people were gone and still no Papa! "It's so hot!" I cried. "My stomach hurts me, I have to go to the toilet, I'm tired, I'm nauseous, and where's Papa!" And I started to cry.

My mother had no patience for me. She was not only worried about my father, but by now she was very upset about the time. "It's almost *Shabbes,*" said my mother. "Soon it will be time to *bensch likht* [light the Sabbath candles] and we will be lost somewhere here in wild America."

The immigration officials, seeing that no one had come to claim us, took us to another, smaller boat and told us we would have to wait for my father on Ellis Island. I started to hate America right then and there.

We had just about made ourselves comfortable in one of the wire-mesh cubicles when a short, fat, balding man with a red face, sweating profusely, rushed into the cubicle. On seeing us, he burst into tears. My mother seemed to know him, as she went into his outstretched arms. They both stood there weeping and holding each other. I, sitting on my stool, observed this scene with a feeling of shock and disappointment. Then my father turned toward me, looked at me lovingly with his red-rimmed eyes, which now matched his face, held out his arms to me, and said, "*Nu,* how do you like your papa?"

I stared at him in disbelief and burst into tears. "Are you sure he is my papa?" I asked my mother through my tears. "My papa is handsome, and this man doesn't look like him." At first my mother and father looked at me unbelievingly, then they both started laughing.

"How do you know I was handsome?" asked my father as he pulled me toward him.

"You don't look like the pictures you sent us," I answered while being hugged and kissed by this laughing, crying little man.

"No," said my father. "Well, I'll see if I can do something about looking better, more like those pictures, some other time."

You see, throughout his absence my father had written letters to us, sent us money and, what I liked best of all, pictures of himself.

The father of my pictures was always dressed in a double-breasted pin-striped suit with a fedora felt-brimmed hat, spats on his shoes. He held gloves in one hand and a cane in the other. To top it all off he wore dark horned-rimmed glasses. He looked tall and handsome, not at all like this father. I knew it was hot and he couldn't wear all those clothes, but at least, I thought resentfully, he could have put on his glasses.

My father, on the other hand, was also disappointed in me. He told me this years later. The photos my mother sent to him of me were that of a pretty blond curly-haired little girl with a winning smile. What he saw was a chubby seven-year-old with a boy's bob, which had been given me to make sure I would not be carrying the lice most every child had in their hair in the *shtetl*. My short hair was now straight, dirty blond, no curls, front teeth missing, and on my face a constant scowl.

All in all it was a poor beginning. My father, however, took it all in stride. He told us he had gotten lost on the way to the pier and had gone to some other place. "However," he said, "now we are going to go home in a taxi, no more getting lost."

In the taxicab on the way home, he held on to my mother with one hand, and with the other, he reached into his pocket and took out a long yellow object. He held it up and with a satisfied grin asked me if I knew what it was. I shook my head—no!

"No? It's a banana," he said merrily, only he said "panana." "In America," said my father, "all the children eat pananas. You want to try one now?" he asked with a definite plea in his voice. "It's very tasty."

I felt I had already done enough damage to our relationship, and I wanted to please him. After all, no matter how disappointed I was, it seemed he was my real father. I took the banana. "First," said my father, "you have to peel it, only halfway." He showed me how. "Then you hold it with the peel hanging down like an umbrella. Now," he said, "take a bite."

I took a bite. It had a strange texture that was unfamiliar to my pallet. It felt squashy, gooey, and cloyingly sweet; it reminded me of my nausea, and I start to gag. My mother put a handkerchief under my mouth and I threw up. My father took the half-peeled banana and didn't know what to do with it. So, he arranged the peel to cover the exposed half and sadly put it back into his pocket. Then, as if a brand-new thought entered his head, he lifted up his hand and, with a finger pointing up to heaven, said with eyes twinkling, "Someday soon, you'll be able to eat a whole panana and then you'll be a real American girl!"

Actually it's only recently that I've been able to eat one. You see, the doctor told me that at my age I need the potassium.

VISITOR: MARVIN SAKOLSKY; RIVERDALE, MARYLAND

LAND OF BANANAS

When he first came to America, my grandfather said he had heard of bananas, but he didn't quite know what they were. So his cousins, who had been here a while—a grand total of about three months— and who were wise to the ways of the world, decided to pull a joke on him. They gave him a banana, and speaking in Yiddish, they used the word that has kind of two meanings. It can either mean "Bend it" or "Do you like it?" And they set him up by asking him to bend it gently because he didn't want to break it. And it snapped. Then he realized that they were playing a joke on the green cousin from the old country. And he said, "Oh, this is a banana, everybody knows how you break them and you eat them." And then he proceeded to eat it—skin and all—saying every last bit was delicious. Thinking back on it—every time my granddad saw bananas he'd crack up.

MY FIRST THANKSGIVING

When I was a new third-grade student at Public School Number 66 in the Bronx, I found out that a play about the Pilgrims was going to be performed in the auditorium for Thanksgiving. All interested third-graders were invited to audition for the various parts. The play was to be *The Courtship of Miles Standish*, written by a very important writer whose name was Henry Wadsworth Longfellow. Our teacher told us the story.

I liked the play very much, so I asked my mother if she thought I could try out for a part. My mother said, "Absolutely, you are a born actress, and besides you have a lot of stage experience. You appeared in all the dramatic presentations of your nursery school in our *shtetl*."

Not being so sure of myself, I checked with my teacher, Mrs. Holstein, who looked a little doubtful but then said, "Why not." Something in my childish heart warned me against doing this, but the lure of the stage was too strong to resist, and I raised my hand in the auditorium when the teacher in charge, Miss Delaney, asked for volunteers. She asked each of us which part we wanted to play, and I asked for the part of Priscilla, the heroine. Miss Delaney hesitantly gave me the page with Priscilla's few precious lines. I took the text home and studied hard. My mother went over the lines with me word for word. When it came to my turn to recite I was one of the few children who did not have to look at my paper.

My heart beat fast as I went up on stage. With my head erect, my eyes sparkling, I was determined to be the best Priscilla in the entire third grade. John Alden had now asked his famous question. Will the fair Priscilla consider the request of the outstanding Captain Miles Standish and be his bride? I bowed my head coquettishly and answered in my most endearing manner: "Vhy daunt you spick for yorself, Jaun?"

All the teachers of the entire third grade started laughing. I stood there looking at them with astonishment. Why were they laughing? Had I done something wrong? I looked at my own teacher, Mrs. Holstein, and I could see the anger in her eyes. Miss Delaney tried not to smile as she spoke to me. "That was very good, Roslyn," she said. "You are certainly a fine actress, but I'm afraid this part is not for you. You see, the Pilgrim maid Priscilla would never have spoken with a Yiddish accent." So that was why everyone laughed. They were laughing at me, and the humiliation cut deeply into my childish soul. Tears came to my eyes, and I ran off the stage.

Mrs. Holstein managed to get me into the chorus of the play, and we sang "We gather together to ask the Lord's blessing." However, my heart was broken, even though Mrs. Holstein assured me that someday soon my accent would disappear and then I could become a great actress if that was what I wanted. I then and there resolved never to ask my mother to help me with anything that had to do with school, because I knew that her accent was much worse than mine. And I also resolved never to speak Yiddish again. I was going to become a real American girl.

Many long years would pass before I realized that my mother knew a great many things that were very important even though she spoke with a Yiddish accent. Many years would pass before I realized my loss in giving up Yiddish, my mother tongue. It has taken me a great deal of time and effort to reclaim it, but I did it—*Ikh hob dos geton!*

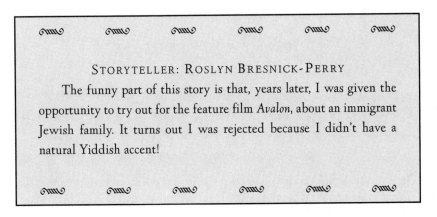

STORYTELLER: ROSLYN BRESNICK-PERRY

The funny part of this story is that, years later, I was given the opportunity to try out for the feature film *Avalon*, about an immigrant Jewish family. It turns out I was rejected because I didn't have a natural Yiddish accent!

BARBARA KIRSHENBLATT-GIMBLETT

Doris and Mayer Kirshenblatt, parents of the folklorist, Barbara Kirshenblatt-Gimblett, immigrated from Poland to Toronto in the 1930s. Because of the strict quotas on immigration to the United States, instituted in 1921 and 1924, Canada attracted increasing numbers of newcomers. In this period between the two world wars, Toronto was the home of a large immigrant community with a thriving Jewish social and cultural life. They were immigrants at a time when the city was filled with immigrants. They continued to speak Yiddish with friends and were part of a garrulous community that had a body of shared experiences—and later a body of stories—about their immigrant days. The stories range from getting off the boat, to experiences as greenhorns, to establishing businesses and then moving to the suburbs. In Canada, as in the United States, a body of immigrant lore grows out of periods of extensive immigration. This lore, Barbara notes, comes "not from the small, isolated, rural communities, but rather from the heart of the big cities, where the Jewish population is found in greatest concentration."

The Kirshenblatt family revels in their stories about their early immigrant days. According to Barbara, Martin Shanoff, Doris's brother and a master raconteur, calls these stories "classics," in contrast with his other stories, which are "oncers." Classics, he says, are funny even after you have heard them many times, whereas oncers are funny only once. Barbara's family stories illuminate the transitions that constitute the immigrant experience.

STORIES ABOUT STORIES:

FROM IMMIGRANT TO ETHNIC IN A FAMILY'S TALES

The minute a ship arrives at the port of entry, the new immigrant has experiences that figure in his narratives. Traditional humorous anecdotes and personal narratives describe the problems of making oneself understood in a strange land and foreign language. A misunderstanding between the immigration official and greenhorn provides the basis for many of these stories, the most common of which involves garbling the immigrant's name:

This one is sort of poking fun at immigrants, particularly Jews, arriving to the United States or to Canada, trying quickly to assimilate themselves, change their names, shorten them, shave off the beard, and just get to be like everybody else. Now in Jewish *shoyn fargesn* means "I just forgot."

So, one day Abie meets Hymie on the street. He says, "Hello, Hymie."

He says, "Please don't call me Hymie. My name isn't Hymie anymore. My name is Shawn Ferguson."

Abie says, "Good heavens. How did you ever arrive at a name of Shawn Ferguson? You have only been here three weeks."

"So I'll tell you how it happened. As you know, my name at home was Podalowski. They told me on the boat, with a name like that, when I come before the immigration inspector, I'll never make it. So they say, 'Remember, change your name right off the bat now. Don't tell them your name is Podalowski. Tell them your name is Smith. Just remember when they ask you your name, you say Smith and everything will be fine.'"

So I kept repeating to myself, "My name is Smith. My name is Smith. My name is Smith."

Finally the fatal moment arrives. I get to the immigration inspector. He says, "What's your name?"

And I say, "*Shoyn fargesn* [I already forgot]."

He says, "Oh yes, Shawn Ferguson."

Rose Shanoff swears that this is a true story and that a friend of hers knows the person to whom this happened. Certainly there were numerous cases of similar confusions and mishearings being permanently recorded in strange spellings and misshapen versions of immigrant names.

FIRST WEEKS AND THE EARLY YEARS

Although there is a tendency for many years of the period of initial contact to be telescoped into the first week, some personal narratives situate the action on the very first day. In the case of traditional jokes, setting the action on the first day of the immigrant's arrival in Canada serves to intensify his greenness, the one characteristic that is indispensable to this type of anecdote. Mayer describes his adventures the first morning in

Toronto. Imagining that the town was the same size as his hometown of Apt (Opatow, in Polish), he started chasing a fire engine, imagining he could run to the fire. "When I was a child," he said, "the fastest thing we knew was the speed of a horse."

In contrast with personal experience stories, the traditional anecdotes are considerably more elaborate and many of them revolve around the ultimate social embarrassment of not being able to find a toilet. The immigrant, being a foreigner, is an unsocialized being vis-à-vis his new cultural environment and is therefore symbolically a child. Since one of the first steps in socializing a child is toilet training, the crisis of not being able to find a toilet highlights the idea that the immigrant is an unsocialized being suffering the trauma of having to learn all over again how to behave in a culturally appropriate manner. Thus the protagonists in the jokes of the period of initial contact are generally bunglers rather than tricksters, bearing such names as Moyshe Pisher (Moses Pisser). The following legend, sworn by Jack Starkman and Doris Kirshenblatt to be a true story, corroborates:

Jack: That reminds me . . . I must tell you this story. This actually happened in the thirties. There was a slow immigration to Canada, and when the Jewish boys came, not being married at the time, there was a woman, they called her a Jewish mother. She lived on Cecil Street. Her name was Mrs. Mandel. So she used to boarder them all together . . . in the top room upstairs.

Anyway, there was this one immigrant, Hershl, who ate all day. There was nothing to eat, so he ate green apples and at night his stomach was driving him nuts. . . .

He started running and looking for the toilet. He couldn't find anything. So he had just finished reading the *Forverts* (a Yiddish daily newspaper). In those days, the *Forverts* used to appear in eight pages. So he did it in the *Forverts* and he shoved it underneath the bed. Sure enough, the next day, the same thing happened again. So he had an old *Tog*, also a Jewish paper. So he did it in the *Tog* and shoved it under the bed. Finally, Mrs. Mandel couldn't stand it anymore. She liked the boy, but she said she must approach him and tell him about it.

Doris: Because in the morning she came to clean up the room and she found the bundle.

Jack: So she says to him—diplomatically, you know, charitable, see—she says, "Hershl, tell me, everytink all right wit you?"
He says, "Yes, Mrs. Mandel, everytink is fine, jost fine."
She says, "Are you a little bit sick or sometink?"
He says, "No, I'm fine."
"How's your stomach?"
Then he realized that she probably found the big *metsiye* [bargain] underneath the bed. He says, "How did you know I had a loose stomach, Mrs. Mandel?"
So she says, "I read in the paper. I read in the *Forverts*.
So then . . . he realized she knew. He says, "Mrs. Mandel, if you won't show me tonight where the toilet is, tomorrow you'll read it in the *Daily Star*."

When Mayer and his brothers came to Canada, they worked at a variety of jobs for the first year or so, giving their earnings to their mother, who gave them a dollar each for spending money. In this way she saved about seven hundred dollars, which the family used to open up a paint store and go into business for themselves. This was the avenue that many people felt was most productive, because once in business for yourself you were more in control of the situation and you could really make some progress. It is therefore not surprising that many of the jokes about making a living in the immigrant phase focus upon being in business for oneself:

Martin Shanoff: When the Jewish people first came to Canada or to America, for that matter, everybody was looking for a job. A man who could sew carried a sewing machine on his back and would carry it up eight or ten or twelve flights of stairs into a loft and he would ask for a job, and if they didn't have a job, he'd walk down the ten or twelve flights of stairs with the little sewing machine on his back and he'd go to another place until he found a place where he could work for a day and they gave him a quarter for the day or whatever he could get. It was better than nothing. And he took it home, and this is the way he went and he lived.

In these days there were many sweatshops. People worked seven days a week, twelve, fifteen hours a day, and the pay was very poor. The working conditions were very, very bad. And if anybody was lucky enough to get into some business where they could make a half decent living, where they didn't have to feed a horse to support them and have a stall and buy oats—they were doing well.

Everybody was supporting everybody else. Everybody was trying to help everybody else. So somebody was lucky enough to get into a business where he was making a nice living, he always had fifty people who wanted to become partners with him because everybody wanted to be a partner in a good business—which reminds me of a story I once heard about a fellow who was in New York. He goes into the subway and there are millions of people going into the subway in New York. He suddenly finds he has to go to the washroom.

He says, "Reb Yid [Mister], I was in da vashroom and dey heven't got any toilet paper."

The man says to him, "I know. I sell it here."

He says, "How much is it?"

The man says, "Three pieces for ten cents."

What can he do? He buys. He goes. While he's in the washroom he starts to think. Millions of people use the subway every day in New York. Millions of people. Three pieces for ten cents. He walks out.

He says, "Tell me, Reb Yid. How many pieces on a roll?"

The man says, "Three hundred and sixty."

The little man starts figuring out. He says, "Three hundred and sixty pieces divided by three. That's a hundred and twenty times ten. That's twelve dollars. Tell me, Reb Yid," he says, "how much is a roll all together?"

The man says, "*Se kost zibetsn sent a rol.*" [It costs seventeen cents a roll.]

He says, "*Zibetsn a rol?* [Seventeen cents a roll?] You get twelve dollars. Millions of people in the subway every day. *Siz dokh take a gite biznes. Efsher zikht ir a partner?* [It is really a good business. Maybe you're looking for a partner?]"

The man looks at him and says, "*Git nor a kik. A gantsn tug geyen pishers. Kimt eyn kaker, vil er shoyn zayn a partner.*" [Just give a look. All day long pissers come and go. Comes one shitter, right away he wants to be a partner.]

Having finally found the washroom, the immigrant, who in previous anecdotes was relieving himself in milk bottles and on pieces of newspaper, now wants to go into the toilet paper business.

THE TRANSITIONAL PHASE

Many of the Toronto narrators learned English, established themselves in their own businesses, improved their financial state, bought their own home, moved from the old immigrant neighborhood in downtown Toronto to the new Jewish suburbs in the northern part of the city, sent their children to the university to become doctors, lawyers, pharmacists, and accountants, and sensed with each advance they made just what a long way they had come from their lives in Poland to the suburbs in Toronto. In many cases, this happened in the lifetime of the immigrant himself rather than in the second generation. Therefore, the sense of being between worlds, neither a greenhorn nor quite an acculturated ethnic, is felt very dramatically by those individuals who have made the longest journey.

With social mobility and the desire for the social acceptance of the dominant group came conflicts about changing values: the sense that no matter how many of the externals of the new social status one acquired, one would always be an immigrant. The following traditional anecdote was received with uproarious laughter:

Ralph Taube: In Kensington Place, there was a *shnayder* [tailor] who worked hard day and night. In fact, he used to work as a "cloak operator," and on the side he used to do a little sewing. And he used to have hanging in there dress "patterns" on the wall . . . and people used to come for him, to sew a little bit and do a little sewing on the side, *shnayder*. Anyway slowly but surely he worked himself up, and eventually he became rather wealthy. And he saved, he moved into a very wealthy district. And he started living high off the hog, and he bought shares and all kinds of stocks.

One day, he was sitting with his wife and he says, "You know, Rivke, such a long time we lived downtown. We were so poor. Let's make a party and we'll invite all the friends from downtown and we'll show them how rich people live."

So she says, "Fine. I think that's a great idea. It's a shame I didn't think from that," she says. "That's nice."

Anyway, they invite all the people from Kensington Place, the old immigrant neighborhood. And they have a maid, and they have the butlers and everything.

Suddenly she comes running. "Sruel!"

"What's the matter?"

"No toilet paper. A *khorbn* [catastrophe], no toilet paper."

So he says, "You know what? They're from Kensington you know. I've got the old paper dress patterns. I'll cut them up and they won't know the difference."

What could they do? They cut up the old patterns. They put them in the johns. They got about fifteen johns all over the house. They put the patterns in.

Next day, there's a lady meets another woman downtown.

She says, "Oy, Mrs. Green. It's a shame that you weren't there by the party."

"My Jack was by me sick and I couldn't go," she says. "So tell me, how was the party?"

"Oh, ah, ah, ah, such a party. Foooooooood, food everywhere. And they are modern."

She says, "What do you mean, 'modern'?"

She says, "Well, to give you an example. They're so modern that even the toilet paper tells you front and back."

VISITOR: MILDRED TRENCHER; NEW YORK CITY
IF I WERE RICH AS ROCKEFELLER

This takes place about 1910, when my family was living on the Lower East Side, going from gaslight to electricity. They had a toilet in the hall and it was shared with another family of eleven people plus our six. With so many people waiting on line, you had to go fast. Mother found it very difficult with four children, and she'd always say, "If I had a toilet in the house, I'd be as rich as Rockefeller."

So the day came when they moved to Hell's Kitchen, on West Fifty-second between Ninth and Tenth Avenues, and she got a toilet near the entrance. Thus, when you come in the apartment, she would tell you to look up and say, *"gib a kick"*—just look—and you'd look up and you'd see a brown box against the wall with a pull chain hanging on the side, and she'd pull the chain and you could hear the water trickling down. And then she would say, "Look, I'm as rich as Rockefeller." And then she'd show you the rest of the house.

Eventually the American dream took over, and we moved to Riverside Drive and we ended up with two toilets in the house. She was in her eighties then. And then she said, "It's got two toilets, but I can't go"—because she had stomach problems. You don't know whether to laugh or cry. You could do both.

The toilet theme returns, again in a highly appropriate manner. The status symbol in this culture is the number of washrooms one has, as the narrator indicates when he says, "They got about fifteen johns all over the house." Just as not being able to find a toilet was associated with being an unsocialized being in the immigrant jokes, so in the jokes about "making it," the more refined one is the greater the number of toilets one has. How appropriate of the transitional phase that people with fifteen toilets should be using old dress patterns for toilet paper and that greenhorns wanting to move up should be impressed with their modernity.

Physical acquisitions, elegant living quarters, lavish Bar Mitzvahs, and weddings are only part of what it takes to move up. The acquisition of social graces, especially a refined way of speaking, is also important, and people who are overzealous in this regard find themselves in ridiculous situations. Mayer's anecdote makes this explicit:

Mayer: Abie and Rosie lived in Toronto, for instance. This used to be the heart of the Jewish district on Spadina Avenue and College Street. They lived there for many years. They prospered. They made a bit of money. They said, "Well, it's time now we made a move."

And they moved. They moved up to Eglington and University or Avenue Road in Toronto.

One day they were just getting settled down. Abie said to Rosie, "Rosie, let's go for a walk."

Rosie said, "Abie, that won't do at all. On Spadina and College Street you can say, 'Let's go for a walk.' Up here, with better people, you say, 'Let's go for a stroll.' Understand? A stroll."

He said, "Fine. Let's go for a stroll."

They passed by a very fancy restaurant called the Noshery. Abie said, "Rosie, let's go in and have a bite to eat."

She said, "Abie, this is impossible, you can't speak like that. Down on Spadina Avenue, you can say, 'Let's go in and have a bite to eat.' Here you say, 'Let's have a snack.' Understand? A snack."

"All right, Rosie, let's go in and have a snack."

They had a snack and went home. Things were going pretty good. Belly's full. Abie got in the mood and he said, "Rosie, would you like to make a little whoopie?"

She said, "Abie, this is terrible. If the neighbors should hear that, that's it. They'll kick us out of here. Now up here you don't say, 'Let's make a little whoopie.' Up here you say, 'Let's have sexual intercourse.' Understand? Sex-u-al in-ter-course."

He said, "All right, let's have sexual intercourse."

Well, as the affair was progressing, Abie wanted to know how she was "coming along," you see. And she said, "Well, you know, you don't say it like that. Here you say, 'Are you sailing?' "

So he said, "Rosie, are you sailing?"

She said, "No, not yet."

He said, "Bon voyage. I'm sailing without you."

VISITOR: CHARLENE VICTOR; BROOKLYN, NEW YORK
FIFTY THOUSAND DOLLARS CASH

When I do a Yiddish accent or any kind of accent, I do it with the same kind of love and care that I would use to keep the character of a neighborhood or of a people alive—because there are certain things said in a Jewish way or an Italian way or in another way that can only be explained in that sort of a way. For instance, there was a Jewish man, and he loved this woman very much. One day he was talking to her and he said, "Etl, how I stand here, how you look on me, I vas voith fifty thousand dollars . . . cash." You can't describe it, isn't that marvelous?—fifty thousand dollars . . . cash.

The changes in lifestyle as symbolized by the new residence, refined ways of speaking, and lavish displays of wealth are part of a more general attempt to change one's identity, which is perhaps symbolized most dramatically by a change of name. Name-changing jokes set in the period of initial contact stress the "foreignness" of the name rather than its Jewishness. Thus Podolowski, a Slavic name, becomes Shawn Ferguson. The motivation for the change of name in the initial period is difficulty of pronunciation, strangeness, confusion because of language barriers, and other factors having to do with the immigrant as foreigner.

In contrast, the name-changing jokes of the transitional period are associated with attempts to conceal one's Jewishness. In one traditional anecdote, a man changed his name from Cohen to Jones to Smith so that when people asked him what his name was before he changed it to Smith, he could say Jones. The absurdity of efforts to conceal one's cultural identity through a change in name is especially apparent in the anecdote about Cohen and Rosenberg, who, when they went into business together, decided to call themselves Jones and Jones. A customer called and asked to speak to Mr. Jones. The secretary answered, "Which Jones do you want, Cohen or Rosenberg?" The impossibility of changing one's identity is stressed again and again.

THE ETHNIC PHASE

If the period of initial contact is marked by culture shock and the transitional period by the incomplete mastery of one's new role, then the ethnic phase is characterized by ambiguity. Language is no longer a problem. Name changing is a thing of the past. To a large extent, the culture of the dominant group has been acquired. Although there is a diminishing of cultural differences, the Jewish community retains a sense of itself as a distinct ethnic entity. But the fear of assimilation is strong. An example:

> **Ralph Taube:** Three mothers were standing on the street, talking. They were talking about their sons, naturally.
>
> "My son, the doctor, he makes a hundred thousand dollars a year, lives in a ranch house, beautiful. Three servants, beautiful!"
>
> So the second one says, "Oh, my son is an accountant and he makes seventy thousand dollars a year. He fixes the books. He's got a beautiful house."
>
> And they turn to the third one finally, who's been, you know, hesitant, "Nu what does your son do?"
>
> "My son, he doesn't earn so much like your sons. He's a rabbi."
>
> "Huh, what kind of job is that for a Jewish boy?"

The major theme in the anecdotes of the ethnic phase is that the price paid for acceptance is too high. Whereas in the earlier periods the immigrants were anxious about being Jewish at all, now the fear is that they are not Jewish enough. Whereas in the earlier periods we hated ourselves for being Jews, we now hate ourselves for not being Jews.

COMMENTATOR: STEVE ZEITLIN

A young man named Shlomo Shlomovitch decides to change his name to Shawn Smith. He becomes a successful broker on Wall Street. One day, he arranges to meet his father for lunch at the country club and reserves a table in the restaurant. Shawn arrives, and his father is five, ten, fifteen minutes late. Finally, half an hour goes by and Shawn starts to panic. He rushes into the lobby downstairs and finds his father wandering aimlessly about. "Dad," he says, "is anything wrong?"

"No," his father answers. "I was going to ask for your table, but I just couldn't remember your name."

RUTH RUBIN

For years, I had heard that my friend Ruth Rubin, an independent but preeminent Yiddish folksong scholar, by now in her late seventies, had written a wonderful story about her grandmother. Try as I might, I couldn't get Ruth to show me a copy of it. At that point in her life, she was less interested in being published than in rustling up some friends with whom to spend a few hours of sociability. She made a bargain with me: "You'll come, bring some people, and I'll read 'Grandma,'" as she called it, "out loud."

For Ruth, a gathering of scholars, a literary circle, is her idea of family. It is an image rooted in her days as a young Yiddish poet who had come to New York in the 1930s. So on March 21, 1994, I spread the word to some of my friends and colleagues that I would buy a Chinese dinner and we'd meet and listen to Ruth's "Grandma" story. On a rainy Monday evening we visited her in the one bedroom apartment on Gramercy Square and ordered up a Chinese dinner.

Somehow Chinese food seemed the perfect appetizer for her "Grandma" tale. During dinner, the jokes were about Chinese food. A history professor was giving a lecture on the history of civilization. When he finished, a student raised her hand

133

to ask, "You say that Chinese civilization is three thousand years old, and Jewish civilization is five thousand years old. So what did the Jews eat for the first two thousand years?"

When the laughter died down, we settled into Ruth's "Grandma" tale. As we listened to the story, all of us were deeply taken by this feminist family story, the powerful narrative of a woman establishing individuality apart from her family. What seems clear only in retrospect is how the tale is also about a woman rebelling against ageism, against the role cut out for older people in a society that sees them as useless appendages who have outlived their time.

GRANDMOTHER ELKE:
NEXT YEAR IN JERUSALEM

Word that Grandfather Nukhem-Ber, Grandmother Elke, and their two youngest, my mother's two youngest brothers, Mottele and Arele, were sailing across the ocean reached us in the New World. They were to arrive by transatlantic liner, and Uncles Samuel and Hyman were going to Halifax by train to meet them. The whole family was to gather for their arrival in Montreal, at Windsor Station on Peel Street.

I pressed against the ropes separating us from the tracks, upon which the boat train from Halifax was soon to arrive. I strained for the first glimpse of the new arrivals, whom I had never met. The train announcer's booming voice suddenly filled the station waiting room. There was a surge of people pushing up against the ropes. The train had arrived and was already expelling a stream of passengers, laden with bundles, baskets, odd packages, parcels.

I continued to gaze intensely through the iron-grilled gates, now flung wide open. I stared hard at each arrival, searching for the faces of Uncles Samuel and Hyman, who had gone to Halifax to meet the European branch of the family. And then my heart leaped as I saw them! Uncle Hyman, gesticulating excitedly, was walking beside a tall, stately old man with a flowing white beard, in a long black coat and high-top leather boots. His eyes were kind, his smile was gentle, and his teeth were as even as pearls. Yes, that was indeed Grandfather Nukhem-Ber, as Mother had described him to us!

Beside him, held under the arm by Uncle Samuel, and trying to keep up with them with short, hasty steps, was a sturdy little woman in a tight-fitting long jacket. Her cheeks were flushed, her dark brown eyes were flashing, her peruke-covered head was half-covered by a kerchief that had slipped on the back of her head. Grandmother Elke! There was no doubt about it! Walking beside her briskly were two young fellows, short in stature, in marine caps with patent-leather peaks and tight-fitting jackets. They were excitedly gesticulating and talking to the four adults with them, laughing, waving their hands, nodding their head, raising and shrugging their shoulders.

We jumped over the ropes and became one moving group of crying, laughing, weeping, shouting, greeting individuals. There was well-wishing and hugging, kissing and questioning. I clung to my grandfather Nukhem-Ber, hugging his arm, crying into his long coat, kissing his hand. He bent over me, took my face in his hands, and kissed me thoughtfully, tenderly, several times. I wept into his beard, which was soft and bushy and smelled of train smoke and the salt of the sea.

We had all entered the station waiting room by now, and Grandmother Elke, short though she was, was embracing her sons' new wives, her new daughters-in-law. She was lifting them up in her sturdy arms, exclaiming, as she was hugging and kissing them in greeting, "My precious treasures, my newfound joy!" Aunts Hannah and Dora were flushed with embarrassment and pleasure, laughing and giggling for all they were worth, as they found themselves pressed to the bosom of their sturdy little Bessarabian mother-in-law.

Then Grandmother Elke turned to me, her "oldest" grandchild at the time. "My eldest granddaughter, my jewel, Rivkele, my poor little orphan." She was breathless as she clasped me to her high, firm bosom and covered my face with hearty kisses. Her flushed cheeks were wet with tears. Wisps of her graying hair showed from under her dark brown peruke. Her kerchief had fallen from her head and was now around her neck. Everybody was weeping, openly and joyfully. Mother was crying softly as she clung to her father, Grandfather Nukhem-Ber.

Then there was a calm, and Grandmother Elke straightened her hair and tied her kerchief neatly under her chin. There was a brief consultation, and Mother and Aunt Bertha and some of the other women left for the flat, which Uncles Arthur and Hyman had rented and furnished a month ago for their parents and younger brothers. The women were to prepare the festival meal for the whole family on this wonderful day.

We climbed the flight of stairs to my grandparents' new home on St. Urbain Street, near Villeneuve, and entered upon a houseful of hustling, bustling friends and family members. Tables were set with long white tablecloths and good things to eat and wine to drink. Never had I seen the family so gay, so whole, so numerous! The air was filled with boisterous laughter and the merry recall of old occurrences—both joyous and somber, as many were inquiring about near and dear ones still in the old country.

The very next day, Grandfather Nukhem-Ber had a talk with Grandmother Elke's brother Hersh, who was a *shokhet*—a professional slaughterer of fowl and cattle. Right then and there, they decided that Grandfather would join the association of *shokhtim* and become the main provider of the family he was now responsible for—Grandmother Elke and the two youngest sons.

In the New World, the men were the main providers. This was made clear to Grandfather Nukhem-Ber, who in the old country was an active Hasid of the Sadigurer dynasty. He was always very helpful to Grandmother Elke, who was the main person in charge of their dry goods stall on the village square. Grandfather was also wonderful with the children —especially when they were ill. But now things were different.

It did not take long for Grandfather to assume the main role of breadwinner in the new land. He missed his old cronies, to be sure, and the merry visits to his favorite rabbi of Chortkev, "back home" in Bessarabia, where he reveled in his rabbi's words of wisdom, along with the beautiful sweet melodies, the *nigunim*. Still, Grandfather was content, putting down roots and establishing himself in this tremendous and beautiful land.

But what about Grandmother Elke?

Grandmother Elke was not happy in America. Her children did not need her support anymore. She felt useless and unnecessary. Two of her sons were now married to nice girls, but she had had no hand in their selection of their mates. She hardly knew the parents of these young women. She had never met her so-called in-laws. She barely understood her daughters-in-law and hardly knew anything of the life from which they sprang.

The city was large and bustling, and she walked the streets gingerly, cautiously at first. Not until she had located the little synagogue around the corner, and established herself with a kosher butcher and grocer, did she feel more at home. Most often, she trod the path to the synagogue. The once hurrying, bustling *eyshis khayil*, the bulwark of the home and her family, now walked slowly and thoughtfully every day to the little synagogue to pray for strength.

On the Singer sewing machine, which the family had bought for her when she arrived, she made her own clothes and did the mending for her three unmarried sons and sewed pretty curtains for the windows and spreads for the beds. Uncle Samuel was now courting a handsome young girl, but Grandmother was not too impressed with the girl's family. The girl herself was healthy and wholesome, but her family seemed crude and ignorant of Jewish learning and traditional ways. Indeed, the New World generally appeared that way to Grandmother.

"Hyman, my son," she would say to Uncle Hyman, "must you work on the holy Sabbath, too? Isn't the rest of the week enough for you?"

Grandmother even missed Grandfather's old Hasidic cronies, whom she had actually resented in the old country. Here, there was no longer the gathering in the house to sing and dance together, to revel in the songs of the Lord. Here there was no favorite *rebbe* to go to on foot those many long miles, just to listen to and bring back his sacred words of wisdom, and the sweet sad tunes and pensive melodies and gay dancing songs, which embraced and regaled the Hasidic followers of their favorite *rebbe*. Here, in the New World, the house was strangely silent and the daily domestic chores did not absorb her heart and her mind. Grandmother felt that her roots had been severed. The days hung suspended and heavily on her hands and heart. She sought about for an anchor in the new environment.

"Here in America," Uncle Hyman said to her, "the man of the house carries the main burden of supporting the family."

Said Uncle Sammy: "Here in America, woman's place is in the home."

Said Uncle Arthur: "You've worked hard enough all your life, Mother. Now you can spend the rest of it being a good wife, a loving mother, a doting grandmother."

Grandmother looked at them, bewildered. Her eyes took on a sadness, and a subtle smile played around her thin lips. Her children spoke of her life as if it were entering its closing chapter. But in her heart she felt that her life, now that her children did not need her anymore, would really just be beginning, though in another way. This realization, that life for her could begin anew, swept over her like a joyous wave. She prayed fervently and sat for hours poring over the Holy Writ, reading and rereading God's sacred texts.

Her restlessness could not be stilled, and one day she made an important decision. She decided to spend the rest of her remaining life, whatever the Lord would grant her, in Palestine, in the holy city of Jerusalem.

At last she could realize the dream of her lifetime! For had she not reiterated and repeated in her prayers "L'shana haba-a b'Yerushalayim"—the yearning that in the coming year, God willing, we might all be in Jerusalem? Well, now she would go there, where the Lord needed her most. Here, she would hardly be missed. Every one of her children and children's children were now living a life in which she had no part. In fact, she felt their resentment about her persistence to remain as she always was, independent and studious, pious and frugal. A long life of endless toil, it appeared to them, had deprived her of the attributes of a doting parent and grandparent.

Grandfather Nukhem-Ber had no such conflicts within himself. He readily assumed the responsibilities of being the breadwinner, as a *shokhet*, accompanying his brother-in-law Sherago to the slaughterhouses, to observe and learn and carry out his various duties in that capacity. Twice weekly they went together to the slaughter sheds. The rest of the week he assisted a fellow *shokhet* on Main Street, slaughtering fowl—chickens, hens, and roosters—for Jewish households. Grandfather still had contact with a few cronies—Hasidim and followers of their old rabbi in the old country. He also belonged to a loan and aide society and had already taken care of his own and Grandmother's burial needs, for when the time came.

He was liked and respected in the synagogue and on special occasions was invited to lead the congregation in song and prayer, for Grandfather had a sweet, clear tenor and sang most beautifully. "Your grandfather Nukhem-Ber sings with great *m'sikes* [unusual sweetness]," Mother would say to me with a benign expression on her face.

But Grandmother's mind was set, and one day she began preparing in earnest for her long journey to the holy land. And on that day, too, she said to Grandfather:

"Next year, God willing, I shall be going to Jerusalem."

Grandfather looked at her but said not a word.

"Will you come with me?" she asked.

Grandfather continued staring at her in silence. But then he said quietly: "But our children are here. Have we then waited all those years of separation and crossed the many seas and lands, just to leave them now?"

This time Grandmother was silent, deep in her innermost thoughts, and then she said, shaking her head with a sigh: "Yes. But I have lost my roots and I yearn to spend my remaining years in the land of our fathers. Here I am not needed anymore. There, I am needed."

Grandfather knit his brows and walked up and down, up and down the room, thinking deeply. Of the two, he was closer to the children. With Grandmother bearing the main burden in the old country, he was the one who had spent more time with the children as they were growing up— supervising their studies, nursing them through their illnesses. He had taught them the simple rules of sanitation, to wash their hands before their meals, to rinse their mouth with warm water in a salt solution when they rose in the morning. He had taught them to brush their hair and keep their clothes in order. He had guided them in the strict ways of the Lord's will.

She had been the one to rise early, rushing in and out of the house, maintaining order both at the stall and in the kitchen, where my mother, who was the oldest of all the children, had been instructed by her in the food preparations. It was she who had taught my mother in the handling of the supplies and the cooking and the managing of the occasional young peasant help, in this large household. It was she who had held the economic reins firmly in her steady hands. But the deepest affection from the children appeared to be rendered to him, to Grandfather. . . .

None of the children seemed to recall Grandmother's ever being in childbirth or ever being too tired to get up and rush to the stall at the marketplace. But they all warmed to their father's good-natured sweet smile, his long, bushy white beard, his straight, tall stature, and the little comb he kept in the upper-right-hand little pocket of his long black frock, the little comb that he would take out from time to time to comb his lovely bushy white beard. His trousers were tucked neatly into his high boots, which were always polished. Grandmother's garb was rarely noticed. She wore the garb of toil.

In their conversation that special day of Grandmother's decision they were both silent, for a very long time, with Grandmother waiting for Grandfather's final reply to her query of "Will you come with me?" And then he finally did, saying:

"I cannot leave the children. My life is with them."

Grandmother sat down and was very still, her hands in her lap, a sad haze covering her usually bright brown eyes. Finally she said: "Then I shall have to go without you."

Grandfather was taken aback. "You would leave me alone?"

"No. You will be here with all the children. It is I who will be alone."

Grandmother was then sixty years old. In the autumn of her life, she had chosen the path of her dream. And once her decision was finally made, she went about her preparations for her journey, methodically and calmly. She bought a new trunk, and each day, as she completed another garment of white, cotton or linen, she would place it into her "treasure chest." "Palestine is full of heat and light," she remarked. "One must wear lightweight garments of bright colors."

She skimped and saved every penny from the money her unmarried sons paid for their room and board. And when she had enough, she went downtown by herself one day and paid down the deposit on a one-way steamship ticket to Palestine. She never ceased her studies, or her prayers, and the closer the time for her departure approached, the higher her spirits rose.

One bitter, wintry day, she took sick with influenza. Uncle Arthur, already a practicing physician, became deeply disturbed at her serious illness. At her age, he feared the complications that could develop. In addition to that, two years earlier, his wife's entire family in Quebec City had been stricken by a flu epidemic. That was when Aunt Hannah, his wife, lost both her parents. Uncle Arthur feared to leave Grandmother alone in her flat all day, with Grandfather at work, with no one to tend to her. So he decided to bring her to his home, so that he could personally watch over her until the crisis was over.

Grandmother was carefully bundled up in many blankets and shawls and taken to Uncle Arthur's home on Esplanade Avenue, not far from where we lived at that time. For several weeks uncertainty hung in the air, until at last the crisis was over and she began to recuperate. Soon she was out of bed and tending and cooking for herself, for she had brought her kosher utensils with her when she was taken, bundled up, to Uncle Arthur's home. She continued to pray and read the Holy Writ, keeping to the little room they had given her, apart from the active household in Uncle Arthur's home.

One day Uncle Arthur said to Grandmother: "Mother, you are now fully recovered. Tomorrow, you can return safely home. Father hasn't had a decent meal since you took sick."

Grandmother was silent for a moment, and then she said: "I'm not going home."

Uncle Arthur opened his pale blue eyes wide, startled and confused. "Why not?" he asked, bewildered.

"Because from here, I am going on to Jerusalem."

Uncle Arthur was a gentle and controlled man, the wise and understanding member of the family, to whom each one had one time or another come for counsel and advice. As a child he was a sickly little boy, suffering from rickets. As an adult he was the peacemaker and counselor to the family, through the years of separation from the other half of the family, which had remained in Europe during World War I. Even after the family was united, he still retained that role. His gentle manner and sweet disposition, his sympathy and understanding, endeared him to both family and friends—and, in his medical profession, to his patients. Even Uncle Hyman, now already a successful owner of a growing business in ladies' wear, would seek him out for advice in his planning and procedures.

But now Grandmother's reply upset him considerably. He knew about her deep yearning for Jerusalem and had even talked with her about it on several occasions. But he had not ever believed that she would be resolving her dreams in this way. . . .

Uncle Arthur was a sympathetic and understanding man, but he also felt that Grandmother's place in her life, especially now, was in the New World, reunited with her children and grandchildren, with Grandfather, within the harmony of the whole family. He pleaded with her gently: "Mother, how can you go away and leave Father alone, at his age, at your age?"

"The Lord will provide for him, as he will for me," she replied softly.

"And are you content to leave us all here—and heaven only knows if we'll ever see each other again?" pleaded Uncle Arthur.

Grandmother heaved a deep sigh and then spoke slowly and at length.

"I am an old tree which has been uprooted. I don't even know whether I shall be able to find a place for myself—where I am going. Here, I feel like a stranger, even at moments from my own children, my husband, my flat. I think perhaps I was removed from all these considerations long ago, in the rush and bustle for a livelihood, where a livelihood was hard to achieve. Back home, there was so much to do—running the dry goods stall on the marketplace, supervising the household chores through my oldest and hardworking daughter, Rukhele. The time for the Lord, and the sweet moments of serenity in the glow of his teachings, kept me balanced and whole. Here, I feel alone and unknown even in the little synagogue around the corner. I go to Jerusalem to dedicate my last remaining years to God. I want to go there to live my remaining years, not to be buried there, although that, too, will come in its own time."

Grandmother was silent, flushed, almost trembling. Uncle Arthur sat there looking at her, sensing deep inside himself, very definitely, that yes, this little room in his house, was Grandmother's first stop on her long journey to Jerusalem.

The imminence and certainty of Grandmother's departure weighed on everyone's heart. Some wept. Some shouted in anger as the day drew nearer. And then, like a clap of thunder, it reverberated over the entire family. Those who had come to plead with her found a calm, gentle, even tender mother, comforting them and speaking softly to them—almost pleading herself to be forgiven for having created such a whirlpool of concern and emotions. It was almost as if she were realizing for the first time in her life how much she had meant to everyone—a realization that had no room to flourish in the midst of all the intensities of living, "back there" and, now, here.

Grandmother's voice was never raised in anger throughout this whole period of distress. But others did not restrain their sentiments. Said Aunt Hannah (Uncle Arthur's wife): "I'll be happy when she's gone!" Aunt Bertha, Grandmother's younger daughter, my mother's sister, was bitter. She felt that Grandfather was being abandoned. She wailed: "How could she do this to our father, at her age? At his age?" Her lips trembled and her eyes were full of tears. As for Hyman's young wife, Dora, who came from a wealthy family and was shy and withdrawn—all she could do was whisper to each one in turn: "What a disgrace! What shame!"

Grandmother quietly continued putting her house in order, filling the "icebox" with food for Grandfather and "the boys," gathering her things for the journey, and saying her prayers. Uncles Arthur and Hyman assisted her all the way. Hyman presented her with a wristwatch as a "going away" present. Arthur would stroke her hand gently between tasks.

By now it was evident to all that her departure was definitely going to take place and that all preparations would have to be completed by then. There were still two basic problems that needed to be finalized: What would happen to Grandfather alone, and how would Grandmother manage in faraway Jerusalem, economically?

Finally Grandfather tried once more. "Elke," he said, "I am still thinking—how will you manage so far away, alone? And I, I too—what will happen to me, all alone in this flat? Who will take care of me?"

Grandmother looked at him, and for a moment it seemed she had a twinkle in her eye. "I'll tell you, Nukhem-Ber," she said. "My aloneness is of no consequence here. As I said to you the other day, God will take care of me. As far as your aloneness is concerned, I have a good suggestion: I will give you a *get* [a divorce], so that you can remarry, and then you will have someone to take care of you." As Grandfather stared at her in astonishment, she rose from her chair and continued putting things together.

But the problem of economics was also not neglected. The two sons

Hyman and Samuel, who were already then on the road to financial security for themselves and their burgeoning families, sat down with a large sheet of white paper and wrote out a contract for themselves: to provide for their mother for the rest of her life. Every month her check would come, to keep her mind at rest and in peace, to fulfill her dream — in Jerusalem.

When Grandmother's departure was but a few days off, Uncles Arthur and Hyman consulted with Great-Uncle Hersh Shragge, grandmother's brother, the *shokhet*, and together with Grandfather Nukhem-Ber, they all went to the rabbi, where my grandparents were divorced according to the established laws of Israel and Moses.

And the day of Grandmother's departure was almost upon us when Uncle Arele, my youngest uncle, only three years my senior, and I hurried to say our good-byes to her. We sat together in the tiny room she had lived in those past months of deep family turmoil. When we arrived she was sitting quietly, poring over a book, dressed neatly and ready. She was flushed and seemed entirely content. Her straw trunk was packed and tied up. She was wearing her new wristwatch. Yes, she was ready.

I sat on the narrow cot, where she slept, looking at my beloved grandmother. We were bewildered at her behavior, but we were proud, too, and quite overwhelmed at her courage in undertaking that remarkable voyage across the seas, alone, just like our great rabbi Yehuda Halevi, who in the Middle Ages did likewise, leaving his home and family in Spain to undertake the dangerous journey to the ancient land of Judea. Oh dear, I thought, the great poet and medical doctor Judah Halevi was never heard from again! What will happen to our grandmother? I blurted out: "*Bubbe*, what will you do in Jerusalem? Where will you live? Don't forget us!"

Grandmother smiled. "I will do the work of the Lord, my child. There are many *yeshivas* [talmudic academies] and *batai midrashim* [houses of learning], and all those students need to be housed and clothed and fed, and I will help them."

I was deeply grieved that Grandfather was being left alone. I was also hurt to think that our home in the New World could not become hers as well. But her glowing spirit was contagious, and Uncle Arele and I jumped up and hugged and kissed her. A tear fell from her eyes and rolled down her cheeks. But her eyes were shrinking, and she said: "Ah, but you, my dear children, you understand me, don't you?"

One last hug and kiss and we hurried out, shouting: "Tomorrow we will come to help you with all the luggage to the station!"

That last night before Grandmother's departure, Mother and I were sitting in the kitchen as usual, talking about this and that, when Mother said, shaking her head and on the verge of tears: "Rivkele, daughter, what do you think, huh? A long and very full life—many children—many worries—endless work—oh dear . . ." She left her sentence hanging in the air.

I waited as we both sat deep in thought, and then I asked Mother: "Mama, were they happily married?"

"Happily married? People got married by arrangement. Young girls and boys were "married off" to each other by contract. There were *shadkhonim* [marriage brokers] and *badkhonim* [marriage entertainers], and all the trimmings of the engagement period and then the wedding itself and the feasting thereafter. Oh, my child, there was a great to-do, but, happy? That was always in God's hands. When young children were married off like that, there was much fumbling and strangeness, and sometimes this strangeness went right on through life. Because men and women were actually leading different lives. Although that didn't prevent them from raising big families!"

"But weren't Grandfather and Grandmother happy?" I persisted.

Mother wrinkled her brow. She was thinking hard, trying to recall the signs of happiness or unhappiness in that long and full life of twelve children birthed, with eight surviving, with a war and separation and an uprooting and a resettlement. "It's difficult for me to talk about it, and I don't even know how to talk to you about such matters," she said uneasily. "I suppose their marriage was like many others back home, although I do recall some of their bickering about little things, it seemed to me. I don't recall any serious quarrels. They must have hidden those from us children. But being the oldest, I saw more. I remember a 'silent' quarrel, which took place at the samovar. It was a winter evening. Grandmother, chilled to the bone, had hurried in from the stall at the marketplace. Still wearing her padded jacket—it had snowed that whole day—she was tired and cold, so she eagerly approached the steaming samovar for some hot tea.

"Grandfather had just prepared the samovar and happened to be standing there, drawing the first hot glass of tea. Preoccupied and intense, Grandmother hurried over to the samovar, glass in hand, noticed Grandfather there, and hastily and impatiently pushed his glass out of the way! Although not a word had been uttered by either one, I could feel their anger in the clink of the glasses. I knew they were quarreling!"

I simply was not able to understand all of this. "But they had so many children, so they must have loved each other!" I blurted out.

Mother tried to explain things to me. "Rivkele, I too wondered about such things, but not in the same way as you do, somehow. I remember a Saturday evening. Twilight had gently floated into the house, where Grandmother was sitting and chanting a soft prayer on the outgoing of the Sabbath. The house was in middarkness, and I had posed the same question to your grandmother then. It seemed to have slipped out quite accidentally.

"When Grandmother had finished her prayers, I must have blurted it out, just as you did to me just now. She was silent for a little while, and then she began softly, as if she didn't want to wake anyone up—she began to speak softly about her life.

"She looked at me tenderly and said, 'The term "love" was not part of our vernacular. Love was a term we knew well, but it was the term of King Solomon's Song of Songs, the *Shir Hashirim*. Such love was not known to us humans. Marriage didn't go with love. Marriage went with security and the birthing of children, and the proper raising of children and then marrying them off to do likewise. Children were "contracted"— engaged and then married. Their parents did the mating with each other! If the parents liked each other, they sat down and signed papers that legally bound the children together, first in an engagement and then in a marriage.

" 'And because of the awful poverty everywhere and general insecurity living under the czars in Russia, these young child couples at first lived with their parents. These terms went into the engagement contract, too. And before we grew up, we were already giving birth to children.

Yes, life was difficult, and we had babies like a cat has kittens—many babies, continuously! I had twelve.' " Your grandmother's voice then faded out, and we sat close together in the darkening room. And the Sabbath was gone and a difficult week was on its way, and it wasn't for a long time afterward that she ever spoke about these things again."

And suddenly the day of departure was upon us. The night before, I dreamed a strange dream—that a huge eagle had descended from the top of Mt. Royal and was hovering, his big wings, widely outspread, over all of us, but searching for Grandmother—to take her away on her long journey!

That day the entire family gathered at Windsor Station. Everyone was nervous, dazed; some wept. At the same station only five years earlier, we had all gathered to greet our grandparents and youngest uncles, who had survived World War I and who had come happily to be united with us in the New World. This time Grandfather was not among us. He simply could not bring himself to come. Till almost the last moment, the feeling that perhaps she would not leave hovered over us, like that eagle in my dream. But something strange was among us, too, for along with the kissing and soft weeping, the hugging and caressing, we, the younger children, were also starry-eyed and excited and proud of our grandmother. We felt that something unusual was happening there. Along with this, we were also frightened to let her go off alone, fearing for her precious life, wondering at the wisdom of her brave decision.

And then there at that scene, which remains clearly imprinted on my memory, Uncles Hyman and Samuel, the two who had signed a contract to support Grandmother to the end of her days in Jerusalem—they each took her under her arms, and when all the good-byes were over, they strutted with her through the gates, out to the platform, and got on the train with her. And thus they escorted her to Halifax and put her on the steamship, with their blessings, and ours—back home—and waved their good-byes for all of us!

Grandmother lived twelve years in Jerusalem and was buried on the Mount of Olives.

Grandmother Elke's departure left a gap within the entire family, a space that almost seemed awesome. A pall seemed to hover over each meeting of the different members as they discussed matters personal and otherwise. But the low cloud of wonderment as well as confusion—admiration as well as anger—seemed to sit over all stubbornly. Grandfather soon shook it off, however, and with the help of a fellow *shokhet*, was introduced to a "little old lady" who readily agreed to marry him and "take care of him."

But several questions remained: Did Elke arrive safely at her destination? Where did she settle in Jerusalem? Not knowing anyone there, how did she manage? The whole family waited impatiently for her first letter. The first news about her safe arrival came indirectly, following the bank notice that the first check sent to her had been properly cashed. They had an address but knew nothing about the people who were housing Grandmother. One little note did come through, in which Grandmother wrote briefly that she was well and content but saddened by the fact that Uncle Hyman, her successful son, worked on the Sabbath. "Hyman, her son," she wrote, "surely, of the seven days of the week, you could afford to render one of them to God."

One Friday evening, when her brother Hersh Shragge had gone to his synagogue—a small intimate *shilekhl* around the corner—he found the limited space packed with an intense gathering, eagerly awaiting to hear —at the end of the service—the words of a *sheliekh*—a "messenger"— from Jerusalem. Such "messengers" usually came from time to time to solicit funds for the Talmudic academies in the Holy Land.

When the visitor from far-off Jerusalem was finally invited to "say his piece," he made his appeal as usual. But when he seemed to be finished, he hesitated for a moment and then said: "Dear friends—in my home, living in one room, there resides an elderly woman. I know that her family comes from this city, because each month an envelope comes to her, which contains a remittance for funds. I have been able to help her establish her contact with my bank. She seems to be quite alone in Jerusalem. But she is not lonely or despondent. Each morning she rises, *gist op negl-vaser* [laves her fingertips], says her morning prayers, eats modestly, and then goes about her "business," which seems to be: attending services in the synagogue, visiting the local houses of learning—the Talmudic academies. I know that she assists them out of what she receives from her family here.

Her name is Elke. If anyone knows of her, come forward or let me know and I will be most happy to tell you more about her."

Great-Uncle Hersh Shragge stood up, flushed and agitated. "That's my sister!" he said. He went up to the *sheliekh*, shook his hand vigorously, and invited him to come home with him for the Sabbath meal.

At Great-Uncle's house, his whole family was assembled at the Friday night Sabbath meal—Great Aunt Sosy and their seven children. All eyes were turned on this special "messenger" from Jerusalem, eager to learn something about their great-aunt, their father's sister. "How does she live? What does her room look like?" they asked.

The *sheliekh* was smiling, happy that without too much effort, in this large Canadian city, he was fortunate to have so quickly made this contact. He began to describe Bubbe Elke's daily life. "Her life is very simple. And so is her room. She has a narrow bed, a small dresser, a small table, and two chairs. On her dresser a number of personal things are arrayed: a hairbrush, a comb, some hairpins, a change purse, a handkerchief, and an array of different-size snapshots—pictures of the family, her children and grandchildren." He was silent for a moment, then continued: "Every morning, upon rising, she greets each child and grandchild in her "photo gallery." 'Good morning, Rukhele; good morning, Alteri; good morning, Khayiml'—she goes on like that until she has mentioned each one."

What specially pleased the *sheliekh* was the fact that the very *yeshivas* —the Talmudic academies—that he represented included one or two that Grandmother Elke was personally interested in and was helping out with funds she was receiving from her caring family so far away.

Grandmother Elke had left Canada in 1928. According to the *sheliekh*, she had never been ill, was completely content and died peacefully in her sleep in 1940. Very few were the letters she had written to her family in Canada. And no one had managed to make the trip to Palestine in the twelve years that she lived there.

After the Six Day War, I visited Israel. Cousin Norman, Uncle Arthur's son, who had settled in Israel some years ago, met me at the airport. His first words as he hugged and kissed me were: "Tomorrow, we go visit Grandmother Elke."

The next day, we went to the Mount of Olives (*Har ha-Zeytim*), the prestigious graveyard on the slope overlooking the Wailing Wall, the remaining wall of the Temple. Norman located her plot easily, although he told me how difficult it was for him to finally do so after the Six Day War, since there had been vandalism and the tombstone had been dragged off somewhere else.

We stood there, communing with the stone, the carvings on it, the words etched in, and the breeze that was hovering over us as he touched the lettering tenderly: "Elke, daughter of Yitskhok and Sheyndl, of Khotin." Two Hebrew words puzzled me: *Kaniti b'khayay.* Unfamiliar with their meaning, I asked Norman to translate them for me. "It says," he told me, "I took care of things in my lifetime."

VISITOR: TOM MILLER; NEW YORK CITY

A similar story is told in my family. My grandmother got married at fifteen, and she was married for seventy years. Finally, she came over to her husband one day and said, "I want a divorce."

He said to her, "But you've been married to me for seventy years."

She answered, "Enough is enough. You can cook your own chickens."

STORYTELLER: RUTH RUBIN

In 1967, just a few days after the Six Day War broke out, I gave a performance of Yiddish folksongs at the World's Fair, and also at Maimonides Hospital in Montreal. My whole family came to the hospital performance, many of whom I had never seen before. And when I was through with my work and was coming down from the platform, there was an old crone there, walking with a cane.

And I noticed near her, my aunt Bertha, my mother's younger sister, who was blushing up to the roots of her hair. You see, she had always been angry with Grandma for having gone away, never forgave her. So I said, "Bertha, what are you getting so pink about? Who is this old lady?"

"That's Grandpa's second wife," she said, pushing her away as she said it. Oh my. Then I went over to her and shook her hand; she must have been in her nineties by then.

It would be easy to condemn Elke for leaving her husband to go settle in Israel. Although I'm not sure she did the right thing, I do think it's important to see her perspective. You have to understand the deep yearning of Diaspora Jews to return to Israel ever since the exile. It's not just an individual wish, but a collective longing, expressed daily in our prayers. When she had the opportunity to live in Israel before she died, it was apparently too hard to pass up.

The lore of many Jewish families is deeply connected to Israel. I remember my mother telling me about the establishment of the state of Israel in 1948. That happened by a vote of the UN. She and her family were all glued to the radio as each member country cast its vote. Once the vote was in, my grandfather called up all of the Jewish intellectuals and Zionists to invite them to come over and drink a *l'chaim*. My mother and her brother got to stay up late with all the grown-ups, because her father wanted them to understand that they were participating in a great moment of Jewish history. She had a sip of schnapps, which she didn't like, and my grandfather ended up leading a chorus of "Hatikvah."

After my mother graduated from college she decided to go teach high school in Israel for a year. On the boat to Israel, the Israeli officers told her, "You can't arrive in Israel with the name of Shayna —that's a *galusdikeh* name [a name of the Diaspora]. You have to have a modern Israeli name." Since "Shayna" means "pretty" in Yiddish, they gave her the name Navah, which means "pretty" in Hebrew. She first met my father in Israel, so everyone who knew her before she met my father calls her Shayna and everyone who met her afterward, including my father, calls her Navah.

ROSA KUINOVA

Born in 1952 in St. Petersburg, Rosa Kuinova immigrated to the United States from Russia in 1981. Her great-grandmother's sisters and brothers left for America around 1905. Her great-grandmother stayed behind because she had two hemophiliac sons who would never have been accepted by U.S. immigration officials.

"Since the Communist regime took over," she told me, "it was a very big secret that we had relatives in America. It could harm the family. Our relatives wrote us until 1952, the year I was born, but by then it was Stalin's time and extremely dangerous for the family even to receive letters. My family moved to another apartment, and letters kept coming to the old address. Neighbors would bring letters to my parents and my grandmother, but they would refuse to accept them, and say it was a mistake. They even took the pictures and old letters to a friend of my great-grandmother's, who, I believe, hid them under the floor. She died unexpectedly, and by the time my parents arrived in her apartment, strangers were already there. They couldn't get them back, so the pictures and letters and addresses of the family may still be under that floor."

The experiences of the recent Russian immigrants leaving both prior to and following glasnost are very different from those of immigrants who left at the turn of the century. Rosa's immigration stories are filled with twisted intrigue and tales of the KGB.

THE REFUSENIK

When I was growing up I didn't even know I was Jewish. Everybody I knew was Russian. When I was eight years old, a little girl called me *zhidovka*, which is a derogatory word for a Jew; it's like calling someone a "kike" in English. I didn't know what it meant, but I realized that it was worse than calling me "stupid." So I beat her up. I was always fighting. I was famous for fighting.

So the teacher put me in front of the class and started screaming at me for beating up this little girl. "Why did you beat her up?" she yelled.

I said, "She called me a *zhidovka*."

Suddenly the teacher looked confused and, instead of punishing me, just sent me back to my seat, and that was the end of it. But I knew something was up.

The school also had a big book that was arranged according to classes. Each teacher had a separate page, and that was where the grades were recorded. One day, I snuck into the classroom and looked through it to find my grade. Each teacher had a separate page, and next to our names there was a nationality listed. As I read down the list it said Russian, Russian, Russian, but against my name was written Jewish. I brushed it off as a mistake, but I started to suspect.

Sometimes as a girl, I would visit the very beautiful Russian Orthodox churches near my house to listen to the music. Many of the churches were turned into factories or swimming pools, but some remained. Although they were actually illegal, elderly people would continue to go, because they wouldn't be punished for it. The Russian Orthodox churches are like a museum, gorgeous, with precious icons—and the voices of the choirs are very, very beautiful. There are no chairs. Everyone stands or kneels, and they burn myrtle. I bought a cross for myself there, and my grandmother found it under my pillow. She started yelling at me, "You of all people!" She still didn't tell me I was Jewish.

When I was older and knew that I was Jewish, there was a tiny, frail, elderly woman who lived on the second floor of our apartment building. Once I was picking up my mail, and she said to me, "I'm so afraid."

"What are you afraid of?" I asked.

"There's a man who lives across the hall, and he's a Jew."

"So?"

She said, "Don't you know, the Jews put the blood of Christian babies in their matzoh?"

This tiny lady couldn't tell that I was also Jewish. And I said to her, "If I were you, I would run away very quickly."

And she said, "Why?"

I said, "I'm Jewish, too, and I prefer the blood of elderly ladies."

She got so scared, you wouldn't believe it. I swear to God that's true. I didn't think anything of it. She was honestly scared. Poor woman, these were the beliefs she grew up with.

But I didn't leave Russia because I was Jewish. I had political reasons.

My first husband turned me in to the KGB because I had some illegal literature against the Communist regime. Anyone who had a brain in Russia was in trouble. I petitioned to leave, and I became known as a *refusenik*. It took me three years to finally get out.

It's a very long story, but let me tell you just one episode. At the time, the only way to leave Russia was to get an invitation from a relative in Israel. I had a friend who managed to leave Russia for Israel in 1972 or 1973. But when I wanted to leave, there was a regulation that only three phone calls were allowed each day from anywhere in St. Petersburg— population about six million—to Israel. One call was allowed from the local post office, the other from the main post office, and one from a home phone.

From home, I called day after day. One minute before nine, it's too early, one minute later it's busy, and then it's too late. So I went to the post office at six P.M. one night and I stood at the window the whole night, until nine A.M. in the morning so I would be there for this one phone call.

When I finally got through to my friend in Israel, it turned out that he was out of town. I had to speak to his wife. My heart sank. I didn't even know in what language to talk with her, but I made myself understood, and she had heard about us and sent me an invitation in her name. I claimed to the authorities that the young woman was actually my grandmother's sister and that the name was different because it was her maiden name—I was lying through my teeth, but I believed it myself. Actually, my grandmother didn't have a sister, but I swear I could have passed a lie detector test, I believed it so strongly.

Then I set about to prove this whole story. I went to Ukraine, to the small village where my family was from, and I asked for a copy of a birth certificate for my grandmother's sister. They told me that when the Germans invaded Russia during World War II, all the documents were burned. So I asked for and they gave me a document that the birth certificate for my grandmother's sister was destroyed in a fire. At the same time, I asked them to give me the birth certificate of my grandmother. And they gave me a paper saying that it didn't exist.

Then I came back to the visas bureau in St. Petersburg (which was a bureau of the KGB), and I handed them the document saying the birth certificate for my grandmother's sister had been burned. And they said, "This is no good."

I said, "It's not my fault the Germans burned it."

They said, "It's not our fault, either."

I said, "What? You don't believe that my grandmother's sister exists?"

And they said, "No."

And I said, "What about my grandmother, does she exist?"

And they: "What are you talking about? Of course she exists, we've talked with her on the phone."

So I gave them the second paper, which said my grandmother's birth certificate didn't exist. I said, "According to this, my grandmother's papers don't exist, either. So, do you believe my grandmother doesn't exist?"

And remember, they don't talk to you, they yell at you. It sounds funny now, but it was a very deadly game. They can do anything to you. At any moment they can put you in jail or in a mental institution. But in that way, over a long period of time, hundreds of letters, a little flattery, I wore them down, and in 1981, along with my younger sister, my mother, and my grandmother, we set out for Israel. When we reached Vienna, we visited the American consulate, where we were granted political asylum to come to America, where we were planning to come all along. It took four years in the United States before we finally tracked down my great-grandmother's sister and her family, who came to America at the turn of the century. In our first visit with my cousin, he showed us a photograph. It was a picture of my grandmother holding my mother as a little girl. We then pulled out a copy of the same picture.

S E C T I O N   F O U R

THE LOWER EAST
SIDE AND BEYOND

When waves of Eastern European Jewish immigrants began to flow into the Lower East Side in the 1880s, solid blocks of newly developed tenements awaited them in a neighborhood that was soon to be more densely populated than Calcutta. By 1890 the neighborhood had more than five hundred persons per acre, more than seven hundred by the century's turn. With no toilets, baths, or running water, the tenements consisted of the infamous "railroad flats," their rooms lined up with only the front and back receiving direct sunlight. The 1905 census showed that a group of six tenement houses on Cherry Street, for instance, housed about 675 people, living with an average of almost 6 people in each three- or four-room apartment. The streets were unpaved, sanitation was abysmal, and working conditions were appalling and unsafe. Into this *goldeneh medina* (golden land) the Jewish immigrants straggled.

"Could this have been a truly happy time?" writer Harry Golden wonders about the nostalgic glow that settles over the Lower East Side immigrant neighborhood. "Have some of us overromanticized the ghetto of New York's Lower East Side? The garbage littered the streets. The tenements could not be heated in the winter and were brutal in the summer. The poverty was all-encompassing. Peddlers with a houseful of children checked their pushcarts at ten o'clock at night, went home, and put the day's earnings on the table—all two dollars and seventy cents of it in coins—and the peddler and his wife laughed and told jokes to celebrate this good fortune. My mother walked from Eldridge and Rivington Streets to the market under the Williamsburg Bridge, a distance of one mile each way; she made the trip twice a week because butter was one penny cheaper there—one penny cheaper. But our life was measured in those pennies. . . ."

In addition to the immigrant neighborhoods of New York, I have selected four other settings that are particularly rich in Jewish stories: the American South, the Catskills, the Yiddish theater, and Jewish summer camps. I have chosen them not because they were more significant than other locales, but because they provided especially fertile soil for folklore and stories.

The American South is home to a diverse community of Jews. As Howard Simons suggests, "Charleston's Jewish community, for example, is rooted in its pre-Revolutionary Portuguese and Spanish heritage, old and very proud. So, too, is Richmond's German Jewish community, tightly connected through marriage. . . . New Orleans's Jewish community appears to be more genteel, largely German Jewish, very insular." In the South, Jews share a love of storytelling and oral tradition with southerners of Irish, English, Scottish, and African backgrounds. For this book, I have chosen the memories of a lawyer and politician from a small town in South Carolina to suggest a bit of the flavor of at least one Southern locale.

At the turn of the century, when the *shtetls* of Eastern Europe were pouring into the Lower East Side, when the sweatshops were at their most intolerable, the Jewish Agricultural Society began to finance Jewish settlers in Sullivan County with the hope that they would become truck or dairy farmers; when the crops didn't grow so well, many turned to the resort business. From this grew the *kokhaleyn*, or bungalow colonies (the term is Yiddish for "cook yourself" as guests did their own cooking), as well as the larger Catskills resorts, Grossinger's, the Concord, the Nevele, and many others that were already in their heyday by the 1930s. Jews, like most people, are at their most revealing when they take themselves least seriously, and vacations were rife with humor and self-expression.

The Yiddish theater is often traced back to a performance of a musical composed by Abraham Goldfaden in 1876 in a wine cellar in Jassy, Romania. The first Yiddish stage production in New York took place only a few years later, on August 12, 1882, on East Fourth Street between Second and Third Avenues. Itinerant and oppressed everywhere they traveled, the Yiddish actors and playwrights straggled into New York, and by the turn of the century Yiddish theater was thriving in a number of playhouses on the Lower East Side. This distinctive theater tradition generated its own folklore. Some of it revolved around its stars—Jacob P. Adler, David Kessler, Molly Picon, Boris Thomashefsky—but much of it was rooted in the raucousness of the theater and the intense involvement of the audience in its melodramas.

The Yiddish theater purveyed the notion that "life on stage should be grander than on the street." "Applause," notes Irving Howe, "could be secured by ranting from the stage, 'A Yid bin ikh, un a Yid vel ikh blaybn.'" ("A Jew I am, and a Jew I will remain.") Howe compares Yiddish theater to Italian opera. "For what counted in Yiddish theater, as it counted in Italian opera, was the sheer display of virtuosity, a talent driving past its material in order to declare itself all the more vigorously. Hit the high C no matter what happens to the plot of the opera, do the bang-up scene where father banishes errant son no matter what happens to the story of the play.... What counted was the virtuosity with which archetypal characters were rendered: Jacob Adler as the towering, heartbroken father; Bertha Kalish as the steely Jewish heroine; Ludwig Satz as the clown; Aaron Lebedeff as the high-spirited rascal; Maurice Schwartz—well, as Maurice Schwartz." Charlene Victor, a Catskills performer and longtime director of the Brooklyn Council on the Arts, captures the melodramatic spirit in one apocryphal line heard from the balcony: "Die louder, Thomashefsky!"

The Yiddish theater stories are followed by tales from Jewish summer camps. Hundreds of Jewish camps sprang up in the United States between the 1920s and the 1950s, ushering in a heyday of Jewish camping. They included Boiberik, a coed camp where children lived in a Yiddish-speaking secular environment and learned the values of Yiddishkeit; Massad, a Hebrew-speaking Zionist camp; and Habonim, which took Zionism even further and related all physical activity to khalusiut, building the land of Israel; Camp Ramah for Conservative campers; and Kinderland for the progressives. Each provided a "very intensive Jewish education without the campers realizing it." As curator Jenna Joselit states in the catalog to a recent exhibit on Jewish summer camps, they "produced several generations of young American Jews knowledgeable about and confident in their Jewish identity, whether as cultural Jews, observant Jews, secular Jews, Yiddishists, or Zionists."

In the same way that the camp names were silk-screened onto T-shirts, the memories of Camp Ramah, Boiberik, Dalmaqua, Modin, and Shangri-la are emblazoned on the memories of the grown campers. As Alan Feinberg states: "Camp Hatikvah has been the primary influence in my life. I came of age spiritually, athletically, socially, sexually, and religiously at camp. Every pleasant memory I have of my 'under twenty' years is associated with this camp. I'm thirty-seven years old and every June I still daydream of going to camp."

A.
TENEMENT LIFE

SAM LEVENSON

On Sam Levenson's fifth birthday, his father put a hand on his shoulder and said, "Remember, my son, if you ever need a helping hand, you'll find one at the end of your arm." His mother, too, passed along her share of proverbs: "A penny is a lot of money if you haven't got a cent."

"I lived in a folk civilization, a folk culture," Sam Levenson said in an oral history interview conducted by the American Jewish Committee in 1976. "I've always liked that image, and when anybody lists me as a comic or comedian, I kind of cringe. That's not my style. I have deep roots in the folk. For twenty-five years I have saved little statements and words and proverbs and sayings—the wit and wisdom of the ordinary guy. My next book I'm going to call Anonymous by Sam Levenson. I find that anonymous voice on little temple bulletins when they've got an inch to fill—now that's a voice. I've cultivated a folklorist's mind."

Born in 1911, Sam Levenson became famous as the Spanish teacher from Abraham Lincoln High and Samuel Tilden High who succeeded as a stand-up comedian. He graduated from teacher to dinner speaker and television talk show guest. For a while he even hosted his own show. He died in 1980, but in his writings, Levenson compiled the largest number of jokes and one-liners ever assembled to explain how family love and good immigrant values can overcome poverty and adversity:

At our house, "The line is busy" meant that Mama was hanging out the wash. On Monday at dawn you were wakened by the twittering of hysterical sparrows trying to reply to the squealing of the clothesline pulleys. By noon all the women had hung their laundry. All light was shut out of the yard by the hundreds of garments crisscrossing each other to form an impenetrable forest of wet wash. . . .

Clothing was always en route from one kid to another. . . . Ma hated *holes the way nature abhors a vacuum. A rip was followed immediately by a patch. The colors of her patches were brilliant, and no two were alike. When brother Bill bent over, he looked like a stained-glass window.*

In the process of philosophizing, Sam Levenson also told some good stories and chronicled the ethos of the Lower East Side in memory.

VISITOR: ABE LASS
THE MUSICAL DOG

Abe Lass was the principal at Samuel Tilden High, where Sam Levenson taught Spanish. He tells of this wonderful exchange:

"We had a dog in our family, and my brother took violin lessons, and there's nothing more painful, incidentally, than the sound of a young, beginning violinist—it's excruciating. Whenever my brother started practicing, wherever the dog was, he would come out, set himself right at my brother's feet, and begin howling. In our own primitive way, we thought we had a musical dog. I mean, how else do you interpret it? We didn't know, as we found out much later, that what was happening was that the dog was responding to these higher vibrations, which are physically painful. We thought he was accompanying my brother.

"Many years later, when I got to know Sam Levenson, we were both reminiscing about our youth and boyhood, and we got off on music lessons. And I told him this story about my dog and my brother. And he, as you know, was a violinist, too—he took lessons. 'You know,' he said, 'I had just more or less the same experience. One Sunday morning I was practicing, and my dog was at my feet, howling his poor little heart out. My father was in a room off the practicing room, trying to read the *Forverts*, and the combination of the screeching of the violin and the howling of the dog, well, my father couldn't take it anymore. And he walked out and, 'For God's sake, Sam,' he says, 'please, play something the dog doesn't know!'"

THE TAX MAN IN
THE TAILOR SHOP

My first encounter with the Internal Revenue Service (at that time called the Bureau of Internal Revenue) occurred long before I became one of their clients. I was in college at the time.

A man from the government came to Papa's tailor shop to investigate him. Washington could not believe that a man with so many kids could live on so little. We knew that Papa had not evaded the income tax; he and the income had evaded each other. He was the head of a nonprofit organization.

I saw poor Papa's face go white. I understood. He had never lost his fear of "government," even the U.S. government, which in his mind still represented Them, not Us. His memory went back to when government meant czarist officers, Cossacks, and *pogroms*. Papers and investigations meant trouble. This man in his dark blue suit (Papa could recognize government cloth) carrying papers was enough to make Papa quiver. But I was not afraid, not me. This was my government.

The government man politely inquired whether he could ask a few questions. Seeing Papa in his skullcap, he turned to me and asked: "Does your father speak English?" I answered simply that I had better act as an interpreter. Papa knew enough English to get along, but he had no intention of getting along with this man. There was no point in explaining Papa's ethnic resistance to giving up his ways for "their" ways. Let *them* learn Yiddish! How could anybody live in this country so many years and not know Yiddish!

There was a secondary anger in Papa that was directed not against "them" as government, but against "them" as the entire industrial civilization. Papa had been trained from the age of six to be a master craftsman in the old guild system. By the time he got to America he was a superb artist with a needle; but what was needed here was not men who could turn out the work good, but fast. "They" had destroyed his pride in his workmanship. To Papa this was an attack on his person.

So the day that man came to Papa's shop I knew right away the government was in trouble. In the old country Papa had no alternative but to answer questions. In America he could refuse.

The government opened its case with, "How much does your father earn a week?"

I knew the answer, if not the exact words. Papa never even told Mama. He was going to tell this stranger? Why does he have to know how this poor Jew is doing? What business is it of *his?* I translated the question into Yiddish and got an answer in Yiddish, which I retranslated into English for the government.

"My father says that his worst enemies should earn what he earns."

The investigator studied his standard answer sheets but obviously found nothing remotely resembling "Enemies, worst."

He tried again.

"Ask your father how much rent he pays."

I went through the process of translation again, with this result: "My father says the landlord should have so many boils on his neck as how much rent he pays."

I could see the beads of sweat collecting on the government's forehead. He stepped outside, studied the store window, checked the number on the door, obviously wondering whether he was in the right place. He didn't even look at his answer sheets again.

"Just one more question, son. Ask your father who owned this store before him."

"Papa, the man wants to know who owned this store before you."

"Tell him some other poor *shnook* with a house full of loafers."

By the time I turned around to deliver the translation the G-man was heading for the door, mumbling in what sounded like Yiddish. He didn't look sane to me, but Papa never looked better. He was beaming. He had defended the Bill of Rights.

"It's a good country," Papa said in perfect English.

VISITOR: MAURICE SAMUEL

A PHILOSOPHY OF *SHMATTES*

Maurice Samuel's Uncle Berel ran a small cleaners on the Lower East Side:

Uncle Berel feels himself to be a sort of economic barometer or, rather, a recorder of barometric readings. Mr. Michelson's grocery store is the barometer, and the mercury Uncle Berel watches is represented by Mr. Michelson's suits. When the operators, cutters, hat makers, pressers, and salesgirls on the block are out of work or on part-time, their diet is low in lox and high in potatoes; then Mr. Michelson's takings are poor and his suits lose heart and acquire luster in longer absences. When times are good and lox is again in the ascendant, Mr. Michelson's suits pick up joie de vivre and come in as often as every other Thursday.

"I tell you," says Uncle Berel, "it is a marvelous world. I stand here and reckon it out. When people are out of work they don't have their clothes mended and pressed very often, and therefore I too earn less, which is only right. Good! But you might think I am in danger of starving to death. Not at all! For if people have no jobs they can't buy new clothes; so the suits and skirts grow older and older, and it has been cleverly arranged that the older they get, the more often they need mending and pressing. The mind of man can't look through the deepness of it all."

CRUCIFIXION

I was crucified: yes, Sammy, me, Sammy Levenson, Sam Levenson was crucified. The Irish kids grabbed me in the schoolyard after school, a bunch of them. We called them the Irishers. I was alone and they grabbed me, and they pulled me up against the steel fence, you know, like the chicken netting fence. Two kids held my arms apart, and another one pulled down my pants to show the others what a Jewish kid looked like. The terror was more than I could bear.

As I looked back later, I could see the position with my arms out-stretched—I didn't know then that I was being crucified. I know it now, now that I look back upon it. When they left me I went crying home, and I told my mother what happened.

VISITOR: ROBERTA SINGER; STATEN ISLAND, NEW YORK
THE CHRIST KILLER

My sister and I were the only Jewish kids in the school, and, being Red diaper babies and being Jewish, we always had to fight our way home. One day, I was coming home from school—I was about eight at the time—and a teenager on a bike threw a rock at me and called me a "Commie kike Christ killer." At the moment I was not impres-sed with the alliteration. He hit me between the eyes on the bridge of my nose, and I went running upstairs with the blood coming out of my head. And my mother said, "What happened, what hap-pened?" as she dabbed blood off my face. And I kept asking, "Who's Christ?" I knew what a Commie was, I could figure out what a "kike" was, but I'd never heard of Christ.

So my mother said, "He was some hero who lived two thousand years ago."

And so I asked, "Then how could I have killed him?"

And I saw this terrible pain in her eyes, that I thought I had put there.

VISITOR: LENNY BRUCE
THE ONE WHO KILLED OUR LORD

You and I know what a Jew is—*One Who Killed Our Lord*. I don't know if we got much press on that in Illinois—we did this about two thousand years ago—two thousand years of Polack kids whacking the shit out of us coming home from school. Dear, dear. And although there should be a statute of limitations for that crime, it seems that those who have neither the actions nor the gait of Christians, pagans or not, will bust us out, unrelenting dues, for another deuce.

And I really searched it out, why we pay the dues. Why do you keep breaking our balls for this crime?

"Why, Jew? Because you skirt the issue. You blame it on the Roman soldiers."

All right. I'll clear the air once and for all, and confess. Yes, we did it. I did it, my family. I found a note in my basement. It said: "We killed him. Signed, Morty."

And a lot of people say to me, "Why did you kill Christ?"

"I dunno . . . it was one of those parties got out of hand, you know."

We killed him because he didn't want to become a doctor, that's why we killed him.

Storyteller: Baruch Lumet
A God Cannot Be Killed

One Christmas in the *shtetl* where I grew up I remember the windows were covered with ice, there were beautiful white flowers in the windows, and I heard children walking from house to house dressed in long white gowns made out of sheets with wings and paper crowns. They went from house to house singing Christmas carols, and they collected money. I was very much enchanted by the whole picture. When these children went into a house to sing the carols, I opened the door and I asked the girl from our neighbors', "Can I come in and listen to them sing?"

She said, "No, you cannot come in. You're Jewish, you killed our God." And that was the first time I heard that, "You killed our God." I was very much hurt inside me, so I asked my father, "What does she mean that we killed their God?"

He said, "No, don't listen to her. We didn't kill any God. A God cannot be killed."

Gus Tyler

On November 22, 1909, a sixteen-year-old girl named Clara Lemlick barged up to the podium at a workers meeting in the Great Hall at Cooper Union in New York City. As Gus Tyler told me, she said in passionate Yiddish, "We've heard the words, we have plenty of words, words will get us nothing. I move that we go on strike." Her words are credited with helping to start the American labor movement. Gus Tyler was not born for another two years, but he was there with her in spirit. A Socialist from the age of thirteen, a fierce labor organizer and labor historian, he retells history as if he were present for all of it. At the age of eighty-three, he is still assistant president of the International Ladies Garment Workers Union.

Gus spent much of his youth listening to the soapbox Socialists who set up outside the Socialist Party headquarters on Tompkins Avenue in Brooklyn. "There were some great soapboxers who spoke on that corner," he told me:

> Oscar Ameringer was a member of the populist movement from Oklahoma. He was editor of a paper, and he had a marvelous, marvelous sense of humor. He was terrific on a soapbox. He toured the country, and I remember him standing on a little soapbox right near 167 Tompkins Avenue in Brooklyn, near the Socialist building. And I remember his wonderful, wonderful stories. "Money is like manure," he used to say. "If you spread it around, it makes things grow, but if you pile it up in just one place, well, it just makes a great big stink." It was the best argument I ever heard for Socialism.

Gus Tyler was never quite sure if he wanted to be a philosopher or a gangster. His home was filled with books, but the learning at home was counterbalanced by knowledge acquired from the streets, where he learned about sticking by your friends, doing favors and getting favors in return. Both perspectives proved useful. His learning at home supplied the philosophy and the long range goals; the streets taught him how to get things done, inch by inch, with occasional setbacks and occasional beatings. "All in all," he said, "I think I had a good education for a union man."

VISITOR: GERALD SIEGEL; NEW YORK CITY
CROTONA PARK

I grew up in the east Bronx, a lovely section that's been destroyed now, around Crotona Park. The park was the center of the world basically. It was divided up in a curious way. There's a lake in the center called Indian Lake, which was always full of rowboats in the summer and ice skaters in the winter. And this was where the anarchists argued. Different political groups argued in different places. If you wanted to argue or agree, you'd know where to go. I'd go with my father. There were anarchists, there were Communists, there were miscellaneous Socialists, there were Zionists. And if you weren't interested in politics, you might be interested in religion. There were a whole series of synagogues there. And if you weren't interested in either one, then you were probably interested in making money. Those were the basic distinctions.

I'll tell you a story that gives the flavor of the thing. I got a goldfish when I was around eight years old, and my father took me to buy a goldfish bowl. The Sino-Japanese War had started, and the five-and-dime was being picketed because the detente with the Communists and China had just broken up; in the Bronx that meant you picketed the five-and-dime. We started into the store to get the goldfish bowl, but meanwhile the goldfish were sitting in a cardboard container on the sink. And someone stopped my father and said, "Comrade, why are you crossing our picket line? Do you want to support the fascism of Japan?"

And my father very carefully said, "Comrade, what am I to do? Do you want to be responsible for the death of a goldfish? Where else can I get a goldfish bowl?"

He said "Pass, comrade."

VISITOR: CHARLENE VICTOR; CHICAGO, ILLINOIS
THE RENT STRIKE

There was this rent strike led by my mother-in law, with whom I had a marvelous relationship—of pure hatred. She lived with me for twenty-one years—but we really had a good, healthy hatred. We admitted it and we got along—there were times that we wouldn't speak—she could get me so mad. But she had a sense of humor, and she was so bright! Soooo bright, you have no idea. So I respected her. She was the same way, she respected me. But we used to laugh together—a lot, because she had a delicious sense of humor. She's the one who led the rent strike.

And who turned out to be the landlord? The local butcher. This was in the heyday of Jewish radicalism in the 1920s. The two radicals Sacco and Vanzetti had been unjustly arrested and charged with a crime they didn't commit, and my mother-in-law and her friends were picketing the local butcher that they wanted he should give more light and more security.

And where were they picketing? In front of his butcher shop! And he was just dying, 'cause it's not only the rent—he really didn't care what he was making on the rent—but the butcher shop! So one day, he got hold of my mother-in-law and he called a meeting, and he said, "All right, I'll give up, I give up. I'll give you more security here, I'll paint, I'll clean up the garbage, but *free Sacco and Vanzetti, I can't!*"

Now she swears to God this is a true story.

171

"THE STRIKE OF THE SCHNORRERS" REVISITED

There is an old Yiddish story called "The Strike of the *Schnorrers*" by Mordche Spektor, which has always lingered in my mind. I'm the assistant president of the Ladies Garment Workers Union. I've helped organize many strikes, and I've researched the history of many strikes. And this story seems to capture some essential quality of the Jewish labor movement.

This is the story of the *gvir* in a small town. The *gvir*, of course, is the wealthy man, and he's highly respected, and his daughter is about to get married. Now in the small towns of Eastern Europe, when the wealthy man had any kind of major celebration, it was customary for him to invite all of the beggars in the area—there were a certain number of beggars who were Jewish, and they were known as the *schnorrers*. And, customarily, they would be invited to weddings.

One day the *gvir* sent one of his emissaries to the beggars and invited them to the wedding ceremony. They could come and join and eat and dance. Now I find that a very fascinating concept that it was an obligation of a rich man to invite the beggars—true, it's an act of charity, but if he did not invite the beggars, he would, in effect, be disgraced, because he was not abiding by Jewish tradition.

It comes down to a word, *tzeddakah*. *Tzeddakah* means charity. *Tzeddakah* also means justice. And it's fascinating that, in Hebrew, the same word is used for those two separate English words. As a matter of fact, in our Western way of thinking, charity and justice are almost opposites. Justice comes under an act that you *must* perform; charity is something that you *may* perform. Charity comes from you, the sense of justice is something imposed by the collective, by the society, or by the state or sometimes by the courts. In the Hebrew language it's one word.

And here is the *gvir*, the rich man, giving this great wedding for his daughter, and he feels that he must invite the beggars. So he sends one of his emissaries to the beggars. And the emissary comes back and says, "No, they refuse to come, they will not come. The beggars have decided to call a strike." In the original story, the worst of the beggars were Shmelke the cripple, Feitel the lame, and Yankel with the flat nose. The others might have been willing to come, but those big shots wouldn't let them!

And the rich man says, "What do you mean, they 'will not come'? They're beggars and this is a great event, and I'm inviting them."

And the emissary says, "No, they refuse to come. They say that if you want them to come, you'll have to pay each one a ruble apiece. They insist that they will not come unless you actually pay them for coming. They claim that this is something they're doing for you, they're doing you a great favor in coming." They want to be rewarded for the favor they are rendering unto him.

Well, the *gvir* explodes. He says, "What's the matter with these people? They're beggars, *schnorrers!* They can't go on strike! A few pennies like this means something to them!" He doesn't quite appreciate the irony —it means a lot to them, it doesn't mean very much to him. But he's enraged! "What's the matter with these people? No! We'll just have to do without them."

But then he thinks about it and he thinks about it. And the story goes into all of his ruminations and all of his questions, and he says, "Okay." And he sends another emissary to the beggars. And finally it turns out that he bargains a little bit—"Why so much? Maybe it should be a little bit less." But in the end he says, "All right!" In the final analysis, the beggars go on strike and he does reach a settlement with them. And they come to a wedding and everybody has a great, good time. The music is playing and the rich dance with the poor, and everything is settled.

I found that a very, very fascinating concept, that the obligation of the person of wealth in the Jewish community is to contribute to the beggars. And the whole notion that a beggar out of a sense of self-respect stands up and makes demands upon the rich person. They don't come crawling to him. It's a concept of charity that says, "You owe us! You owe us." It's not an act of charity; they are our people.

I love the story because, in a sense, all workers are *schnorrers.* You come to me and beg, and I might give you another penny. But you strike? You make demands on me? What do you mean, you make demands on me? I'm the boss! Yes, we make demands, because charity and justice are not distinct ideas. When the rich give to the poor, it's their obligation— because they've been living on the backs of the poor all these years.

It goes back to a concept of charity that Moses Maimonides developed. You don't give charity so you can be a big shot in your community, you don't give charity so people should say thank you, you don't give charity so they should treat you like a God, you give charity because you've got it and there are people out there who need it. You give charity because it's your obligation. Period. And the recipients don't have to say thank you. They need it.

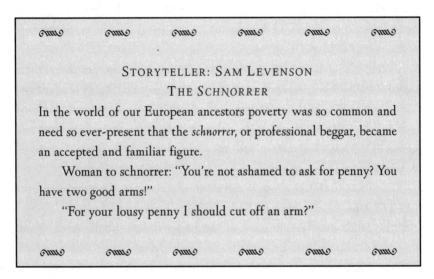

STORYTELLER: SAM LEVENSON
THE SCHNORRER

In the world of our European ancestors poverty was so common and need so ever-present that the *schnorrer*, or professional beggar, became an accepted and familiar figure.

Woman to schnorrer: "You're not ashamed to ask for penny? You have two good arms!"

"For your lousy penny I should cut off an arm?"

JACK TEPPER

Jack Tepper refers to himself as a "displaced Palestinian." His father was a freedom fighter in Palestine in the 1920s who was arrested by the British along with Vladimir Jabotinsky (the charismatic Zionist leader). With no future in Israel while it was under British rule, the family immigrated to Brooklyn, where Jack was born in 1931. His father taught him to shoot a rifle, and in his business dealings in rough Brooklyn neighborhoods, he always carried a gun.

But as a boy, sitting around with his father's relatives and friends, he was swept up in an undercurrent of Ashkenazic, Eastern European Jewish culture. He tapped into it, and it carried him. It provided a different way of fighting back: "Jewish humor is very, very similar to the Oriental martial art of jiujitsu; there is some humor that confronts, but the old humor rolls with the blows, it rolls away to deaden the impact of the blow, and make something funny out of the hatred and despair."

PAZAMENTRY

During the 1930s my uncle needed work, and somebody got him a job in the garment center. He became a presser. It was during the Depression, and during the Depression things were very hard. If you came home with $10 a week, you really did quite well.

As a matter of fact, I have a story that's connected with it. There was Sam Cohen, and he was a salesman of pazamentry. Are you acquainted with what pazamentry is? Pazamentry is the thing in the garment trade where you don't deal with the fabric, but what you deal with is the lace trim, the embroidered trim, the fancy buttons—it's the decoration that's added to a garment, and it's manufactured separately and applied to the gown—that's pazamentry.

Well, Sam Cohen was a salesman of pazamentry—very successful, forty years. And a successful salesman doesn't even have to sell anymore, all he does is come in and say, "Haven't gotten an order from you in a long time," and he gets the order. They're very successful.

Well, after forty years Sam is going to retire, and he's talking to another salesman, and he says, "What I really want to do is, there's a Mr. O'Connell who owns a dress house, and he would never buy anything from me 'cause he hates Jews. And to me, the highlight of my career, is before I retire I could sell him an order."

So he goes to Mr. O'Connell to sell him an order. Mr. O'Connell looks at him and says very sardonically, "I hear you're retiring, Cohen. You've been bothering me for years, and you know I don't deal with Hebes. But, okay, you want an order, I'll give you an order—token order." He says, "You have any red ribbon?"

Cohen says, "Sure we got red ribbon. What width?"

He says, "Half inch."

"We got half-inch ribbon."

"You got it."

"How much you need?"

"All you need is an order, right? Just to show you sold me. I want a ribbon that will reach from your belly button to the tip of your penis. That's as big a piece of ribbon as I want." And Mr. O'Connell throws him out of his factory.

Six weeks later, Mr. O'Connell goes to open up his factory, and in front of his door are five trailer trucks. And they are unloading thousands and thousands and thousands and thousands of yards of ribbon. He runs upstairs, gets on the phone, and says, "Cohen, you miserable animal, what the hell did you send me?"

He says, "Look, Mr. O'Connell. Exactly what you asked me is what I sent you. My belly button, everybody knows where it is. You said till it reaches the tip of my penis. Fifty-five years ago I was circumcised in a little town outside of Warsaw, Poland . . ."

Why did God create *goyim* (non-Jews)?
Someone has to buy retail.

SHIRLEE KRESH HECKER

Shirlee Kresh Hecker was born in 1929 and grew up in Brownsville, Brooklyn. Her two family stories in this book, "Papa's Sukkah" and "Ike the Pike," are based on incidents and memories from her girlhood. Only years later, when she became a grandmother, did Shirlee begin to retell these stories. "My grandchildren are half Italian and half Jewish, and I wanted them to know how I lived as a little girl. I would show them pictures, and they would say, 'Who's this?' They love these stories because they can picture me as a little girl. My mother, father, and two sisters are all gone," she told me. "I am keeping their memories alive, I'm the only one left."

"Ike the Pike," which won a prize in the Legacies contest for stories by older adults, is a hilarious family tale about a carp which her mother kept in the bathtub for Passover, and which her father refused to kill. *"It's a ritual now,"* Shirlee says, laughing. *"We read it each year as part of the Passover celebration."* Like *"Papa's Sukkah,"* it's a resonant tale about her father and his complexities.

Shirlee first told me the story of her father's sukkah on the phone. When she sent me a copy of the tale, only recently written down, it didn't have a title. I called it *"My Daddy's Sukkah"* and sent it down to her home in Delray Beach, Florida, for her to look over. I received a phone call back saying that she called her father Papa, not Daddy, and asking that the name be changed to *"Papa's Sukkah."*

"Sure," I said.

"Thanks, tootsie," she said, and laughed as she hung up.

PAPA'S SUKKAH

This is a story about my father and a *sukkah* (a temporary hut open to the sky built in order to eat, pray, and celebrate the harvest holiday of Sukkos). The *sukkah* was located on the roof of a one-hundred-foot extension in the rear of our two-story house in Brownsville, Brooklyn. (The extension was originally my grandfather's thriving sweater factory, but the business failed soon after *Zayde* died.)

The roof of the extension became my playground. It was tarred and smooth, held three skylights, an old kitchen table, a double swing for when I was really young, a lot of potted plants, and a big box filled with sawdust for the cats. When I was an infant, Mama gave me my airing on the roof and was never worried, as she was able to watch me from the kitchen window while she was busy inside.

My father was what was known in the family as "not such a successful businessman." He worked as a painter when he could, but it was a Depression economy, and there just wasn't too much money in that, so on the side he fixed watches. He also bought and sold jewelry. (He was well-known in the neighborhood as "Izzy the jewelry peddler.")

Even though he didn't earn enough to support his family, he was a marvelous human being. To me, his adoring daughter, he was the most wonderful, caring person, especially when it came to animals and birds.

177

My mother was not too happy about my father's love of birds. Each day the birds in the neighborhood flocked to our roof to eat. The feed was special, as it came from my father's *landsman* (member of his hometown society), the chicken flicker, who worked in the marketplace nearby. They were fat, happy birds and would rest on my father's shoulders and hands as he threw the feed all over. Not only didn't they want to fly south each winter, but they nested under the roof of the *sukkah* and made our home their home.

In the early 1920s, *Zayde* (Grandfather) built the *sukkah* on the roof. It was my father, however, who added the wonderful extra touches. He made colorful eggshelled birds flying from the ceiling. He would sip the raw yolk from the eggs through a pin hole and then delicately apply a different color to each bird. He made the beaks out of dough and painted lifelike eyes. The wings were painstakingly pasted together from chicken feathers. He suspended these beautiful decorations with string, and I imagined that real birds were flying overhead. He also made little flowers out of paper napkins and placed each on a toothpick. We had the most delightful and unique *sukkah* in the neighborhood.

Then one day, right before Sukkos, my father took ill and went into the hospital. He told me he would never live to see another Sukkos, and soon after he passed away. I was so angry at him for leaving me that I went straight to the *sukkah* and pulled all the birds and flowers down and stomped on them. I was sixteen years old when he died, but I cried like a baby.

Now, each year when Sukkos comes around, I can't help but smile as I think of my early years with Papa. No one had such a remarkable and beautiful *sukkah*. It left me with so many wonderful memories. My father taught me to appreciate life and nature by living the lesson, and the *sukkah* was my classroom.

IKE THE PIKE

Almost two weeks before Passover my father brought home a live fish in order for my mother to cook it for the holidays. Of course, he knew this fish would be of the finest quality, since it came from his *landsman* on the

East Side. Papa made the trip from Brooklyn by a trolley car that passed right in front of our house. He had this fish in a bucket and presented it to my mother so she could put it in the washtub and fatten it up until she was ready to prepare it.

This fish became the family's new pet, and soon it had a name. "Look how he knows me," my father said after just one day, as "Ike the Pike" settled in the washtub in his new home.

Each time my father lifted the washtub's lid, the fish perked up his head and opened his mouth. My father would feed him little pieces of bread and talk soothingly to him, and every time my father would approach the tub he would say, "Watch how he greets me." Sure enough, the fish would jump up to the direction of the light and open his mouth. Ike seemed to know that my father would be there to feed him.

My father was fascinated with Ike's intelligence, and soon Ike became one of my father's favorite pets. Papa would show off this fish's so-called talents to whoever came to the house.

Although I was very young, I knew that my father had a way with all animals. I also believed this fish to be just what my father claimed— "very smart." I knew nothing of the word "conditioned."

One day, my father beckoned me over to the tub to look at Ike. "Can you see how much he looks like my friend Levine?" he whispered. "The eyebrows, the one larger eye that held his monocle, the thin lips with the cigar always in place, and the high cheekbones?"

Why, he really does look like Mr. Levine, I thought, being as imaginative as any five-year-old should be.

"You know," added my father, "when people die, they can come back as anything or anyone."

"Even a fish?" I asked.

"That's what Levine came back as," my father said convincingly, and I truly believed it.

Then came the fateful day when Mamma asked my father to kill the fish.

"Kill him, are you crazy?" my father said. "That might be Levine. He stays in the tub forever."

My mother just stared at my father and then said quietly, "Take that fish out in the yard and bring it back dead so I can cook it, and stop telling that child that the fish is your friend. Your friend is dead, and that's how I want that fish."

But my father refused, and he walked out of the house, muttering that he would never, as long as he lived, lift a hand to his friend.

This went on for almost two days, and I stared from one parent to the other, wondering who was going to win the battle. I counted on my father, but my mother would not relent.

"Izzy," she said, "if you make me kill this fish, I will never forgive you."

"Well, Rosie," my father replied, "if you want to see him dead, you be the murderer," and he sadly left the house.

I watched my mother as she picked up a big towel, walked over to the tub, caught the fish in the towel, and went out to the backyard with it.

"Stop!" I screamed. "Don't kill him. Please. Please!" But to no avail.

My mother raised the hammer and aimed for the fish's head. I screamed, "Murderer!" at the top of my lungs and held on to her, but she pushed me aside and struck the fish's head again and again. But the fish wouldn't stop moving and jumping around.

"Die, Levine, die!" she pleaded, and with the third blow, the fish finally stopped moving. It was then that my mother, whom I had never seen in real tears, burst out crying and ran in the house with the fish.

When Papa came home he passed by the tub, but he didn't lift the lid to look inside. He knew, just looking at my mother's face, that his friend was really gone.

The first *seder* was the next night, and after what seemed like endless praying, Momma got ready to serve. By that time everyone was on edge. I got yelled at a dozen times for various things I claimed I didn't do to my sister, and my sister almost got hit for the things she did do to me. As for my oldest sister, she said she wasn't very hungry and left the dining room.

It was then that my mother brought out the gefilte fish platter. When she uncovered it, there on the very top was a fishball with a face: horseradish for a mouth, a carrot for a nose, and raisins for its eyes, and on one eye was my Charlie McCarthy doll's monocle, just like the one Mr. Levine wore. In its horseradish mouth was a small piece of celery in place of a cigar. My sister had done a real good job on the face, but no one appreciated it, no one laughed, and no one ate any gefilte fish.

My father left the table, saying he didn't feel good. My mother did nothing but mutter under her breath about how she was going to kill my sister (who had locked herself in the bathroom).

Needless to say, the fish was not eaten, nor was it saved the next day. As far as we know, my mother, who never wasted food, threw it in the garbage. As for my father, he never brought home a live fish again.

VISITOR: LILA ZEIGER
THE FISH

I had about as much chance, Mother,
as the carp who thrashed
in your bathtub on Friday,
swimming helplessly back and forth
in the small hard pool you made
for me,
unaware of how soon you would
pull me from my element
sever my head just below the gills
scrape away the iridescence
chop me into bits and pieces and
reshape me with your strong hands
to simmer in your special broth.
You bustled about the house
confident in your design,
while I waited at the edge
imploring you with glossy eyes
to keep me and love me
just as I was.

HANK HALIO

Born in 1917, Hank Halio grew up in the Bronx and worked in the garment industry in New York until 1977, when he retired with his wife, Phyllis, to Delray Beach, Florida. In Florida he joined the local Sephardic social club and began writing a column for the newsletter. The column was picked up in New York by the Sephardic Home News, which comes out of the Sephardic Home for the Aged on Cropsey Avenue in Brooklyn but goes out to Sephardic communities across the country.

He is currently gathering together his columns for a book called Ladino Reveries; *among them are the stories of his eccentric and physically powerful uncle Joe. Once, in the early part of the century when the subway cars had open windows, someone tried to steal Uncle Joe's hat off his head as the train started moving. He turned around and almost killed the man, yelling, "Hijo de un asno"* [son of an ass]*.*

STORIES ABOUT STORIES

A JEW WHO DON'T SPEAK YIDDISH: ASHKENAZI/ SEPHARDIC CULTURAL DIFFERENCES

Let's go back a few years to our grade-school days. That's when we first became aware that we, the Sephardim, were different. The first days in school were not easy for us Sephardic children. That was when we came to realize that we were different from our Ashkenazi co-religionists. I, for one, could not speak English when I entered kindergarten—I spoke Ladino, the language of the Sephardim. For the first time our last names were brought to our attention—names like Aboulafia, Abrevaya, Amira, Candiotti, Cherasi, Crespi, Forma, Gormezano, Halio, Massa, Motola, Penso, Roditti, Sarfati, Saporta, Strougo, Susi, Toledano, Varsano, Yohai, and many more, most ending in a vowel that set them apart and gave the Ashkenazi reason to believe we were not Jewish.

We took off from school on Rosh Hashanah, Yom Kippur, and other Jewish holidays. When we returned to school the next day, our teachers would ask us why we were absent. We said we were absent because it was a Jewish holiday. Both the Jewish kids and the gentile kids would laugh at us. They didn't believe us. "With your name, how can you say you are Jewish?"

Which of us at the age of six, seven or eight knew about the Spanish Inquisition or the Expulsion? Which of us knew how to explain it to our teachers? We just insisted we were Jewish. The next step was, "Bring a note from your parents." That was when panic set in. Many of our parents had little schooling, and most couldn't read or write English well enough in those days to write a comprehensible letter.

Now comes the kicker. When we became old enough to appreciate the charms and fascinations of the opposite sex, our troubles really began. We rarely made dates with Sephardic girls, although many of us married them. If we were seen with a Sephardic girl more than once, the whole community would have us engaged and ready for marriage. Most of us dated Yiddish girls. Can't you just hear our folks say, "*Mira hijo que se esta indo con una Yiddisha. No puede topar una de las muestras?*" (Look at that nice fellow who's going with a Yiddish girl. Can't he find one of ours?) Hardly any of us ever dated non-Jewish girls.

A new problem arose. The parents of the Yiddish girls would want to meet the "boyfriend." Can you picture what happened at the first encounter? We were introduced by our first names only. Then the parents would speak to us in Yiddish. When they saw the blank look on our faces they turned to their daughters and asked, "*Er is nit a yid?*" ("*El no as Djudio?*" Isn't he Jewish?)

"You say you are Jewish, but you don't speak Yiddish, how can you say you are a Jew?" Some of us had the urge to say, "You don't speak Spanish, how could you be Jewish?" Being well-brought-up Sephardic boys, we didn't. To try to prove we were indeed Jewish we recited some Hebrew prayers, but our pronunciation of Hebrew is different from that of the Ashkenazi, and they didn't believe us. A certain perverse thought crossed the minds of some of the wise guys, a surefire way of proving that we were Jewish, but I don't think any of us tried it.

STORYTELLER: JOE ELIAS

Till the day that she died, my Ashkenazic mother-in-law wished that my wife had married a "real" Jew. As a youngster I would often meet the parents of my Ashkenazic girlfriends. They would speak to me in Yiddish, and of course I stood there with my mouth open. Or I would answer in English if I thought I could guess what they were asking, and they would turn to the daughter and say, "I thought you said he was Jewish? Why are you bringing me a Puerto Rican? What kind of a Jew don't speak Yiddish?" Of course, Hitler understood who was Jewish. He had no trouble accepting us as Jews. He decimated the Ladino-speaking population in the Balkans.

Once the reality that the Sephardim were actually Jewish was established, the language barrier was surmounted and the parties involved were convinced that we were in fact Jewish, we thought our troubles were over. Far from it. It was inevitable that there would be "mixed marriages." At the turn of the century it was tantamount to marrying out of the religion. There was much speculation how the bride and groom were going to get along. *Como se van a pasar?* A lot more was said about how the *kosuegros* or *mahatunim* (in-laws) were going to relate and communicate with one another. The Ashkenazim were as apprehensive as the Sephardim in trying to cope with the myriad problems the bride and groom were going to face. Our customs and culture were literally continents apart. Our cuisine was different. We, the Sephardim, celebrated the Jewish holidays in a slightly different manner. The way our services were conducted in the synagogue was not the same.

The greatest conflict in relations among the husbands, wives, and in-laws was when it came to naming the children. The Sephardim named the progeny for the living and the Ashkenazim for the departed. With a good deal of research, I was able to understand the merits of both sides of the question. I am always asked, "Why do you name your children for the living?" My answer is typically Jewish. I answer the question with another question, "Why not?" There is no Hebraic law that dictates how the children are to be named in either culture. It's a matter of superstition and custom.

It was the custom of the Sephardim for the firstborn boy to receive the name of the paternal grandfather, the firstborn girl to receive the name of the paternal grandmother, the second-born boy to receive the name of the maternal grandfather, the second-born girl to receive the name of the maternal grandmother. This was done whether those individuals were living or deceased, thus the phrase "they name for the living." This was considered sacrilegious by the Ashkenazi and was the hardest thing to reconcile.

I was named for my grandfather, who was alive at the time. I was born in America, and he was living in Turkey. Even though I had never seen him, I always felt I was somebody. I had an identity. I'm looking forward to the day when a little Hank will be named for me. My mother was very proud when my first daughter was named for her. So was my wife when our first grandchild, Phoebe, was named for her. When our second daughter was born, I suggested to my mother-in-law, a wonderful Ashkenazi lady, that it was her prerogative to name this child. Her answer was, "By all means, give her my name."

VISITOR: PHYLLIS HALIO; BORN 1925, BROOKLYN

My dad was the editor and owner of *La Vara* (*The Yardstick*), a Sephardic newspaper in New York. He was Mr. Sephardic in the community, a real Sephardic man. My mother came out of an Ashkenazi Jewish home, and they had different customs. In my mother's family we did not name our babies after living relatives.

But I was named for my father's mother, who was still alive. My brother was named for my father's father, who was alive. Both were later killed in the Holocaust in Greece, but they were alive when we were born. My mother's mother didn't argue with her son-in-law. She told my mother simply, "You don't argue about a name."

B.

THE AMERICAN SOUTH

SOLOMON BLATT

When Solomon Blatt died in May 1986 at the age of ninety-one, he had served in the South Carolina House of Representatives for fifty-four years and as Speaker for thirty-three. He lost only one election, in 1930. "Did my Jewishness have anything to do with it? It always did. It always did. It became more minor as the years went by." His reminiscences were recorded by Howard Simons, who in the last years of life set out to "trap memory," carrying a tape recorder across the United States for four years and interviewing Jews from every walk of life.

WHAT MR. BLATT CAN'T EAT

I live in Barnwell, South Carolina. I've been practicing law in Barnwell since 1917. It's going to be difficult for me to tell you the place where my parents were born. I can remember something of a place that sounded like Brest-Litovsk or something like that. I don't really know the correct name, but that's my recollection of where my father was born. My father and mother were married over there before he left and came to the United States.

He got enough money and got on a ship. Of course, he couldn't speak English. They tagged him for New York. My recollection of what happened is that a group of Jewish people met the ship and took him and housed him somewhere, and then they sent him on a boat that used to run between Jacksonville, Florida, and New York—it doesn't run anymore. They put him on that ship and tagged him for Charleston, South Carolina. There, another group of Jewish people met him. They took care of him for a few days, and they decided he was going to peddle. A company by the

VISITOR: CAROLYN LIPSON-WALKER;
BLOOMINGTON, INDIANA
ZIPKY

Great-uncle Julius Levy, born and raised in the small Louisiana town of Slidell, already a graduate of Tulane University Medical School, had never been exposed to Yiddish or the more traditional practices of Judaism. Attending his first traditional wedding in New Orleans, he dimly recalled that there was an appropriate Jewish phrase meaning "Congratulations." As he neared the receiving line Uncle Julius overheard someone saying, "*Zipky.*" The word seemed to ring a bell, and Uncle Julius made his way down the receiving line, greeting the newlyweds and their families with "*Zipky,* it was a beautiful wedding." "You were a beautiful bride, *zipky.*"

As Uncle Julius neared the end of the line, my aunt Jeannette overheard her husband's congratulatory remarks. In alarm, she whispered to him, "Julius, what in the world do you think you're saying?"

He answered, "Why, *zipky,* isn't that the Jewish word for congratulations?"

My great-aunt retorted, "My God, no. That's the bride's maiden name."

Ever since, "*Zipky*" rather than "*Mazel tov*" is the congratulatory comment used by my family.

This story has always said a lot to me about being Jewish in the South and trying to maintain traditions in the absence of a large, fully formed, Yiddish-speaking community.

name of M. Hornig and Sons operated in Charleston, a little wholesale place there, and they sold him a pack of merchandise without any down payment.

He started walking. He told me, many a time, that in the coldest of winter people wouldn't let him in the house. He had to sleep on the frozen ground, and he was very lucky if he got in a hay barn and they let him sleep out there under that hay, where he could keep warm.

He didn't know a nickel from a dollar. He carried a little merchandise like socks and ladies' stockings and handkerchiefs and whatnot. He trusted the honor of the people who bought from him to give him the correct amount that was owed on that merchandise. It was marked. They could have given him a dime and taken a dollar and a half worth of merchandise. He wouldn't have known the difference.

In those travels he came to Blackville. I understood this—sometimes he'd go down toward Savannah and go over to Augusta and maybe get some merchandise there and walk back to Charleston and load up again. From here to Charleston is a hundred miles.

My father stopped peddling and got a little store not too much bigger than my office. I remember the store well, because when I came along I could see it there. It had a fireplace in the back, and that's where he built a fire and cooked his meals. And then they had a counter about like this desk, and the bottom of that counter was open and he would put a little mattress down there and sleep under that counter.

Then my mother came. They had one child who was born in Europe, and his name was Jake. He was about three or four years old. She couldn't speak English, either. They got her off at New York and sent her on down to Charleston. At Charleston they put her on a train and tagged her for Blackville. My father met her, of course. He had a little house rented. After my mother came to Blackville, he got into a little larger place. . . .

My parents were religious to the extent that my father went to Charleston and they taught him how to kill chickens and all that. On the holidays, he closed and went to synagogue, either in Charleston or Augusta. I can remember, of course, Saturday they had to keep open because that's the only day they did any business. Some days he wouldn't take in ten dollars. He wouldn't smoke on Saturday. I remember this: My mother would come to the store to help, and she would not tear the paper off the paper rack on Saturday. She'd make the customer do it.

It was difficult to maintain our Jewishness. When I was a child, Blackville had about fifteen hundred to two thousand people. I'd say there were three or four Jewish families.

My mother and father tried their best to be kosher in everything that they did. They observed the holidays, sacred Jewish holidays. But it got to the point where they had to buy meat that wasn't kosher. My mother did the best she could under the circumstances. And I'll tell you one thing about it, there is one thing I am right proud of, and I'm that way, too: They didn't hesitate to let everybody know they were of the Jewish faith, and I think the public knew it generally, too.

I have proclaimed on many a stump and many times that I am of the Jewish faith and I'm proud of it, because I love my mother and daddy, and I couldn't love them unless I was proud to be a Jew.

I'll tell you. This is a little funny experience. I don't know if it has any value or not. There was little town up the road, between here and Augusta, Georgia, called Dunbarton, and when the Savannah River Plant was constructed, it swallowed the town of Dunbarton. But every other year in the political campaign they had a meeting at Dunbarton and they spoke in front of the freight depot platform. Well, when they had the meeting then in those days—not like it is now—every country church would invite the candidates to come speak. Then they would go to each candidate and ask him for a contribution to buy the hogs to have a barbecue. Then, after you made the contribution to the purchase of the hogs, the church members would come and sell tickets. I had to buy ten tickets or whatnot.

I was at Dunbarton at a campaign meeting, and I spoke last. The fellow who was presiding at the meeting was a good friend of mine. He introduced everybody else and they made their speeches, and I was the last one and he was introducing me. So he told the audience, he said, "I regret that we are having something today that Mr. Blatt can't eat," referring to the barbecued hog. He said, "I just overlooked the fact of his religion, and I'm sorry and I regret it." He went on. He apologized. It was a very kind statement he made. But I didn't know exactly how that thing was going to go with people up there saying, "Well, we eat it. Why the devil can't that Jew eat it?" But they didn't say that. When he got through introducing me, the first thing I told that crowd, I said, "Ladies and gentlemen, don't you worry about what you got here to eat today. Don't let it give you any concern, because I'm going to eat it, too, and call it goose." They applauded, and I got a terrific vote up there.

C.
THE CATSKILLS

JOEY ADAMS

In his wonderful book The Borscht Belt, Joey Adams describes a "Night of Stars" benefit at Madison Square Garden. Over a million dollars' worth of tickets were bought to see a group of entertainers who had all cut their eyeteeth in the resorts of the Catskills: David Kaminsky, Aaron Chwatt, Al Dabruzio, Philip Feldman, Pinky Perlmut, Moishe Miller, Jerome Levitch, Bernie Schwartz, Milton Berlinger, and Murray Janofsky, with Joseph Abramowitz as master of ceremonies. They don't sound like big names, but Joey Adams captures something about the era when he provides us with their assumed, far more goyishe stage names: respectively, Danny Kaye, Red Buttons, Robert Alda, Phil Foster, Jan Peerce, Robert Merrill, Jerry Lewis, Tony Curtis, Milton Berle, Jan Murray, and the MC, none other than himself, Joey Adams.

Much of what has been written about the Catskills are show business stories about the legion of American comics who got their start in the "Sour Cream Sierras." But they can be read elsewhere; for this book I am interested in the way ordinary Jews experienced the mountains. But Joey Adams provides that, too, in the wonderful personal anecdotes about visiting the Catskills as a child in the early 1920s. Better than anyone, he captures what it was like to spend summers in that distinctive milieu created by the immigrants from their moments of "slack," or downtime, from the sweatshops on the Lower East Side.

THE KOKHALEYN

The first eight summers of my life I spent strictly under the open fire hydrant on my block. I was nine years old when my father the tailor decided his family would "summer by the country." What a thrill for a kid from Brooklyn who had never penetrated deeper into the bush than Ocean Parkway!

In the *Daily Forward* Papa had read of a small boardinghouse that advertised "Rooms and Bungalows and Apartments to rent for the summer. Do your own cooking; Rates very reasonable; Beautiful view; Private lake nearby; Heller's Bungalow Colony—Monticello, NY." This sounded great. Papa immediately dispatched a special-delivery postcard for fuller details. A few days later, although it was only the first week of April, Mr. Heller called personally to set the deal. The way he described his *kokhaleyn* it sounded like Monte Carlo instead of Monticello. Mr. Heller even offered to cart us up to see this paradise "anytime in April or May before the season starts so you can choose the best place."

How could Pop refuse? Here was a chance for a free ride to the mountains on Sunday, and "You could even take the kids along; there's no obligation on your part." Of course, if you didn't hire the rooms, there was a small charge for the ride, but this you didn't find out until later. Even if you did take the rooms, Heller still tried to chisel gas and food expenses for the big trip. Heller was a local merchant in Monticello who ran the shoe store. For the price of two pair of sneakers he had bought a hunk of property with a farmhouse. He added some rough cabins, hung out his roadside shingle, and was in business. The colony consisted of twelve rooms in the main house and three bungalows, with one big community kitchen.

Mama's cousin, who was going to share the bungalow and expenses, came along for the ride. She loved the place. A Monte Carlo it wasn't, but it was the country and Heller promised to take her into town twice a week to buy her kosher meats. He also pointed out the convenience of Relleh's grocery store just across the road. He didn't, however, find it convenient to point out the Relleh's was Heller's spelled backward.

But I wanted to know, "Where's the lake you promised? You said the bungalow colony was near the lake. It's about three miles away."

"I said it was *near* the lake, not *on* the lake," he explained.

One season, circumstances dictated that Mama and I and my older sister, Yetta, drive up by hacker a week earlier than the rest of our chic ensemble. Mama had reserved the three backseats for us. The rest of the car contained an elderly lady and a young man who were squeezed together with the hacker in the front seat. A tubby bleached blonde sat on a jump seat, with most of her hanging over both sides. The other passenger was a completely different smell altogether. He was a bald-headed man who was reverently carrying a jar with such care that it could've been the crown jewels except that the wrappings around a jar of crown jewels are rarely fastened with a rubber band. As the sun came up full we came to know its contents: garlic pickles.

Seven minutes past the toll the bleached blonde started. "My Sam and I don't like formal hotel-type life. Every year we just prefer to hire a simple bungalow at Madame Geretsky's Villa. Who wants to get dressed three times a day? I get enough of that all winter," she said, balancing the pots and pans on her lap.

"You're so right," agreed the pickle man, who was going to Heller's Bungalow Colony. "I'm so busy all year round that all I want to do is sit in front of my bungalow and dangle my feet in the lake." It occurred to me that if he was going to Heller's, his feet had better be three miles long.

"I far prefer the more relaxed tempo that one finds at the bungalow colony. And this way, like my Sam and I always say, you can eat what you like. You don't have to be a slave to food three times a day," said the bleach job, who looked like Fatso Farouk after a heavy meal.

I was but a youngster on the green side of my Bar Mitzvah, but even I knew this was a crock. Nobody actually preferred a *kokhaleyn* unless he couldn't afford anything better. We all knew it. She knew we knew it. And wherever her Sam was, it figures he knew it, too.

When the hack arrived at our destination it was near midnight. We had been the first ones to be picked up and were the last to be dropped off. Since our luggage and bedding were on the bottom, the hack man naturally waited until all the others were removed.

The joy of the whole world for a *kokhaleyn* wife is her first morning in the community kitchen. As our GIs fought for every inch of land on Guadalcanal, so did each woman fight to establish a beachhead at one of the two sinks. Armed with Brillo pads and scouring powder, each lived by the motto "Take the sink—*and hold it!*" Even the two ovens and the breadbox became battlegrounds. Everybody fought for the best spot in the icebox, too. The status symbol was the two cubic inches assigned to you, and the top shelf on the front was equivalent to a triple-A rating in Dun & Bradstreet.

Every jar of goodies had a label. The little lump of farmer cheese, already turning yellow, was tagged "H. Potkin." The pickled lox in the wax paper said "J. Traum." One always heard such anguished cries as "Somebody's been at my stewed prunes"—"Who spilled and left the shelf so dirty?"—"All right, so it was a little yellow, but did I give you permission to throw out my farmer cheese?"

VISITOR: DAVID KOTKIN; HARTFORD, CONNECTICUT
KESL GARTN!

Each summer during the 1920s, my parents, my four sisters, and I escaped from our steamy flat in Hartford and went to Ocean Beach on Long Island Sound. In those days, none of the immigrant families could afford to rent a whole house, so we rented two rooms in a large cottage with three or four other families. I remember bringing our own pots, pans, and food and splitting the cost of ice with the other families. You can imagine the scene as four women, all used to their own kitchens, tried to fix three meals a day for their large families in one tiny kitchen. "My husband's coming home at four. I must have dinner ready!" "Thief! You used our milk." "That's *my* chopped liver!"

Finally, my mother had had enough. She threw up her hands, exclaiming, "I don't need this kesl gartn." This, undoubtedly, was a reference to the confusion that characterized Castle Garden, the immigrant processing station that preceded Ellis Island. "Kesl gartn" became an expression used to connote chaos in our family.

THE TUMLER

The farmers turned hotelmen stayed away from regular paid entertainers as long as possible. "It's thrown-out money," they whined. "The only thing they do good is eat."

But as the hotels grew, so did the complaints from the guests. If a girl didn't find her Prince Charming the first day, the food was lousy. If the boy didn't score the first night, the hotel was from hunger. If it rained and Charlie Feldman couldn't get up a ball game, the boss was a bum.

That's how the farmers were forced into show business. Each had to get a specialist to calm his nervous customers. As the owner burrowed deeper into his kitchens to hide from his newfound troubles, the social Director, better known as "the *tumler*," came into his own.... The name *"tumler"* comes from one who makes tumult. A "tumult maker," alias "tumulter." But with the czar's English as spoken by the proprietors, tumulter became *tumler....*

The social Director took over all of the activities day out and night in. He had to sing, dance, tell stories, arrange parlor games, plan hikes, organize the community sings at the campfire, *kibitz* with the fat old women, and entertain in the dining room during meals. Finally, if he had any strength left, he crept into a few bedrooms here and there.

My first job was at the Olympic Hotel in Fallsburg. I was combination bellboy and assistant bookkeeper. On the side I was the house *tumler*. When the rains came I was pressed into active service. With the first drop I went on "red alert."

One early morning in the middle of August I was awakened by a frantic banging on the partition that served as my door. "The rains are here," yelled a voice. "The boss says to hurry up and amuse the guests. The lobby is full and they are mad."

I dressed hurriedly and looked out at the worst storm the mountains had all summer. I quickly donned my raincoat for the long trek to the lobby. It was then I knew what they meant in the ads when they said "spacious grounds." My quarters were two miles from the main building. As I splashed into the lobby, soaked from head to foot, the boss growled, "What the hell are you doing wearing a raincoat? And rubbers yet!"

"But, boss," I pleaded, "don't you know it's raining?"

"I know it's raining," he barked. "You know it's raining. But must you remind the guests it's raining?"

No matter how soaked, every employee was trained to smile and say to the guests, "This is nothing. Just a little mist. It'll clear up in a minute." According to the weather bureau they had fourteen inches of mist one summer.

VISITOR: SAL RICHARDS

FROM *IT HAPPENED IN THE CATSKILLS*

In most of those places there were no spotlights, just lights stuck into the ceiling. I was performing at the SGS Bungalows near the Stevensville Hotel. [When I] opened my mouth to sing, a giant moth flew in. I almost choked. I spit the moth out.

"That moth," I told the audience, "does that every week. He loves that song."

D.
YIDDISH THEATER

BARUCH LUMET

Baruch Lumet was born in Ahata, a suburb of Warsaw, on September 16, 1898. As a young boy he developed a longing for the stage. His hilarious efforts to break into the fledgling field of Yiddish theater at the turn of the century paint a fine portrait of its early history. In an oral history collected by the American Jewish Committee in 1976, he recounts his first job as an assistant to a traveling magician and his early apprenticeship to an actor, a wonderful teacher and mentor, who is rounded up as a revolutionary shortly thereafter and slain for killing a Russian officer.

In Warsaw, he sees the early Yiddish theater melodrama Pinteleh Yid *and develops a crush on the daughter of the troupe's famous director, Misha Rapell; he seeks out a Gypsy fortune-teller and asks for a potion to make this little girl fall in love with him. She tells him to pull some hairs from her head and bring them to her so she can mix a love potion. After one of her performances, he runs up behind her, pulls some follicles from her pretty head, and brings them to the fortune-teller. As he holds out his bounty, the Gypsy seductively begins unfastening his pants. He runs away.*

When he returns, the Gypsy and her storefront are gone, but he spies a sign for a "Parisian tailor" in the same building. He gets a job as an apprentice to the tailor, and the kindly man ends up buying him a piano, helping him launch a musical career.

During World War I, he sees babies with swollen bellies starving to death on the streets of Warsaw and comes close to being arrested for singing a song against the czar (he is saved by a shmeer, or bribe). Finally he joins the famous Vilna theater troupe when they perform in Warsaw and rehearses for the part of Chonen in The Dybbuk. *When he meets Ansky (Shlomo Rappoport), the famous playwright and folklorist, the author tells Baruch, "When I wrote the part of Chonen, I must have thought of Baruch Lumet!" But it is precisely then that his long* awaited ticket to America finally arrives. With a brother recently drafted into indefinite military service, he uses the ticket, never opening in the part.

In America, he moves to Philadelphia, where he obtains work as a salesman of musical instruments, even though he can't speak English (the boss gives him the Yiddish-speaking clients). Yet the urge to act never leaves him, and he finally breaks into the American Yiddish theater when Boris Thomashefsky brings his famous troupe to perform at the Philadelphia Opera House. He goes on to become a respected Yiddish actor, and the father of Sidney Lumet.

At the age of seventy-eight he recalled this hilarious, telling episode from his performance for Thomashefsky.

STORYTELLERS: MOSHE WALDOKS, WILLIAM NOVAK
SLEEP WITH A BAKER

Boris Thomashefsky, a star of the Yiddish theater, was as famous for his romantic pursuits as for his acting, and there was always an attractive woman waiting for him at the stage door.

One night, the story goes, Thomashefsky went home with an alluring young lady. In the morning, he handed her a gift—two front row tickets to that evening's performance.

The young lady was evidently disappointed, and she began to cry.

"What's wrong?" asked the actor in astonishment.

"Oh, Mr. Thomashefsky," she said. "I'm very poor. I don't need tickets. I need bread!"

"Bread?" cried Thomashefsky. "Thomashefsky gives tickets. You want bread? Sleep with a baker!"

PLOTTING TO KILL HARRY

Little by little I said, "What am I doing as a salesman, what happened to my acting?" And I took a few trips to New York—they had one-day excursions to New York—and a man came over to me, Zaslavsky was his name, a Jewish composer who had conducted in a Yiddish theater in Warsaw. He knew me from one of the old vaudeville houses. He says, "Baruch Lumet, what a coincidence. I just finished a score for a beautiful operetta to be opened in Philadelphia at the Philadelphia Opera House by the famous Boris Thomashefsky, producer, star, and director, whatnot. There is a beautiful part there for you; it's a young *yeshiva bukher*, a young *yeshiva* student who falls in love with a *shiksa* [a gentile woman]."

I said, "Well, it sounds good, and I could play a *yeshiva bukher*, whom I missed playing in *The Dybbuk* way back." Now I would have a chance not only to play a *yeshiva* student, but also to fall in love with a Polish girl. The Polish girl was played by the wife of Mr. Thomashefsky, who was perhaps twice my age, but she was beautiful. There was no such thing as age in the Yiddish theater. The star of the company was ageless.

So sure enough, one day I went to my boss and said, "Mr. Goldman, I will take a leave of absence."

He says, "You are crazy! You have accumulated so much money, about eighteen hundred dollars in payments that you have coming." As the customers made their payment for their instruments, I would get ten percent out of it. "You have a job and you are going back to the theater?"

But nothing could stop me at the time. I said, "I'm taking the part," and I began to rehearse in the theater to open in the Philadelphia Opera House. I didn't have to move to New York.

You see, the Philadelphia Opera House was built on Broad Street close to the Academy of Music, because Philadelphians wanted to have their opera house, and they spent an awful lot of money on it. But opera did not go over, the expenses for the building were too great, and they began to rent it as a theater. So who would get it for a show? Mr. Thomashefsky. He was a great showman, everything elaborate, everything big, he himself was a big man. Money was no problem.

We started to rehearse. I have never seen anything like it. A chorus of women, close to sixty women, and an equally large male chorus—on an opera stage, you can just imagine! Thomashefsky went to town, everything —new costumes, new wigs, new everything—all to tell the story of how a young student falls in love with the beautiful girl and her parents and his parents—the old story—they want to take her away from him. Finally she takes on the Jewish religion, and everything is kosher. It had a happy ending and beautiful music. Zaslavsky wrote a beautiful score.

In this same spectacle was another lover, we called him the villain. His name was Harry. I cannot mention his second name because he's still around here in Los Angeles. He took the part of the other lover, and the two of us were rivals in the play. But in real life Harry and I became very, very good friends. He was American born, and he taught me English.

During rehearsals, everything went beautifully. Mr. Thomashefsky threw me more lines, more scenes. Everyone in the cast thought that after opening night this greenhorn would become a star. What else can you ask for, such an opportunity?

Opening night came around. And, I must tell you, the jealousy started to build. Mr. Harry was a very good friend of mine, but jealousy is jealousy, you know. Actors are actors. And it's about five or ten minutes before curtain time, and I was in my dressing room lined with these opera house mirrors. Harry comes in to see me, his face drawn, eyes teary. "Baruch, I am in trouble, maybe you can help me. In fact, you can help me. Help me, please."

I said, "What happened, Harry?"

"Look. Here, read it." He gave me a letter.

I said, "I can't read English."

"All right, I'll read it to you."

It was written, "Harry dear, you know how much I was in love with you. I'm pregnant. You promised to give me money for an abortion, but you turned away from me, you changed your mind. I am desperate, I'm afraid if my parents find out they will just commit suicide. I can't find you and I don't know where you are. I know you rehearse, but you never want to see me. I'm desperate, now I am taking my revenge. Tonight as you appear on that stage I have a ticket in the front row center. I also have a gun in my bag. As you appear on that stage, I will shoot you down like a dog." Signed, "Your girl, who still loves you very, very much, Anna Maria."

"Who's Anna Maria? Harry, go out and get her!"

He said, "Where can I get her? Opening night, the theater is packed. Five minutes before curtain, where can I get her?"

"I don't care. Go tell Thomashefsky to hold up the curtain. You must find her. Shooting in the theater on opening night, the house is packed, people will be killed." I became more desperate than he was.

"Wait a minute," he says, "calm down. I'll tell you. It is impossible for me to find her now. I'll tell you what I'll do. I'm only appearing in one act, the first act. When I come on that stage, ignore me, don't mind, don't mind where I go, it will be changed. The blocking will be changed, and I'll manage to stay behind you."

I said, "Behind me? Are you crazy? What do you mean, you want me to get killed for you? I have a wife and a child, this is my first appearance in America." And I began to cry. "Harry, you must find her!"

He said, "Wait. I'll manage."

I said, "You will not manage. Go out! Go and tell— Oh, get out of my dressing room, get out!" He ran out, I was in tears. You can imagine how I felt.

Then, suddenly, we hear the stage manager calling, "All on stage, curtain going up. Actors, take your places." I didn't know what to do. I walked to that stage, of course, without my glasses, and I'm nearsighted, I didn't know where I was walking. I hear the overture, the chorus on stage, the applause, everything, the lights, I never saw such a thing in my life. And on a certain musical cue I had to walk in. I came in and I walked in different directions, and she came over to me, Regina Tsukenberg, the prima donna. "Baruch, what's happening to you, stage fright? Compose yourself." That's what she could understand, stage fright. And I said, "No, I . . ." In the meantime I missed a musical cue.

All of a sudden I saw Harry on stage behind a tree, like a villain. Then he came up, it was a beautiful set, you've never seen anything like it. And he came on stage and wherever I turned he was behind me. He was scared crazy, absolutely crazy. And we start to sing our numbers and the drums roll—bang, bang. But I didn't hear drums, I heard shots! The bass drum, I looked around, is he dead? I touched myself—am I dead? I said to myself, My God, if I will live through this act, I'll live as long as my mother. My mother passed away at a hundred and seven.

Finally the curtain went down. I ran to my dressing room, the stage manager after me, "Baruch, come! Wait a minute, wait a minute! Hold it, come here! What happened on that stage? Thomashefsky wants to see you."

I came into his dressing room, he looks at me calmly and says, "Mr. Lumet, I gave you such a chance, and what happened on that stage? You lost yourself completely." I didn't know what to say, I couldn't tell him the truth. Finally he began to get a little, or I should say more than a little, unhappy. So I burst out crying and I told him the story. I told him what happened.

He looked at me, and he burst out laughing. He said, "You idiot. You don't know Harry? Harry's a trickster, he likes to play tricks on actors, that's his nature, but this was purely professional jealousy. You believed, pardon the expression, that cock-and-bull story he told you? Go inside, get in your dressing room, wash off your face, put on fresh makeup, and I want to see a second act, Mr. Lumet, you hear me?"

I didn't know what to say. Was it really possible that an actor would do a thing like that? I went to my dressing room. The second act went fine because he wasn't in it. When it was over I was desperately hoping not to meet Harry, because this time there would be murder backstage.

I still got beautiful reviews, but not the reviews I expected. I was hoping to become a star after this performance, and here I fluffed so many things. . . .

During the night I received a telephone call from the stage manager. "Baruch, tomorrow ten o'clock you have a rehearsal." I thought, Of course, we need the rehearsal after what happened last night. "Thomashefsky called New York and another actor's coming in."

That was the end of Harry and his career in the theater. I never saw him again, never, never, until many, many years later, in fact, about two or three years ago. We attended the funeral of Edward G. Robinson, and an old man came over to me with a long white beard and long white hair: "Hello. Remember me? I am Harry. You remember?"

I smiled. He said, "I never went back to the theater again. You know, I came to Los Angeles and I started to paint and I'm still earning a living from my art."

And I said, "Yes, I remember, yes. I didn't forget, but I forgave you."

ZYPORA SPAISMAN

I first heard about the Folksbiene Playhouse because they were nominated for—and then received—a People's Hall of Fame Award, which the nonprofit City Lore presents to honor grass-roots contributions to New York's cultural life. Friends had told me about the theater, the last holdout of the vibrant Second Avenue Yiddish theater tradition. When I arrived at their Fifty-fifth Street address, I discovered it was the posh entrance of Manhattan's Central Synagogue. I asked the security guard where I could find the Folksbiene, and he told me to walk down the hall and look to the right, I couldn't miss them. I walked into the lobby, and it's true, I couldn't miss them—three elderly people sitting at a card table on the right side of the lobby. A telephone plunked in the center told me that this was their office; it is to this convenient location in the lobby that they have been relegated after a financial cutback at the synagogue (they still use the synagogue's auditorium for their performances).

Seated around the table were Elyse Frummer, their new manager, drafted three years ago when Ben Schecter, their revered manager for forty years, passed away; 101-year-old Morris Adler, the president and former leading man (he is not related to the famous Yiddish actor Jacob Adler, though he did know him); and Zypora Spaisman, who became a childhood actress in Poland, was captured by the Russians at the age of seventeen, spent ten years in a Russian concentration camp in World War II, became the Folksbiene leading lady in 1956, and is still passionate, melodramatic, and beautiful at the enduring age of thirty-nine.

The Folksbiene was founded in 1915, with sponsorship from the Workman's Circle as Chapter 555, a status it retains to this day. Originally an amateur, now a professional, company, it has not missed a season in its eighty years. On a good night they have three hundred people; on a bad night they play to empty seats or paper the house. Their main problem is finding actors who speak Yiddish; they actually train many aspiring Broadway actors by teaching them to sound out the Yiddish words phonetically.

"With so many financial struggles, and fewer people speaking the language," I asked them, "Do you worry about your future as the last Yiddish theater?"

"We do not want to say the last," Adler says. "We hope that some young person will take it over, and make it bloom. If Jews don't have hope, they wouldn't be in existence as Jews. There's a Jewish song that was written in the concentration camp: 'Don't ever say you are walking the last mile.'"

When Zypora was being transported to the Russian concentration camp in Siberia in a cattle car, she was called to deliver a baby on the train. She had training as a midwife, and on June 29, 1942, as she remembers, "I delivered a beautiful boy on a moving train. I dream sometimes that I will meet that baby I delivered, here in America, in New York. And I say to him, 'Are you rich?' and he says, 'Yes.' And I say to him, 'Give a fund in your parents' name for the Folksbiene.' I have a dream—this kid will show up some time for me."

THE LONESOME SHIP

In the old days, 1910, 1912, when the audiences would come to the Yiddish theater, they brought supper, chicken and eggs, everything. Second Avenue, they come with the whole family. Why they came? They were lonesome, they were newcomers, and they came to the theater because the theater gave them a place where they could come to cry and to laugh and to eat!

They used to have prompters who sat under the stage in a booth and would tell the actor what he had to say. But the actor ignored them. He talked what he liked. If he saw the people laughing too much and he wanted them to cry, he just put in—from another show—some lines to make them happy. Because this was the one place that the immigrants could enjoy, because they lost their families, they lost everything, they came to our city, to our town, to our world, they're not speaking well English—the Yiddish theater was their home. This was the early early days.

The audience for a Yiddish play is so devoted to you. In one of the shows, I played a very sloppy woman, a terrible gossip—my stockings were torn, my blouse was hooked with safety pins, I looked a mess. After the show I was approached by a woman waiting for me outside the theater. She said, "Mrs. Spaisman, we saw you last week, and we see you don't have a blouse and you don't have stockings. So we brought you three pairs of stockings and a blouse and an apron." The audiences believed what they saw on stage.

In another show I played a woman whose husband had a heart attack and died. And as I was leaving the theater, a woman asked me, "What happened, when will be the funeral?" They believe so much. They forgot my name is Spaisman, they called me by name in the play, Mrs. Rubin. "Mrs. Rubin," they asked, "when is going to be the funeral?" And I don't want to take away the illusion. I said to her, "Tomorrow, read the papers, you will find the time and place of the funeral."

When I arrived in the United States and I went into the Folksbiene, I played my debut in a show called *The Lonesome Ship* that we performed in 1956. You see, in 1939, when Jewish people were fleeing the Nazis, there was a group waiting to leave Europe, I believe it was in Marseille. There was one French captain who found a broken-down ship called the *St. Louis*. He said to the Jews, "I'm going to save you." He took a whole group of them on the ship and sailed for Cuba. He asked for permission to land in the United States, and President Roosevelt would not accept any of the Jews. He sent them back. And the ship never made it, almost all the people were killed. It was a tragic episode that Jews have never forgotten.

This is a true story, and a Jewish writer, Choshe Glushnosky, made a show of it called *The Lonesome Ship*. And when I came to try out, the director said I looked like a German and cast me as a German with a Jewish husband. And in the play I was on the ship with the old people, and they were crying and asking for help, and I was playing the part of a German spy, giving signals to help the German submarines find the boat and torpedo it. And I have signals that this is a Jewish ship.

The play was so realistic that I had to leave the theater disguised; the audience outside wanted to kill me for being a spy. "What the hell is she doing in the Folksbiene?" they asked. Here I was the victim of a concentration camp myself.

And I want to tell you, at the time, in 1956, we didn't have a theater, we played in the Y on Stanton Street. Downstairs, they're playing Ping-Pong. Upstairs they're playing handball. And every time they bounced the balls, it made the ship rock—the vibrations were so strong, the ship would rock. It was so realistic. People wanted to know how we did it! They thought it was part of the set.

AN EXCHANGE BETWEEN ZYPORA SPAISMAN
AND JACOB ADLER, 9/13/95
A LOVE SCENE ANY TIME

Zypora: I was interviewed by Mr. Adler for the Folksbiene in 1954, when I first came to America. He gave me the four commandments of the Folksbiene: one, you come to the rehearsals at seven o'clock; two, you leave when rehearsal is finished, whether you have to go to work or not; three, you don't ask for a part, the director gives you the part; four, you don't get paid. Then you had to sign your name.

Mr. Adler, you know I didn't like you very much for years. You remember? I hated you. Because you were looking for every little thing I did wrong—you were a tough man, and we loved you. We were a family, the Folksbiene was our home. We are proud to have these memories. And I'm very pleased to have Adler around at the age of a hundred and one—maybe we will make a love scene someday, when I will be hundred and you will be a hundred ten.

Adler: A love scene I can make any time.

E.
JEWISH SUMMER CAMPS

RABBI DAVID HOLTZ

At the Joseph and Betty Harlam Camp Institute for Living Judaism, nestled in the Poconos, there is a chapel in the woods. A triple-trunk tree serves as the ark and a large rock in front as the Torah reading table. Each Shabbat morning, the young campers gather for services.

"The campers are out there in the hot sun," Rabbi Holtz told me in his study at Temple Beth Abraham in Tarrytown, New York. "Even though it's under trees, the sun burns down, the bugs swarm around, and the kids are utchy, wanting to run around, nudging each other. So it's certainly not a place for a formal sermon, so I look for more engaging ways of getting a message across—and one is by means of a story."

Rabbi Holtz first came to Harlam (one of nine Reform Jewish summer camps) thirteen summers ago as a student at the Hebrew Union College Jewish Institute of Religion. Each summer he returns to counsel campers, tell stories, play the guitar, sometimes all at the same time.

WATER AND WINE

Once upon a time in the old country (where all the best stories took place), there was a town in a wine-producing region of Eastern Europe. The villagers in this region heard that a very famous rabbi was going to be on a grand tour early the following year and would be passing through their town. So they called a town meeting and said, "We must have some kind of great celebration in the rabbi's honor."

Then one of the villagers suggested, "Since we all make wine, wouldn't it be wonderful if we had some kind of wine festival where we tasted the very best of the wine?"

And then someone countered, "But each family only makes a little wine each year. A big celebration would use up one family's entire supply of wine for a year."

So they devised a plan. They put a big oak barrel in the center of the town, and every week, just before *Shabbat*, every household was to bring a small pitcher of wine and pour it into the cask. Then, by the end of the six months, they would have a great cask of wine.

But in one of the village families, the husband went home and he said to his wife, "Listen, you know that everyone is going to be bringing wine, and we are not a rich family. There's going to be so much wine in that cask, ours certainly will make no difference. Why don't we just fill our pitcher up with water? When I take it to the cask, I'll pour it in right at the lip—I guarantee you that no one will see." And that's what he did, every week.

Six months later the big day arrived. They set up a stand in the center of town and put the cask on top of it. Right on schedule, the famous rabbi appeared. The townspeople were all very proud of their village, their wine, and the rabbi. They presented him with a beautiful, ceremonial *kiddish* cup to taste the wine and inaugurate the celebration. He put the lovely cup underneath the spigot, filled it up, and lifted it high.

Suddenly there was a gasp from the crowd: his cup was filled to the brim with water.

STORYTELLER: RABBI DAVID HOLTZ

This is a community-building story. It's perfect to tell to a group of kids in a bunk. There's only twelve of you in this room, so you're not going to clean the bathroom this week? What if everyone said that?

STORYTELLER: PENINNAH SCHRAM

A few years ago I told this story as part of a *Shabbat* service at Temple Sinai in Los Angeles. One of the many Iranian congregants came up to me afterward and told me that story was a family story his father had told to them and repeated many times over, to teach this important family/community-building lesson. In fact, he was quite surprised to hear this story told outside his family.

THE HOLOCAUST

On November 9 and 10, 1938, *Kristallnacht*, "the night of the broken glass," shattered Jewish lives all through Germany, a horrendous portent of things to come. By the end of the war, two-thirds of all the Jews in Europe had been murdered. The names of the camps symbolize the horror: Treblinka, Majdanek, Belzec, Auschwitz. Following the war, about fifty thousand straggling survivors came to America.

Marc Kaminsky has written brilliantly on survivor stories: "Only through the experience of our nightmares, only through our own descent into a private, psychological hell, can we form any idea of the survivor as storyteller—that of a recurring immersion in a reality that was immediately experienced as unreal, and that continues to isolate the survivor in its incommunicability. This analogy is as near as empathy can come to comprehending an historical experience in which empathetic listening as a source of knowledge must end in failure."

Unlike the stories of survivors, the mass media's treatment of the Holocaust is not so much about remembering as titillating and forgetting. Kaminsky writes, "Photographs of people in anguish are flashed before us by the mass media so that we are always repeating the lesson of turning away. While the stories of survivors never let us forget how much of the event we can never know, the mass media tends to make us wholly ignorant of just how ignorant we are." The stories contain within them silences that the tales have, in the telling, broken.

Since the war there have been numerous projects to collect the stories of the survivors, among them the Brooklyn Center for Holocaust Studies at Brooklyn College, the American Jewish Committee's Oral History Project, the Video History Project of the Museum of Jewish Heritage, and Yale University's Fortunoff Video Archives for Holocaust Testimonies. After the success of *Schindler's List*, Steven Spielberg funded the Shoah Project, the most ambitious collecting effort to date. "Our future depends on our testimony," states Elie Wiesel. "To forget Auschwitz is to justify Hiroshima—the next Hiroshima. It's a paradox: only Auschwitz can save the planet from a new Hiroshima. This is why survivors often overcome their fear and trembling and speak up."

A.
FOLK AND HASIDIC TALES

RABBI ISRAEL SPIRA/YAFFA ELIACH

In the foreword to his masterful collection of tales first published posthumously in 1815, Rabbi Nachman of Bratslav tells that when his great uncle, the Baal Shem Tov, the founder of Hasidism, saw the lines of communication with heaven were severed and it was impossible to mend them with prayer, he restored contact by telling a tale.

The Holocaust savagely threatened all the lines of communication with heaven, but the miraculous tales of the Grand Rabbi of Bluzhov, Rabbi Israel Spira, leader of a Hasidic dynasty, clung to the spiritual and never lost contact with God. His tales chronicle a response to the Holocaust that comes from a point of pure, indestructible spirituality that is at the heart of Hasidic tradition. Beautifully recorded and retold by Yaffa Eliach in Hasidic Tales of the Holocaust, they are filled with the stench of barracks and the feel of barbed wire, but they are set in the human heart. The stories manifest a metaphysical resistance to the Holocaust; the ability to maintain unfettered belief in the face of desolation and destruction.

In his tales of Janowska, Bergen-Belsen, and Auschwitz, Rabbi Israel Spira and his fellow Hasidim in the camps wage a defiant spiritual struggle to celebrate the Jewish holidays. The rabbi, who died in Brooklyn in 1990, tells of lighting the first Hanukkah light and of trying to obtain matzoh for the seder in the Bergen-Belsen camp. The first story, "Even the Transgressors in Israel," tells of the struggle to celebrate Yom Kippur, the holiest day of the year.

EVEN THE TRANSGRESSORS
IN ISRAEL

"This particular story is one of those stories that deserves to be published in a book," said the Rabbi of Bluzhov to his Hasidim as he was telling about his experiences during the concentration camp era.

In the Janowska Road Camp, there was a foreman of a brigade from Lvov by the name of Schneeweiss, one of those people one stays away from if he values his life. He had known Rabbi Israel Spira in Lemberg (Lvov) but was not aware that the latter was an inmate at the Janowska Road Camp. Only a handful of Hasidim who were close to the rabbi knew the rabbi's identity, and they kept it a secret.

The season of the Jewish holidays was approaching. As the date of Yom Kippur neared the fears in camp mounted. Everyone knew that the Germans especially liked to use Jewish holidays as days for inflicting terror and death. In Janowska, a handful of old-timers remembered large selections of persons to die on Simchat Torah and Purim.

It was the evening of Yom Kippur. The tensions and the fears were at their height. A few Hasidim, among them Mendel Freifeld and others, came to the Rabbi of Bluzhov and asked him to approach Schneeweiss and request that on Yom Kippur his group not be assigned to any of the thirty-nine main categories of work, so that their transgression of the law by working on Yom Kippur would not be a major one. The rabbi was very moved by the request of his Hasidim and despite his fears, for he would have to disclose his identity, went to Schneeweiss. He knew quite well that Schneeweiss did not have much respect for Jewish tradition. Even prior to the outbreak of World War II, he had publicly violated the Jewish holidays and transgressed against Jewish law. Here in Janowska, he was a cruel man who knew no mercy.

With a heavy heart, the rabbi went before Schneeweiss. "You probably remember me. I am the rabbi of Pruchnik, Rabbi Israel Spira." Schneeweiss did not respond. "You are a Jew like myself," the rabbi continued. "Tonight is Kol Nidre night. There is a small group of young Jews who do not want to transgress any of the thirty-nine main categories of work. It means everything to them. It is the essence of their existence. Can you do something about it? Can you help?"

The rabbi noticed that a hidden shiver went through Schneeweiss as he listened to the rabbi's strange request. The rabbi took Schneeweiss's hand and said, "I promise you, as long as you live, it will be a good life. I beg you to do it for us so that we may still find some dignity in our humiliating existence."

The stern face of Schneeweiss changed. For the first time since his arrival at Janowska, there was a human spark in it.

"Tonight I can't do a thing," said Schneeweiss, the first words he had uttered since the rabbi had come to him. "I have no jurisdiction over the night brigade. But tomorrow, on Yom Kippur, I will do for you whatever I can." The rabbi shook Schneeweiss's hand in gratitude and left.

That night they were taken to work near the Lvov cemetery. To this very day, the rabbi has scars from the beatings of that night. They returned to their barracks at one o'clock in the morning exhausted, beaten, with blood flowing from fresh wounds. The rabbi was trying to make his way to bed, one level of a five-tiered bunk bed made of a few wooden planks covered with straw. Vivid images from the past, of Yom Kippur at home with his family and Hasidim, passed before his tear-filled eyes that wretched night at Janowska.

Suddenly the door opened and into the barracks came a young Hasid named Ben-Zion. "Rabbi, we must recite Kol Nidre."

"Who can say Kol Nidre now?" the rabbi replied. "The people can't even stand on their feet."

"Rabbi, I used to pray in your *shtibl*. Do you remember the tune?" In the darkness of the barracks, among the rows of hungry, beaten, exhausted Jews, a melody was heard, the soothing, comforting melody of Yom Kippur, as Ben-Zion chanted a prayer:

And pardon shall be granted to the whole congregation of Israel and to the stranger who sojourneth among them. . . .

"Rabbi, the heart wants to hear a prayer. We must say Kol Nidre. . . ." As Ben-Zion was talking to the rabbi, about twenty men gathered around them. How could he refuse? He took out his prayer shawl, which he kept well hidden underneath the straw on his bunk bed, and was about to begin to chant the Kol Nidre.

No one knew how, but the news spread fast: In barracks number twelve they were chanting the Kol Nidre. In the dark shadows of the Janowska barracks one could see shapes against the barracks walls as they made their way to barracks number twelve.

They recited with the rabbi whatever they could recall from memory. When they reached the prayer "Hear our voice, O Lord our God; have pity and compassion. . . ." the voices were drowned in tears.

In the morning, the rabbi and a small group of young Hasidim were summoned to Schneeweiss's cottage. "I heard that you prayed last night. I don't believe in prayers," Schneeweiss told them. "On principle, I even oppose them. But I admire your courage. For you all know well that the penalty for prayer in Janowska is death." With that, he motioned them to follow him.

He took them to the SS quarters in the camp, to a large wooden house. "You fellows will shine the floor without any polish or wax. And you, Rabbi, will clean the windows with dry rags so that you will not transgress any of the thirty-nine major categories of work." He left the room abruptly without saying another word.

The rabbi was standing on a ladder with rags in his hand, cleaning the huge windows while chanting prayers, and his companions were on the floor polishing the wood and praying with him.

> All of them are beloved, pure and mighty, and all of them in
> dread and awe do the will of their Master; and all of them open
> their mouths in holiness and purity, with song and psalm, while they
> glorify and ascribe sovereignty to the name of the Divine King.

"The floor was wet with our tears. You can imagine the prayers of that Yom Kippur," said the rabbi to the Hasidim who were listening to his tale while he was wiping away a tear.

At about twelve o'clock noon, the door opened wide and into the room stormed two angels of death, SS men. The room was filled with an aroma of freshly cooked food, such food as they had not seen since the

German occupation: white bread, steaming hot vegetable soup, and huge portions of meat.

The tall SS man commanded in a high-pitched voice, "You must eat immediately; otherwise you will be shot on the spot!"

None of them moved. The rabbi remained on the ladder, the Hasidim on the floor. The German repeated the orders. The rabbi and the Hasidim remained glued to their places.

The SS men called in Schneeweiss. "Schneeweiss, if the dirty dogs refuse to eat, I will kill you along with them."

Schneeweiss pulled himself to attention, looked the German directly in the eyes, and said in a very quiet tone, "We Jews do not eat today. Today is Yom Kippur, our most holy day, the Day of Atonement."

"You don't understand, Jewish dog," roared the taller of the two. "I command you in the name of the Führer and the Third Reich, *fress!*"

Schneeweiss, composed, his head high, repeated the same answer. "We Jews obey the law of our tradition. Today is Yom Kippur, a day of fasting."

The German took out his revolver from its holster and pointed it at Schneeweiss's temple. Schneeweiss remained calm. He stood still, at attention, his head high. A shot pierced the room. Schneeweiss fell. On the freshly polished floor, a puddle of blood was growing bigger and bigger.

The rabbi and the Hasidim stood as if frozen in their places. They could not believe what their eyes had just witnessed. Schneeweiss, the man who in the past had publicly transgressed against the Jewish tradition, had sanctified God's name publicly and died a martyr's death for the sake of Jewish honor.

"Only then, on that Yom Kippur day in Janowska," said the rabbi to his Hasidim, "did I understand the meaning of the statement in the Talmud: 'Even the transgressors in Israel are as full of good deeds as a pomegranate is filled with seeds.'"

CIRCUMCISION

"I will tell you another story," said Rabbi Israel Spira to his student Baruch Baer Singer, "a story that took place in the Janowska Road Camp.

Janowska was one of those camps about which, if one is to recall the events that took place during one year, one can fill the pages with tales of heroism, suffering, and death. Not one book, but ten volumes. And even then, it would just be a drop in the ocean.

"Many have asked me to publish the stories of Janowska in a book. I told them I am not writing new books. It would be sufficient if we read and studied the existing books. But this particular story is a duty to record. It is a *mitzva* to tell it, for it is a tale about the devotion and sacrifice of a daughter of Israel.

"One morning in Janowska, I was standing and sawing wood with another *katzetnik* [camp inmate]. To humiliate us as much as possible, I was given as a partner a very short man. As you see, thank God, I am not among the short ones. It made the wood sawing both a difficult task and a laughable sight. With each pull of the saw my partner would stretch out and stand on the tips of his toes, and I would bend down till my aching, swollen feet were bleeding. And the Germans stood by and watched our misery and suffering with delight.

"One morning, on Hoshana Rabbah, as we were sawing wood, the wind carried in our direction piercing, tormented cries such as I had never heard before, even in the Janowska hell. The desperate clamor was coming closer and closer, as if the weeping were filling up the entire universe and drowning it with painful tears.

" 'It's a children's *Aktion*, little angels from the entire vicinity of Drohobycz, Borislov, Lvov, Stryi, Stanislav, and others were brought here to meet their Maker,' said a *katzetnik* who passed by, pushing a wheelbarrow, without even glancing in our direction. I thought the cries would shake the world's foundation. We continued sawing the wood as our eyes became heavier and heavier with tears.

"Suddenly, just next to us, I heard the voice of a woman. 'Jews, have mercy upon me and give me a knife.' In front of us was standing a woman, pale as a sheet. Only her eyes were burning with a strange fire. I thought that she wanted to commit suicide. I looked around, and since I saw no German in sight, I said to her, 'Why are you in such a rush to get to the World of Truth? We will get there sooner or later. What difference can one day make?'

" 'Dog, what did you say to the woman?' A tall young German who appeared from nowhere demanded an answer, while swinging his rubber truncheon above my head.

" 'The woman asked for a knife. I explained to her that we Jews are not permitted to take our lives. For our lives are entrusted in the hands of God.' I added hastily, 'And I hope that you, too, will spare our lives.'

"The German did not respond to my words. He turned to the woman and demanded an explanation from her. She answered curtly, 'I asked for a knife.'

"As she was talking, she kept examining the German with her feverish eyes. Suddenly her eyes stopped wandering. Her gaze was fixed on the top pocket of the German's uniform. The shape of a knife was clearly visible through the pocket. 'Give me that pocket knife!' she ordered the German in a commanding voice. The German, taken by surprise, handed the knife to the woman.

"She bent down and picked up something. Only then did I notice a bundle of rags on the ground near the sawdust. She unwrapped the bundle. Amidst the rags on a snow white pillow was a newborn babe, asleep. With a steady hand she opened the pocket knife and circumcised the baby. In a clear, intense voice she recited the blessing of the circumcision: 'Blessed art thou, O Lord our God, King of the Universe, who has sanctified us by thy Commandments and hast commanded us to perform the circumcision.'

"She straightened her back, looked up to the heavens, and said, 'God of the Universe, you have given me a healthy child. I am returning to you a wholesome, kosher Jew.' She walked over to the German, gave him back his bloodstained knife, and handed him her baby on his snow white pillow.

"Amidst a veil of tears, I said to myself then that this mother's circumcision would probably shake the foundations of heaven and earth. Next to Abraham on Mount Moriah, where could you find a greater act of faith than this Jewish mother's?"

The rabbi looked at his student with tear-filled eyes and said, "Since liberation, each time I am honored at a circumcision to be a *sandek* [godfather], it is my custom to tell this particular story."

HOVERING ABOVE THE PIT

It was a dark, cold night in the Janowska Road Camp. Suddenly, a stentorian shout pierced the air: "You are all to evacuate the barracks immediately and report to the vacant lot. Anyone remaining inside will be shot on the spot!"

Pandemonium broke out in the barracks. People pushed their way to the doors while screaming the names of friends and relatives. In a panic-stricken stampede, the prisoners ran in the direction of the big open field.

Exhausted, trying to catch their breath, they reached the field. In the middle were two huge pits.

Suddenly, with their last drop of energy, the inmates realized where they were rushing, on that cursed dark night in Janowska.

Once more, the cold, healthy voice roared in the night: "Each of you dogs who values his miserable life and wants to cling to it must jump over one of the pits and land on the other side. Those who miss will get what they rightfully deserve—ra-ta-ta-ta-ta."

Imitating the sound of a machine gun, the voice trailed off into the night, to be followed by a wild, coarse laughter. It was clear to the inmates that they would all end up in the pits. Even at the best of times it would have been impossible to jump over them, all the more so on that cold, dark night in Janowska. The prisoners standing at the edge of the pits were skeletons, feverish from disease and starvation, exhausted from slave labor and sleepless nights. Though the challenge that had been given them was a matter of life and death, they knew that for the SS and the Ukrainian guards it was merely another devilish game.

Among the thousands of Jews on that field in Janowska was the Rabbi of Bluzhov, Rabbi Israel Spira. He was standing with a friend, a free thinker from a large Polish town whom the rabbi had met in the camp. A deep friendship had developed between the two.

"Spira, all of our efforts to jump over the pits are in vain. We only entertain the Germans and their collaborators, the Askaris. Let's sit down in the pits and wait for the bullets to end our wretched existence," said the friend to the rabbi.

"My friend," said the rabbi as they were walking in the direction of the pits, "man must obey the will of God. If it was decreed from heaven that pits be dug and we be commanded to jump, pits will be dug and jump we must. And if, God forbid, we fail and fall into the pits, we will reach the World of Truth a second later, after our attempt. So, my friend, we must jump."

The rabbi and his friend were nearing the edge of the pits; the pits were rapidly filling up with bodies.

The rabbi glanced down at his feet, the swollen feet of a fifty-three-year-old Jew ridden with starvation and disease. He looked at his young friend, a skeleton with burning eyes.

As they reached the pit, the rabbi closed his eyes and commanded in a powerful whisper, "We are jumping!" When they opened their eyes, they found themselves standing on the other side of the pit.

"Spira, we are here, we are here, we are alive!" the friend repeated over and over again, while warm tears streamed from his eyes. "Spira, for your sake, I am alive; indeed, there must be a God in heaven. Tell me, *Rebbe*, how did you do it?"

"I was holding on to my ancestral merit. I was holding on to the coattails of my father and my grandfather and my great-grandfather, of blessed memory," said the rabbi, and his eyes searched the black skies above. "Tell me, my friend, how did *you* reach the other side of the pit?"

"I was holding on to you," replied the rabbi's friend.

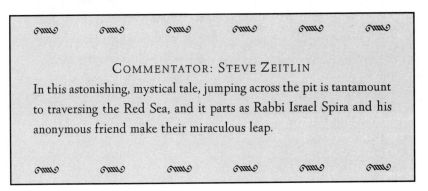

COMMENTATOR: STEVE ZEITLIN

In this astonishing, mystical tale, jumping across the pit is tantamount to traversing the Red Sea, and it parts as Rabbi Israel Spira and his anonymous friend make their miraculous leap.

VISITOR: YAFFA ELIACH, AUTHOR OF
HASIDIC TALES OF THE HOLOCAUST

At one point, while I was listening to the tape of an oral history account, my tape recorder fell off my desk and broke. I rushed upstairs from my study to tell my family. Our daughter, Smadar, who since grammar school has watched me sit at my desk and listen to tapes, said, "Mother, your tape recorder did not break, it simply jumped off your desk and committed suicide. How could you have expected your tape recorder to function till now? It never played a cheerful sound of music, it never recorded ordinary conversation. Even a machine can't bear it any longer."

My tape recorder "recovered" quickly. I could close it, push a button and silence it. But my mind was rarely "off." Tales would follow me and stay with me. The experience overwhelmed me with a sense of responsibility and left me doubting my abilities to fulfill my mission. I constantly sensed that the tale entrusted to me was a living witness, a quivering soul. The painful spoken words were a memorial to a family, to a mother, father, brothers, sisters, the only testimony to their ever having existed on this blood-soaked earth. Now the responsibility rested with me, to pass on the legacy of their lives and deaths. If the tale fails, the only imprint of their existence will be a path of blackened sky and a handful of scattered ashes.

NINA JAFFE AND STEVE ZEITLIN

Storyteller Nina Jaffe and I first heard this story from Rabbi Avi Weiss, who told it at a 1992 Jewish storytelling conference at Stern College for Women of Yeshiva University in New York City. We learned from Rabbi Weiss that he had used it in his sermons for many years and that he had originally heard it from a fellow rabbi at the Laurel Park Hotel in Old South Fallsburg, New York, when he was nineteen years old. We felt that this traditional story could be recast as a foreboding omen to the Holocaust. Nina and I retold it this way for the children's book we coauthored, While Standing on One Foot: Puzzle Stories and Wisdom Tales from the Jewish Tradition, *and the story is now becoming part of Nina's repertoire as a Jewish storyteller.*

IN YOUR HANDS

Walking through the streets of Bremen in the 1930s, anyone could easily see signs of the rising tide of hatred that was sweeping Germany. Everywhere there were soldiers in brown uniforms, members of the new National Socialist (Nazi) Party. Swastikas were painted on walls, and soldiers wore them on their sleeves. Mischievous children painted them on German synagogues. Teenagers in the much hated Hitler Youth Brigades passed by, marching in the famous goose step, kicking their legs up stiffly as they walked.

One gray afternoon, a rabbi walked sadly through the city, where everything was rapidly changing for the worse. He was filled with sorrow at what he thought might lie ahead. He hoped that the young generation would turn away from this Nazi movement that was taking over the country. In an open field, he saw two young men dressed in the dreaded brown uniforms. The rabbi could see the cruel mischief in their eyes as they approached. One of them had his hands cupped, as if he were holding a precious thing that was twitching and turning, struggling to escape. "What do you think I have in my hands?" snapped the young man.

The rabbi glanced at the Hitler Youth's trembling hands. He saw a feather drift gently from between his nervous fingers. "It's not hard to see," the rabbi said, "that you have a tiny bird cupped in your palms."

"Yes," said the young German, his lip quivering with anger and contempt. "But is the bird alive or dead? Tell us the right answer and no evil will befall you or your synagogue."

The wise rabbi realized that if he said the bird was dead, they would release the bird. But if he said the bird was alive, they would certainly kill it. In either case, wrongdoing was certain to befall both him and his congregation—and they would be the very ones responsible! The rabbi saw the history of the Jewish people pass before his eyes. How many times throughout history had they been put in a no-win situation? Forced to choose between two dead ends?

But the wise soul looked straight into the young man's eyes.

"You ask whether the bird is alive or dead," he said. "The answer is in your hands. The answer is in your hands."

SAM LEVENSON

Comedian Sam Levenson calls it "the folklore of oppression," the bitter humor that circulated both in the concentration camps and in America at the time. Humor was often the only possible form of defiance, and it remains part of the legacy of resistance. Some argue that elements of the humor belie too much acceptance of what happened; they point to the stories of two Jews who stand blindfolded before a firing squad. One pulls off the blindfold and begins to curse the German race. His friend pulls on his sleeve and says, "Don't make trouble." Yet most Holocaust humor has the Jews besting Hitler and the Germans.

There is, for instance, the widely known tale of a storm trooper who accosts an old rabbi, points a gun at his head, and asks, "Tell me, who caused all of the Fatherland's troubles?"

The frightened rabbi admits reluctantly, "The Jews." The German officer smiles.

Then the rabbi adds, "And the pretzel bakers."

"Why the pretzel bakers?" asks the German.

"Why the Jews?" comes the eternal reply.

Sam Levenson's story "The Wand" imagines a striking scenario: Hitler, at Dunkirk, standing before the English Channel, supposing that he can make the waters part for him just as they did for Moses at the Red Sea.

THE WAND

Soon after Dunkirk, Hitler makes it to the shore of France. Looking across, he can almost see England, it's about seven miles. That's the next stop, see. But it's a hard one to take—how do you get across and finish up the war?

One of his advisers says, "You know, it is written somewhere in the Hebrew Bible that Moses was faced with crossing the Red Sea, and how did he get across? The waters parted and he walked across with his men and all."

"How did he do it?"

"Well, the Bible says he had a wand, you see; he just smote the waters with the wand and the waters opened and there was dry land."

So Hitler says, "Let's get the wand, where's the wand?"

He says, "We don't know, we don't know where the wand is, see, it's a legend."

So Hitler says, "Well, you've got to ask a Jew."

So his adviser says, "Well, all right, we'll find the most important Jewish rabbi. We know just where he is, he's in Buchenwald, the concentration camp."

So the Nazis get him out and ask, "First of all, was there a wand?"

The rabbi says, "Yes, it is written that he took a wand."

So the adviser tells him, "Hitler says they'll release you, they'll free you, if you tell him where the wand is. All Hitler wants to know is how to get the wand."

The rabbi says, "He's going to have a hard time getting it."

The adviser says to him, "Why? Where is it?"

"It's in the British Museum."

Masterful story, a masterful story that remained in the folklore, the folklore of oppression.

COMMENTATOR: STEVE ZEITLIN
HUMOR OF THE HOLOCAUST

There is a kind of Talmudic sadness in some of the humor of the Holocaust. A Jewish man goes into a passport office and asks for a visa to leave the country. The German officers ask him where he would like to go. Seeing a globe on the desk, he points to the United States. "Impossible," they say, "they're not taking Jews." He points to England. Again, "Sorry, they're not taking Jews." He points to South America. "Sorry, none of those countries take Jews."

Finally, the Jewish man looks up and says, "you have another globe, maybe?"

What a wonderful response to the many people who ask, "Why didn't the Jews just leave?"

I heard a similar story from Elie Wiesel, who told it in one of his lectures at the 92nd Street Y. Some of the humor of the Holocaust is so sad, you really can't grasp whether it's funny or just tragic and bitter. A father and son visit a passport office to acquire visas to leave Germany. The son asks his father before they enter, "Where are we going, Dad?"

His father answers, "Anywhere, anywhere but here."

The father goes into the office. The son waits and waits. When his father joins him again, the son asks, "Father, where are we going?"

His father says, "Tierra del Fuego."

"Tierra del Fuego!" his son says. "But that's very, very far away."

His father answers, "Far from where?"

It's the saddest joke I've ever heard.

B.
BITTER MEMORIES

MELVIN KATZ

Melvin Katz, born in 1916, grew up in the shtetl of Opatow. During the war, he was relegated first to the Opatow ghetto and then to a series of concentration camps in Poland and then Germany: Sandojeiz, where they built roads in Poland; Radom, a munitions factory camp; Auschwitz, where the cattle car he was on stopped briefly to drop off women and children to be liquidated; Weihingen, where at least there was water to wash and slightly more humane conditions; Bissingen, where, in abysmal sanitary conditions, prisoners were used for slave labor to try to extract oil for airplane fuel from shale or "oil stones" (and where most of the stories told here took place); and finally to Dachau, where Melvin was liberated.

He was the youngest and the smallest of three children. Melvin grew only to five feet and was extremely frail. His parents said, " 'What will be with him?' The doctor gave me to take two times a day oil from a fish, cod liver oil. I still don't have an appetite. In the camps, that's what saved my life."

ONLY THE SMALL SURVIVE

That's my observation—the thinner people, the smaller people, had a better chance to survive than the big people. Five hundred calories a day is very little to eat, but my body never required that much. There were people in there who could eat a whole bread in one meal. They couldn't survive because they still got the same rations that I got. I was never able to eat that much.

Most people died from nonsanitary conditions. A person can survive on small portions, on five hundred, or four hundred to six hundred calories, for years and years and years. What happens to the body is that it becomes slowly a skeleton—they did become skeletons, they ate up their own fat. But you don't die right away from it—it takes you years to get to that point. But from unsanitary conditions, you can die in two months.

The other camps, at least, you had a place where you could have washed yourself and kept yourself half clean. The last six months we got into a camp, Bissingen, where we couldn't wash ourselves—at all. Our job there was to break up the stones to get oil for the airplanes, 'cause everything else was closed to the Germans, and they couldn't get oil any other way.

So we walked in mud, and our barracks were mud. You couldn't shave. And you didn't have no water to wash yourself. The only water you had is—we used to go after work over to the kitchen where they used to cook. The Germans looked out the window and they saw already there's a hundred people there waiting for water. Then the men in the kitchen took the hose and put it through the window and let it go. And you had to get some kind of utensil to catch the water, but you tried to get the water and somebody else wanted the water, too, and the water often spilled—it was very hard to get water, almost impossible.

In the morning, when you got the coffee, you put your hand in it to wipe out your eyes, because your eyes were sticking with the mud in between. You worked the whole day in mud. You came home, and you slept in mud because you didn't have where to wash yourself. You slept on wood shavings, and the shavings were not only rough, they were dirty, *farfoylt*, they got rotten. A German guard never stepped into our barracks, a normal person couldn't step in our barracks, because as soon he opened the door the smell hit you, the stench hit you. And in four months—of the 2,200 people in our camp, only 250 were left.

TYPHUS

The people in our camp died from dysentery and typhus from the unsanitary conditions. We were full of lice; the lice ate us up. You cannot imagine, you could put your hand under your arm and pull out a handful of lice.

At one point, me and two friends were the last from our town that were still alive. One already couldn't work, but we brought him with us. We knew if we left him in the barracks, they'd take him out, take him to the hospital, and once you went in there you never came out. I had a friend in the hospital one time. I brought him water. Because when you have typhus, you are in heat, and water makes it a little easier. I brought him some water one night. And he knew how hard it was to get the water. He knew how hard it was. He said, "Melvin, don't bother tomorrow, don't bring me the water."

I said, "Why not, Fischel?"

He said, "I won't be here no more."

I brought him in the water the next night. I came in, he was not there. He knew he wouldn't be there. Because, when the guards saw already prisoners were in the last stages, they buried them when they were still alive. While they were still breathing.

PRETENDING TO WORK

I used to do everything I could to avoid work. Most of the German officers you worked for would beat you if you didn't work fast enough. Once you got injured, you were finished. I worked once for a German, I saw he doesn't hit nobody—he had one eye only, and he was a *supetten Deutsch*, a "folks" German from Czechoslovakia. So I saw he doesn't hit— you work for him and he never picks up a hand—so whenever it was possible I tried to steal my way into his group.

But it was not possible to do that all the time. Once, we were working in the road, and another "master" (we called the officers "master") comes over. He needs twelve people. The man counts up, here's twelve people, take them. I'm among them. He takes us away. I could see it was a heavy turn. What we had to do, we had to carry rail tracks to build a railroad. Here I get with twelve people, to carry railroad tracks on our shoulders, and I'm so short that my shoulder doesn't reach the railroad tracks. So I put my head against the tracks, and I pretend to work. I see the master sees it and doesn't say nothing.

Then, after hours of the work crew carrying the tracks on their shoulders, and me resting the tracks on my head, a guard comes up, and he asks the master if he can borrow a man for an hour to dig foxholes. And the master said, "Take Melvin. Him you can have for a whole day."

And I thought to myself, This is the end. This is one on one, I won't be able to fool around. As I said, I didn't work no more. I just slid around, shuffling. I couldn't walk no more. So how can I take a pick in my hand or a shovel? I could dig a foxhole like I could make rich the heavens.

THE CIGARETTE

Well, I come over there, and he tells me to go over to a shed and bring out a shovel and a pick. Meanwhile, I see the crew, they keep putting the rails down, putting them down. By the time I was ready to do something they were out of our sight.

And I tell you that boy could have been no more than twenty-one or twenty-two years old, a nice young German fellow, blond hair, healthy looking. All of a sudden he said to me, "Now put this away." The pick. And he starts talking to me and telling me stories, and I don't say nothing. He wasn't an SS man. This was 1944, maybe the beginning of 1945, I think. He said his father was in a concentration camp in 1939, as a German—as a writer, his father was a writer. And he was nine months in concentration camps and then they let him come out. And this boy starts to talk—he was a pilot and he was injured, and they assigned him as a guard to our camp.

He wants to find out what I think about the Germans. He's trying me out, I don't open my mouth. He even gave me part of his lunch, and then I went home. He gave me two apples and a few cigarettes. A cigarette in our camp—if you say it's possible for you to get a million dollars, you have more chance than to get in our camp a cigarette.

When I got the cigarettes from him, I figured out that the best thing I can do is go over to the man who gives out the soup and tell him I got cigarettes, what'll I get? He said, "Okay, go through the line a second time." The man had a list, and we went by numbers. I would say, "four, six, three," and he would cross it out. But he didn't cross me out the first time, and I go up the second time.

And this was going on maybe for a month. But all of a sudden, I go up for my second soup, and another man, what was called a *jair* in camp, one who took care of the repairs, said, "You got already your soup today. Why do you go up for a second time?" And the man what had a deal with me said, "If he's going over the second time, I'll kill him." He checks the list and says, "Oh, no, no, no, no—this is the first time." But I saw already this is not going to work anymore, and I stopped going there.

But many days, I got to go back with the young German. It was not all the time possible for me to get there, but when I was working for him I always got something. I became like a businessman in the camp—the people who were the biggest *makhers* (big shots) didn't have what I have. But the most important thing what I got from him was a piece of soap. He told me to go over to the river to wash myself. If I ever thought that I would ever survive, I would ask him his name, where he lives, so I could thank him. But it was silly for me to ask, why would I ask, because I won't survive anyhow. You were only thinking about how do I get that piece of bread, how do you get to sleep, how do you get through the next day. You never thought of surviving.

NEW BARRACKS

Toward the end of the war, when the Germans were already negotiating with the Allies, they built new barracks for us—they tore down the old barracks because they were so contaminated, you couldn't use them. In the wintertime, you walked naked in mud—wintertime, all you had was those pajamas that you see sometimes on television with the stripes. And the stripes had a hundred holes, hundred holes. And there was no heat inside. In the new barracks they even built an oven. And showers with hot and cold water.

And you got assigned to a bed, what you didn't have before. It was as big as a single bed, maybe still narrower, but it was for two people, less than a twin bed. And they give you two blankets, one to put over the wood shavings and one to put over the two of you.

And all of a sudden they connect the water. They gave us soap and water, soap to clean us up, and we go through a disinfection. And then you have two soldiers, a surgeon and an SS man, and they give you a new striped suit, a new blanket, a new hat, a new pair of socks, but most important they give you a pair of rubber boots.

And we go to sleep—and they also built like a sidewalk around all the barracks into the kitchen from wood, from planks, it was about half a meter high—you shouldn't have to go up no more in the mud. My God —we come into a warm barracks, clean, doesn't smell, and we go to sleep —and this is not exaggerated. You fell to sleep, and you couldn't get up in the morning, 'cause normally you didn't sleep a whole night—you worked twelve hours and couldn't sleep, because the lice were eating you up. Either you were in the hospital already with 105 fever, or you couldn't sleep anyhow.

In the morning, the guards had an appeal to get up so they could count us, make sure nobody's missing, but they cannot wake us up— because after so many months not sleeping with everything eating you, you got clean, disinfected, in a warm barracks, the guards had to run around with sticks to wake us up, and I get up in the morning and we go to work, and again I'm telling you this is not exaggerated, I feel the blood circulating in my body. I felt the blood running in my body, and I swear to you I said to myself, My God, under those conditions I can stay with them another five years. Every day, I was able to pick my feet up higher and higher only because of the change of the sanitation conditions—our rations did not increase.

And then, about two months before the liberation, two thousand Jews come from Hungary to replace the ones who died. Two hundred and fifty people come into our barracks. From the original 250 Jews, only 4 Jews remained, and I was among the 4. So after they come in, they complain, how will they be able to survive? And they started complaining, they want this, they want that. And I tried to tell them, "This is no more a camp, you came in now to a fancy hotel."

VISITOR: BORIS BLUM
THE WOUNDED JESTER

In the morning after we were liberated in the vicinity of Dachau there was a shoe factory. The road was strewn with shoes. I found a pair my size, but I had no shoelaces, so I went to the factory. There were so many people dragging around boxes of shoes! I found a box of shoelaces, took out a pair, tied my shoes, and left.

Then we went into a German house. There were no men to be seen; the men had hidden. The German woman thought we had come to rob. We went over to a chest. In the chest lay all sorts of things: tablecloths, sheets. There was a very beautiful large red piece of material. The fellows took the tablecloths and material and spread them on the street, and I walked on a red carpet. I had found a German hat with a feather on it, and also an umbrella like those they use today at the beach.

Imagine me walking along, with a German hat with a feather, wearing a pair of sneakers, with my two friends continually spreading out tablecloths for me to walk on. It was muddy then, and I walked on the tablecloths. It was a kind of kingdom, a kind of *Bontshe Shvayg* parade. This was our way of celebrating.

LIBERATION

Then, at the very end, they took us out on a march, they wanted to take us wherever, because the Allies were already coming from all sides. And they took us in a railroad car. We walked for six days to Dachau, we walked for six days. In Dachau we came in, and I observed that—normally, they were well organized, the Germans. No matter what, they were organized, everything on paper. Here, they bring us into Dachau, and nobody is there to tell you anything. And we don't know, where do you go for soup? Where do you go to sleep? This was maybe the last four weeks before the liberation—and they were not no more so organized. And you run around naked, you possessed only a blanket to cover yourself, nothing else.

And we waited, and from there they said they couldn't take us to any camp, all the camps were controlled either by the Americans or the English or the Russians. And so we traveled on the trains back and forth for seven days, no destination. And finally one night they stopped. Nowhere to go. You just stayed there. And the SS was still with us. All those times when I was in camp, there was never Red Cross, all of a sudden the Red Cross comes, and we all get a package. And the package was a can of dried milk, a can of conserves, something like hash, a can of tuna, and a box of chocolate maybe three-quarters inch thick, covered with wax. When I opened the chocolate the chocolate was white inside, who knows how long it was there. And a package of Camels, Camel cigarettes.

So we opened the package and we ate everything, I ate everything in one shot. But then I get to the powdered milk, what do I do with the powdered milk?

And the Americans come the next morning. We get up the next morning, the SS are not there—all of sudden there are old people, maybe fifty, sixty years old, with carbines from World War I. And they become our guards. The SS ran away, left them in charge. The Americans came, maybe one hundred feet away. Once we saw the Americans we all run out—"Oh, the Americans are here, Americans are here"—and we run over to them, but we stank so bad, they tried to run away from us! At first I couldn't figure out why they were running. We run to them, they tried to run away from us. They couldn't stand the smell.

VISITOR: RENÉE FODOR SCHWARZ
SAVING MY SANITY

In the Auschwitz concentration camp, the constant pain, danger, fear, helplessness, and hopelessness attacked my sanity. Reality became unbearable and my awareness of reality's harshness, slowly reduced my perception, sending it out of focus. My senses grew numb, my energy diminished as if I were shrinking. I felt I was going down. This process took place without my will, and I did not know how to stop it. Feeling my sanity slip away was frightening. . . .

Pens, pencils, and writing paper of printed matter were strictly forbidden in the camp. Yet I greatly desired to tell the world about the life we were living. . . . Before sunset one day, I remained outside while the others entered the barracks from work. I smoothed out a sandy space until it felt smooth as paper. With a twig, I started to write. I was so happy that I had not forgotten how to write and read. With the twig as a pencil, I wrote more and more, but I do not remember what. I never shared my writing. Others avoided watching me for fear of being caught doing something forbidden. Every night, after I finished what I had to say, I carefully erased it, leaving no trace of my forbidden venture. So many parts of me were lost in the war; this precious one I left in the sand.

As carefully as I erased my writing from the sand, I tried to recall it in my mind; however, my fear of being caught made memory impossible. I longed to get in touch with lost compositions, but I could not. What I do remember is the feeling of my mind working again. I was able to think, the blood was flowing in my veins; and I felt my heartbeat increase. I even had momentary glimpses of joy.

A BOWL OF SOUP

Soon after we were liberated, I found a place where they are giving out pails of soup. The Germans run away, the kitchen was still working, the food was still boiling, and there are hundreds of people there. All of a sudden I see one what I knew from home. And he sits like a Turk, cross-legged on the grass. And he sits there eating a whole pail of soup with a ladle. I said, "Joe, give me little soup." He says, "*Geist* away"— don't get close to here. He had been a friend of mine. But I don't blame anybody at that time, because everybody thought only how to survive, it was not a normal time. Because your eyes were so big, you thought you were going to eat it. He's a nice guy, he was a nice guy before, too, but he thought he was going to eat up the whole pail. Today, this guy Marmour, I still know him, but he doesn't remember it.

LISA LIPKIN

Lisa Lipkin, a child of Holocaust survivors, constructed a story from silences. Her mother was a survivor of Auschwitz and the German labor camps, and since Lisa was a little girl, she has tried to interview her mom. The attempts elicited only anger. "My mother," she told me, "is like a fabric that has found a way to stay together."

It's not stitched well, it's not stitched properly, it definitely would be better off if she would open it up and start again and restitch. But she doesn't want the garment to fall apart, and she's found a way with her own precarious stitching to hold it together. I don't want to be the one to snip it open.

Lisa has come to believe that the task for children of Holocaust survivors is not to coax their parents into telling their stories or revealing the nightmare of their experiences. "The biggest task for us," she said, "is to find resolve in dark silence."

Radiant and beautiful, thirty-four-year old Lisa's humor and irony provide a counterpoint to the dark silences. She has traveled around the country, telling the

story of her own response to her mother's quiet and to the storytelling fragments
that slipped out inadvertently. "Even if I never know how my mother was raped or
beaten," she told me, "or how she lay on a bed with rats running over her head,
even if I don't know the specific details of those stories, which I'm guessing probably
happened to her—I know the look on her face when I ask her about them, and I
know the silences, and that's a story to me. That's a very powerful story."

STORIES ABOUT STORIES

WHAT MY MOTHER NEVER TOLD ME: REMINISCENCES OF A CHILD OF A HOLOCAUST SURVIVOR

I am the child of a Holocaust survivor. During Holocaust Remembrance Week everyone wants to remember, so I get a lot of work. Recently I was in Washington, D.C., performing at the B'nai B'rith Museum. I invited the only person I know in D.C.—Yacek, the director of acquisitions for the new Holocaust Memorial Museum in Washington.

I started the show the usual way. I introduced myself by my Hebrew name: Rachel. It's an international name given to me so that, in case I have to flee, it's easily translatable. When I was growing up, my parents told me to become a doctor. That way, when it came time to run, I'd have a skill I could use no matter where I ended up. My mother told me that when she got married she made a conscious decision to have only two children. That way, in case they ever had to run, she could grab one child and my father could grab another.

My American name is Lisa. It's an ordinary name. A common, all-American baby boom name, the kind of name you find on a plastic pen in the drugstore. In school, no matter what grade I was in, whenever the teacher called my name, at least three of us shouted, "Here!" It was anonymous. Anonymous was good. I learned that early. All donations were made anonymously. We weren't allowed to put any bumper stickers on our car—no one should know our political leanings. When my parents bought their house from an Irish family twenty-five years ago, they never changed the front-door mat. It still reads "Maloney."

When I was growing up, camp didn't mean summer camp. In school, during an endless film on fire prevention or in one of Mrs. Medbocker's multiplication drills, my thoughts drifted, and I would see things ten-year-olds weren't supposed to see: barbed wire, piles of corpses, ovens, guns, murderers—at any moment three men in black jackets and black boots could storm into the classroom and tell all of us to lie flat on the floor and then "rat-tat-tat," shoot all of us dead or, even worse, just point them at all the kids while shouting, "Out! Quickly! *Achtung!*" until everyone would file out in perfect alphabetical order and march down the hall and never be seen again. Then the bell would ring, and I'd get my Charlie Brown lunchbox out of my locker and go home on the bus with everyone else.

Ronnie was the first kid I knew who was also the child of a Holocaust survivor. When we were growing up, our families did everything together. Ronnie and I were exiled to the foldout vinyl bridge table at family dinners, since there was no room at the adult table. It sat right next to the grown-up table, though a foot lower. It was covered with the same lace tablecloth, the same chopped liver and chicken soup. And it was from this table that we celebrated every family occasion together. *Yom Kippur:* The upright piano in the corner was covered with so many *Yortzeit* memorial candles (one for each family member who had died in the camps) that the glow was blinding. Thanksgiving: Ronnie's father carved the turkey with a fork stolen out of a Nazi kitchen. It was heavy and silver and had a swastika engraved in the handle. He used to keep it hidden in a drawer and took it out only once a year to carve the turkey. Who would have thought, sitting at that bridge table, looking at all of them laughing, munching, talking in Hungarian with bits of English accidentally thrown in, that those faces had seen more pain than any human being had a right to?

It was at that bridge table that us kids decided our parents weren't quite normal. For one thing, they were all four feet tall, they all had these thick accents, and they loved to freeze food. Food was a big issue in our house. They could never get enough of it. When Shop-Rite had a clearance sale one autumn, my mother bought twenty cans of cat food and we didn't even have a cat. One night I was hungry and I went into the freezer and took out a head of lettuce. I noticed the inside of the head was green and moldy, so I threw it away. The green inside the lettuce was actually a roll of two hundred dollars my mother had hidden inside it. "You never know when it can all be taken away," she said. After that my father conceded that for years he'd been finding money in the strangest places.

During high school, my mother's attempts at bonding with me translated into "ladies' shopping days." We would go either to Lord & Taylor's, where she had a charge card, or to B. Altman's, where, on the sixth floor, you could indulge in date-nut bread and tea sandwiches at the Charleston Gardens.

On one particular occasion the restaurant was packed and our table hadn't been cleared yet. Sitting in front of my mother was a half a sandwich on a small china plate. She glanced down at it, and "that look" took over her face. I knew what was about to happen. On the one hand, I wanted to protect her from her memories. But I was so desperate for these stories, they came out so rarely, that I had to hoard them like crumbs. I let her speak.

"I haven't thought about this for so long. But seeing this sandwich . . . We were chopping wood in the forest in Lithuania, helping the Nazis build railroad tracks to fight the Russians. We used to pick berries off the trees whenever no one was looking and pop them in our mouths. I was working and this laborer in the forest saw me and he threw me half of his sandwich and it landed at my feet.

"I picked it up, and I knew I was just going to have the smallest little bite. Because I knew my mother and sisters were over there working and they were starving and I had to share it with them. I was only going to have a small little taste."

Suddenly she began to cry. The tears were falling with a vengeance, dropping in her lap. "I never meant to eat it all. I just, I couldn't stop."

And then there was silence. A silence so noisy, it kept me up that night. But after a few minutes she said, "Don't you want more cream cheese for that date-nut bread?" And we were back to talking about purses and panty hose, and the subject was never brought up again.

As far as I knew, my mother had no roots or, if she did, that part of her past was so dark, I wasn't allowed to know about it. Her life began in America after the war. To me, she was like a tree that you saw off in the middle, plop into the earth, and hope it grows upright.

At the end of my performance at the B'nai B'rith Museum, the audience started asking me questions about my mother. "What camp was she in?" "How did she survive?" "Did she escape?" Somewhat frustrated, I said to them, "I was told nothing. The only stories I have tumbled out accidentally. For instance, I know my mother and her two sisters were called the 'blue kerchief girls' because while they were in labor camp they had found a swatch of blue fabric on the ground. It was big enough to cut up into four pieces and cut into head scarves, which my mother and her sisters wore over their shaved heads."

I saw a hand go up in the audience. It was Yacek, my friend from the Holocaust Museum, who said, "You know we have that scarf in our warehouse, don't you, Lisa? Your aunt donated it about a year ago, along with a sweater that someone in the camps knitted for her out of old socks. She had it hanging in her closet all these years. I thought you knew."

Knew? Knew?! I used to play hide-and-seek in that closet. Hundreds of times I crouched in the corner of that darkened space. Had the scarf been hanging over me? Had it brushed up against my face?

I was visibly shaken, and as soon as the performance was over I made an appointment to visit the objects at the Holocaust Memorial Warehouse —an industrial building somewhere outside of Baltimore where they, along with everyone else's donations, were being stored. All night long I was tossing and turning, wondering what it would be like to finally come face-to-face with my mother's past . . . my past.

On the way, I got lost on the beltway. By the time I drove into the industrial park, I was sweating and frustrated and cursing. "I just want to get on with my future. Damn those objects!" There was no sign out front, only a number. I could only guess it was to prevent anti-Semitic attacks. I walked up to the front door. It was made of glass, and it was locked. I looked inside and all I could see was a quaint lobby with plush pink carpet, cute rocking chairs with quilted cushions, and a poster, framed and hanging on the wall. In it was a smiling circus clown, and underneath the picture it said "Le Cirque." It felt like the children's room at the library.

I knocked on the door and a woman emerged from behind the corner and opened it. Her smile stretched across her face, and she had huge teeth. "Yes?"

"Yeah, is this the Holocaust Warehouse?"

"Yes! You must be Lisa. Yacek's been expecting you. Come in and head down the hall. It's the room on your right." She reminded me of a student nurse in a root canal clinic.

I started to make my way down the shiny hall. I could tell where the storage room was, even from a distance. A cardboard box sat outside the door on the floor, and as workers came out they peeled rubber gloves off their hands and dropped them into it.

I started to make my way down the corridor toward my destination, and my heart began to beat faster. Inadvertently I dodged into the ladies' room, the way I do at Dr. Thaler's office when I want to avoid the dental chair. But after a few minutes I gathered up my courage, took a deep breath, and made my way into *the Room.*

It was enormous, larger than life, big enough for three hundred Mack trucks. There were massive gray stone pillars rising high into the air. Everywhere ceiling fans whirred, creating a permanent low hum. Everywhere technicians were hovering over tables with slide rulers and compasses, measuring objects. I know they were dressed in street clothes, but somehow in my mind, I picture them wearing white lab coats. There were thin white drawers everywhere labeled with names like "Genetics Experimentation" or "Slave Labor." I felt as though I were in a morgue.

Yacek came up from behind me and placed his hand on my shoulder. "Pretty amazing, Lisa, isn't it?"

I was too disturbed to answer, so I just nodded. As if reading my mind, he asked me if I wanted to look inside one of the drawers. I did. He walked me over to the set of cabinets labeled "Prisoners' Belongings."

"These were objects confiscated from prisoners as they entered the gates of Auschwitz. To me, the contents of this drawer represent the entire story of the war." He opened it up, and lying motionless across a sheet of stark white paper were hundreds of rusted scissors, in all different shapes and sizes. "Look," he said. "This is the barber's scissor. And these, the tailor's. This small one is for a baby. And these, for a seamstress."

He opened another drawer, and this one was filled with hairbrushes —all natural bristles. My eyes hooked on one in particular—made of a masculine dark brown wood with a wide handle. Another was painted delicately with a whimsical white pony and wisps of grass, with soft small bristles with which to comb a child's hair.

We walked along the back wall until we came to a row of giant shelves. They were so tall, they created a shadow in the aisle, like New York City buildings do to their own streets. To my right, unloaded and forgotten about, were hundreds of leather suitcases. Brought by prisoners on transports, these bags were also confiscated upon their arrival at the camps. The leather had eroded, but I could still make out the names on many of them: Rosensweig. Gruener. Braun. Goldfarb.

I wondered which ones would be selected for the museum floor and which ones would remain there, in hiding. How would they even choose?

I almost didn't notice the objects to my left, since they were covered with a long sheet of paper. A wooden handle, edging out into the aisle, caught my attention, and I stopped and lifted up the sheet and slowly looked underneath. The entire shelf was covered with umbrellas. Their canvases had completely disintegrated, so that no trace of their original vibrancy and individuality remained. All that was visible were their wooden slats, warped and sticking out like arthritic fingers. In another corner was an iron gate. It was tall and elegant, and in its center was an intricately carved Star of David, with vines of delicate grapes wrapped around it. But they were slashed with knife marks and its delicate design covered in graffiti. In the center of the room was the "extraction" table. It was made of gray steel with a hole in its center. The table, I learned, was used to extract gold teeth from prisoners. The hole was for the blood to drain.

But I soon saw what I came for. Yacek's assistant, Susie, was carrying the box with my aunt's things to the viewing table and she was waving for me to come toward her. Even from a distance I was amused by the box they stored her things in: it was one of those elegant boxes you would store a prom or a wedding dress in. I watched her lift, layer upon layer, the soft tissue paper, then remove the objects and place them neatly on the table.

I walked slowly up to the table. But when I stood over the sweater I started to laugh out of relief. They had taken the wrong sweater out of storage—someone else's by mistake. I had come to see my aunt's sweater. My aunt was a tall woman. This was a sweater for a small child.

And then it hit me. My God. That was my aunt. That was my mother. My aunt was ten, my mother eight. They were that little when they went through it all. It was a beautiful sweater—solid wool with red and blue stripes across a beige background. The back was a charcoal gray, and the buttons were wooden and covered with gray fabric. I wondered who this woman was who had knitted it for my aunt. Was she still alive? Did she have stories she could tell my family?

I reached for the kerchief. But before I could touch it, the assistant grabbed my wrist. "No, no, Lisa. We mustn't touch the objects. You have to put on these sanitary gloves first. Otherwise the oils on your fingers will deteriorate the fabric."

Not only did I want to touch it, I wanted to lie my entire body down on it, to caress it for hours. It had gone from the inaccessibility of my aunt's closet to the inaccessibility of an archive, a warehouse, and the one place it had neglected to stop was with *us*, the children. Wasn't it our rightful legacy?

I asked Yacek and Susie if I could be alone with the objects, and as soon as they left I misbehaved. I took off the gloves and touched the scarf. It was softer than I had imagined, like faded denim. It had a fringe going down one end and two small holes near the edge, but other than that it was in perfect condition. Just like my aunt to keep it pressed and washed. And it was pale blue.

I put my head down on it and felt it against my cheek for a long time. And I wept. But I'm not sure why. Because, while on the one hand it was larger than life, on the other hand it was smaller than I ever could have imagined.

I know one thing. Touching it, touching my mother's past, was a small flash of insight for me. And that flash gave me just enough light, so that I could once again take my "appropriate" place back in the shadow.

BARBARA MYERHOFF

In her classic book, Number Our Days, *anthropologist Barbara Myerhoff writes about why she turned to the study of elderly Jews following her research on the Huichol Indians (her book* Peyote Hunt *was nominated for a National Book Award). "However much I learned from that was limited by the fact that I would never really be a Huichol Indian. But I would be a little old Jewish lady one day." Although Barbara never did become an old Jewish lady—tragically, she died at the age of fifty in 1985—she did, through her research, put on the mantle of her elders' insight and wisdom.*

"To experience the self as a stable, continuous being through time, across continents and epochs, despite dramatic physical changes," she writes, "is especially important to the old, burdened with such vast and disparate memories." The presence of the past fascinated her and was one of the ideas that underlies all of her work on aging and Yiddishkeit. She uses the term "re-membering" to call attention "to the reaggregation of members, the figures who belong to one's life story, one's own prior selves, as well as significant others who are part of the story." And she suggests that we as humans are, above all else, Homo narrans, *"humankind as storyteller."*

This story "The Shoebox" is from a longer essay assembled by Marc Kaminsky after Barbara's death from tapes of a lecture she gave in numerous settings. She called the talk "Stories as Equipment for Living."

VISITOR: MICHAEL SCHLESINGER

As a folklorist and record producer, I was interviewing an old klezmer musician, and I asked him, "after you're gone, who will be left to pass on these stories and these memories?"

And he answered, "Well, you're listening to them, aren't you?"

STORIES ABOUT STORIES

THE SHOEBOX

You have heard a great deal about the stories that survivors tell. What I want to do is pick up on some of the themes that run through those stories —themes that have to do with suffering and, through suffering, growing a soul. I'm going to talk a little about the impact on the listener of these stories. Because half the tragedy is not to be heard and seen, and the other half is not to be seeing and listening. And the one who tells and is heard can grow a soul through the talk, but the one who listens and sees in some ways also grows a soul.

What is a story? Everyone has talked about this, endlessly. I come back to the minimum definition of story that Ursula Le Guin suggested when she described a little twelfth-century church that she discovered somewhere in Wales, and in it she encountered words scraped on an altar of stone, in runes, and it said: "Tolfin was here." This is wonderful because even as it speaks the words that come to us from afar, it's so close to "Kilroy was here." And Ursula Le Guin comments: "This is perhaps the minimum human tale." She says that the tale contained in those three words tells us: "Human life is short. The material was intractable. What one has to say is: 'Someone was here.'"

It's perhaps not too great a leap to connect that scraping of one's name on the stone to the scraping of a prisoner's name on the walls of the cell, to the effort to leave behind a record of the atrocities one has seen and lived through when a person knows he or she will soon be gone, and to the scrapings on the gas chamber walls—the nail marks, those marks that say, "I was here."

In *The Anatomy of Melancholy*, Thomas Browne said, "The threat of oblivion is the heaviest stone that melancholy can throw at a man." That's not just being being forgotten, that means never having existed.

I worked with a man who was a survivor, and he was a Hungarian. When he was eleven, they knew in his family that the time was limited, everyone knew that, and he was told to pack some things because they would be leaving in a hurry, and he pondered as to what he should take. His pondering of what to take from his little room has always fascinated me.

I watch old people look around their houses and ponder what to take [to the nursing home], and I watch how every object becomes a container and synthesizes an entire lifetime, becomes a reservoir of memories. "And *that* should be left behind?" I mean, we all get shaped when cleaning a drawer. Or you find you can't turn out letters. These are not just things, these are parts of one's life.

So picture an eleven-year-old child looking around his room, knowing his life is about to be destroyed: what should he take? And he was frozen in the dilemma of the choice. And so he made himself two shoeboxes. In one shoebox he put pictures of his family, he put some poetry he had written, he put a postcard from a girl—his treasures, his autobiography-in-things. And in the other he put an extra pair of shoes and some underwear and a hankie and a knife and a watch. And I think he probably put in a toothbrush. And he came home from school one day and he was told, "Now! Run!" And he ran in and grabbed the shoebox. And they left.

When they stopped again, he looked into the box, and he had taken the wrong one. He had the hankie and the shoes and the watch.

And he thought, What did I want this box for? What did I want the other box for? What did the other box mean—to anybody? And he said, "It was as though I were standing at the edge of the sea, and I knew I would be pushed into the sea with my box, and the only thing that mattered was that I not sink with the box. It was as if I would try to throw the box back onto the shore, and maybe someone would catch it."

GOING HOME TO NOWHERE

ROSLYN BRESNICK-PERRY

In the summer of 1991, when I was sixty-nine years old, I went back to my *shtetl*, my small town of Wysokie-Litewskie in what is now Belarus. It was something I had looked forward to since as a child of seven I arrived here with my mother in 1929.

I arranged for a man named Shlomo Gavrilowitz Kantranowitz to be my guide. When I was a child, the town of Wysokie had three thousand people, almost all of them Jews. He was now the only Jew left in the entire area.

We parked the car and started to walk around the "green" when I asked Shlomo where this unpaved little street led. "To the Lunke," he answered (the meadow).

"This is my street," I said. "My house is a little ways down the road."

I started to walk very fast. And there it stood, right where I knew it would be. It looked different now with its painted windowboxes and new fence, but there was no mistaking it was my house. I walked around to the back, and sure enough, there in the corner of the house, behind the kitchen and the bedroom, stood the old crab apple tree I had watched go into bloom so many springs ago. I did not want to go into my house. I couldn't.

I walked farther down the road to my grandparents' house, right across from the old synagogue. "You see this old *shul?*" said Shlomo. "It's the only *shul* left standing in the *shtetl*. The Germans used it as a jail. See the bars on the windows?" I looked closely, and there among the decaying wooden frames I see the bars.

We walked a little farther, past my aunt Goldie's house, which is no longer there. And then I see it, the new synagogue, the one built just before we left for America. I remember how proud everyone was of it. It was so grand and elegant, with its stained-glass windows and wonderful candelabra. It had two awesome golden lions carved alongside of the altar where the Torah was kept. Guardians of the faith. I stand and look at its destroyed walls. Trees are growing out of its center, surrounded by pieces of wall that refuse to give way. I can't stand it anymore. I can't seem to swallow the lump in my throat. My knees want to buckle. I sit down on a stone, my head swimming. And then I see them, my family, my whole family dressed in their holiday clothes for Rosh Hashanah, the Jewish New Year, so proud, going to the new synagogue to pray and to hear my young uncle Avrom-Lieb blow the *shofar* (ram's horn) for the very first time in that new holy place. I sit on that stone for a long time just staring as they walk past me into the ruin.

Much later, after I finally stopped crying, I saw the meadow, the woods, the sky, the stork nests, and the sunflowers. I had not spoken to a single person in my little town. I could not find a single gravestone in what had been the Jewish cemetery. It was now a government housing project. I had come and gone without finding out anything. The records of the Jews, I was told by the city clerk, had been sent to Kiev, where they were said to have been destroyed in a fire. I couldn't wait to leave this tragic place that had once been my whole world.

STORYTELLER: BARBARA MYERHOFF

In my book, *Number Our Days*, the tailor Schmuel talks about the significance of his death in light of the fact that his entire *shtetl* was wiped out in the Holocaust. He talks about the meaning of this, and he says, "It is not the worst thing that can happen for a man to grow old and die. But here is the hard part. When my mind goes back there now, there are no roads going in or out. No way back remains because nothing is there, no continuation. Then life itself, what is its worth to us? Why have we bothered to live? All this is at an end. For myself, growing old would be altogether a different thing if that little town was there still. All is ended.

"So in my life, I carry with me everything—all those people, all those places, I carry them around until my shoulders bend. I can see the old rabbi, the workers pulling their wagons, the man carrying his baby tied to his back, walking up from the Vistula, no money, no house, nothing to feed his child. His greatest dream is to have a horse of his own, and in this he will never succeed. So I carry him. If he didn't have a horse, he should have at least the chance to be remaining in the place he lived. Even with all that poverty and suffering it would be enough if the place remained; even old men like me, ending their days, would find it enough. But when I come back from these stories and remember the way they lived is gone forever, wiped out like you would erase a line of writing, then it means another thing altogether for me to accept leaving this life. If my life goes now, it means nothing. But if my life goes, with my memories, and all that is lost, that is something else to bear."

VISITOR: BORIS BLUM
CONCENTRATION CAMP INMATE 114520
THE FACE IN THE MIRROR

After liberation, I went with two friends to look for a place to spend the night so we wouldn't have to sleep outdoors near the wagons. We came to a German house and went inside. There were already about thirty of us in one room. I saw that there was a mirror on the wall, and I went over to it. I wanted to see what I looked like. In that same mirror were the reflections of others; there were many faces in the mirror. But I didn't know who I was. I couldn't recognize myself in this group of people. So I began to make all sorts of faces and gestures, to stick out my tongue, so that I would be distinguished from the group.

And how frightened I became! Because the person I saw in the mirror was one that I had never seen in my life. I didn't know him. The years I had spent in the concentration camps had apparently changed me, because that person standing there in the mirror didn't bear any resemblance to the person I had seen before the war.

HUMOR IN CONTEMPORARY JEWISH LIFE

No other genre of modern Jewish folklore has received so much attention or generated so many popular printed collections and scholarly and popular articles as Jewish humor. Almost everyone writing in the twentieth century agrees there is such a thing as Jewish humor, but heated debate continues regarding its characteristics and origin. Did Jewish humor develop only in the last two hundred years in Eastern Europe and die with the demise of Jewish culture in Eastern Europe in World War II? Or does it extend from antiquity to the present and across Europe to America and Israel? Is the essential Jewish strategy "laughter through tears" or "self-ridicule" arising out of self-hate? Did Jewish humor arise in response to sociocultural conditions of seclusion and poverty in the ghetto and *shtetl* or as a reaction to the marginality and identity crisis precipitated by emancipation and integration into gentile society? Or is Jewish humor the product of a paranoid and masochistic psyche that Jews inherit as part of their collective unconscious? Are all jokes that Jews tell about Jews examples of Jewish humor, or are there special points of view and peculiar stylistic and structural features that must be present?

———

Folklorist Barbara Kirshenblatt-Gimblett (see page 121) ingeniously poses these questions. I can't provide definitive answers to any of them. In the same way that the Talmud is a sixty-three-volume commentary on the original five books of Moses—I can only add to the commentary on a body of material loosely known as Jewish humor.

To date, collections of Jewish humor have focused on traditional Jewish jokes, the monologues of famous comedians, and, most recently, the work of writers such as Philip Roth and Woody Allen. But Jewish humor is present not only in the jokes and the monologues, but in everyday life—in the sarcastic, fatalistic, and funny way the Jews often approach real-life situations such as fleeing the Old World or making a life for themselves on the Lower East Side. In this book, I hope to show that Jewish humor cannot be reduced to a classic set of jokes; Jewish humor is part of Jewish storytelling.

Typically, joke collectors don't tape-record their raconteurs and joke tellers; they recall them from memory, compressing what is often a five- or ten-minute, carefully layered and detailed story into a brief paragraph, which is the mere skeleton of the tale. Here, I highlight the humor in Jewish American stories, including both jokes and humorous tales and anecdotes from real life; for the best joke tellers are the best storytellers (even when they do compose their stories in reverse, beginning with a punch line and working backward). You want a joke? I'll tell you a story.

MOSHE WALDOKS

Often irreverent and hilariously funny, Moshe Waldoks, coauthor of the classic Big Book of Jewish Humor, *refers to his belly as his "Holocaust memorial paunch": "I carry it around to honor the six million." Traveling across the country as a lecturer on Jewish renewal and "the power of positive Judaism," he talks about the importance of going beyond the Holocaust. A child of survivors himself, he suggests that too often suffering provides the lowest common denominator of what it means to be a Jew. "No matter how pious or not pious you are, what makes you a Jew is that you could have ended up as soap in Auschwitz. We've got to get beyond that. Kids today know more about Auschwitz than about Vilna."*

Most Jewish jokes are not about anti-Semitism, he explains; they run the full gamut of community life. Humor is one of the positive ways to explore and appreciate the fullness of Jewish culture. With a doctorate in Jewish intellectual history from Brandeis University, soon to be ordained as a Jewish Renewal (non-denominational) rabbi, he brings this message to temples and Jewish gatherings across the country.

"The Health Club" is one of the stories Moshe tells in his lectures. Calling his tales "Jewish shaggy dog stories," he elaborates on an old punch line until he creates a masterpiece of narrative humor.

THE HEALTH CLUB

We form these wonderful attachments to our families, and families are important because they, ultimately, do provide a great deal of support. There's a great myth around about the Jewish family as being somehow immune from a lot of the breakdown that we're seeing, but clearly the Jewish family does give a lot of support, and that's one of the qualities that I hope we will continue to instill in our children and in our grandchildren.

The story that I think brings this to light is about a gentleman named Max Gelbert. I don't know if you know Max. Max hangs out occasionally in temples around here. And Max was married for fifty years to the same woman, which today really deserves a plaque, at least. But unfortunately, his wife of fifty years passed away.

And as you know, there is a phenomenon that if a spouse passes away and you've been together for a very long time, there's often a despondency that sets in, and even though the surviving spouse is healthy, they go. But Max was surrounded by a very sophisticated and supportive family—good children, who gathered around Dad and said, "Dad, you know what? We love you, we need you, Mom would have wanted you to carry on." And they gathered around Dad, and they wouldn't leave him alone; and they bothered and they pampered and they made him feel wonderful, and, sure enough, within six months his despondency lifted, and he saw that his kids were right: he had something to live for, and he decided, you know what, he was not taking care of himself—he was going to join a health club.

He goes to the Paris Health Club on West End Avenue and Ninety-sixth Street, for those of you who know New York, and he's feeling good, he's working out. And one day he's walking down Broadway, and a friend stops him and says, "Max, is that you? I didn't recognize you, Max, you look sixty."

And he says, "Sixty, why, if I fooled that *alter kaker*, I'm doing okay. I went to the *Yeshiva* with that guy! You know what, I'll start eating health foods."

So Max goes out to a health food store and he buys ten pounds of granola and birdseed. You know, you got to keep going, right? And he begins to jog. Now in New York if you jog, it's not bad because you get mugged less often if you're running. And he's running in the park, at first very slowly, he's seventy-two, and then he's working himself up to a mile, and then two miles, and all of a sudden he's running to a point where the endorphins are kicking in, and he's high all the time.

He runs out of the park at Fifty-ninth Street and Columbus Circle, a friend stops him: "Max, is that you? I didn't recognize you. You look forty-five."

"Forty-five? I must be doing the right thing." He says, "I got a couple dollars in the account," he pulls out a couple dollars from the account, buys himself a couple of new suits, a toupée—he always wanted a toupée, ever since he was thirty-seven and the hair was beginning to go. He buys himself wonderful hats, beautiful shoes, and he's walking down in his own neighborhood, Forty-seventh Street, where he used to work in the diamond business, and a friend stops him. He says, "Max, is that you? I didn't recognize you. You look thirty-five years old."

He says, "You know what? I think I beat the clock. You know what? I'll move to Florida. You go to Florida, you get a tan, it doesn't matter how sick you are—you look great. People say, 'You look good, you got a tan.'"

So he packs everything up, he goes down to Florida, and the first thing he does, he begins to pump iron on Muscle Beach. And there he is, Max, every morning at six-thirty with the Cuban guys. You know the big Cuban guys, they're about four feet eight and about four feet wide. And he's pumping iron every morning—he's amazing, he's lifting, he's lifting, and he *kvetches*, and he's lifting, he's lifting. Walks down Collins Avenue, friend stops him: "Max, is that you? I didn't recognize you. You look twenty-five years old."

"Twenty-five years old, I must be doing the right thing. You know what? I think I should get married again. You know how men are? They like to get married a lot. But if I look twenty-five, I don't want to marry a woman that's seventy-two. I've been through that. Maybe I should make a deal with one of the grandmothers on the beach. Maybe she's got a granddaughter!

"How many years have I got left? So, I'll sign over the insurance, I'll sign over the Social Security, what could be?"

So sure enough, a couple of weeks later, one of the grandmothers goes over to Max and says, "Max, I've got just the girl for you—my own granddaughter. She's eighteen years old, a recent graduate of Miami Beach High School."

Now here's a man who supported education his whole life, he's very impressed. He says, "Ooo, a graduate. Tell me a little bit about her."

"Well, she was active in many things. And she was a cheerleader."

"A cheerleader?" His eyes began to widen. "A cheerleader, tell me more about that."

"Pom-poms."

Pom-poms did it. He heard pom-poms, he knew this was a girl for him. So he meets her, and quickly they go to a lawyer. The lawyer signs up everything in the girl's name. And he wants to have a wedding—and he's a man of great tradition. And he wants to have perform the wedding the same rabbi who performed *his* wedding fifty-two years earlier. So he combs all the old-age homes down in Miami, looking for Rabbi Hurowitz. . . . Now Hurowitz was connected to an iron lung, but it didn't matter—they wheeled him in.

And he looks down at Max—they were standing in this little chapel—and he looks down at Max, and he says, "Max, I tell you, it's a pleasure to see you here. At first I didn't recognize you. What a *fargenein* [pleasure] it is to be able to perform this. You look like a *khusn bukher*—you look eighteen years old."

And Max, he's smiling ear to ear. You've never seen such joy—pom-

poms, unbelievable! Instead of a *yarmulke*, he's wearing a little Mouseke-teer hat. Right after the ceremony they were going to go to Disney World for the honeymoon. This guy was going to do it right!

And the rabbi says the *brukhes*, and they break the glass, and he goes out and he hires this big stretch limo to take them to Disney World. And he goes around and puts the pom-poms in the backseat, puts the young girl in beside them, and he walks around to the other side of the car to get in—and at that moment a big Checker cab comes along and kills him!

You think you're upset? Max was a little bit upset. And he goes upstairs. And, believe it or not, I hate to break it to some of you, there's a line to get in. Not only that, they're not computerized yet. Everything's on index cards. So there's a line upstairs, you have no idea—it goes on for miles! And Max starts screaming, "There's been a mistake!"

And all you hear is the echo of a hundred and fifty thousand voices, saying, "It's always a mistake."

Finally he gets his turn at the front of the line. They're looking through the files: "Gellerman, Goldstein, Goldberg. Mr. Gelbert, I hate to break it to you, but I think we made a mistake here. But you know what, it's okay, you're here anyway, what's the difference. You know, we don't send people back—we did that once two thousand years ago, we've had trouble ever since. It didn't work out too good."

So Max says, "I wanna see the boss."

"Come on, no one sees the boss, the boss is busy. He's making deci-sions. He doesn't handle the everyday business."

Max pushes the angel aside and starts charging over to the boss's office. He sees a big sign on the door, "the Almighty." And he bangs on it and he bangs on it and he pushes it open, and there is the Lord sitting on the Throne of Glory. And Max looks up and he says, "How could you do such a thing to me? This is Max Gelbert! Don't you realize who this is?"

The Lord looks down upon him. "Max, is that you? You look so terrific. I didn't recognize you!"

STORIES ABOUT STORIES

JEWISH LAUGHTER, GOD'S SENSE OF HUMOR

STEVE ZEITLIN

Sailing into New York Harbor at the turn of the century, the Jewish immigrants carried with them far more than the meager possessions bundled in their arms. They brought their indomitable sense of humor and storytelling, the culture of *Yiddishkeit*. Their culture intermingled with the folk culture of New York City on the streets of the Lower East Side. Ultimately, Jewish humor became synonymous with New York humor and (through early television) with American humor. Through comedians such as Jack Benny, Milton Berle, Fanny Brice, Lenny Bruce, George Burns, Mort Saul, Sam Levenson, Buddy Hackett, Jackie Mason, Myron Cohen, Don Rickles, Joan Rivers, the Marx Brothers, Henny Youngman, and Woody Allen, Jews left an indelible imprint on American humor.

There is even a well-known joke about the way Jews tell stories. Sometimes it's told about an Englishman, a Frenchman, and a Jew, but this version is set in the *shtetl*:

When you tell a joke to a Russian peasant he laughs three times: once when you tell it to him, the second time when you explain it, and the third time when he understands it. A landowner laughs only twice: when he hears the joke and when you explain it, for he can never understand it. An army officer laughs only once: when you tell the joke. He never lets you explain it—and that he is unable to understand it goes without saying. But the Jew, before even you've had a chance to finish, he interrupts you impatiently. First of all, he has heard it before! Secondly, what business have you telling a joke when you don't know how? In the end, he decides to tell you the story himself, but in a much better version than yours.

So what makes Jewish humor so funny? What is the recipe for the humor in Jewish American stories?

COMMON PERCEPTIONS OF CLASSIC INGREDIENTS

When I began this book, I imagined a mythical table—what Marc Kaminsky calls a *tish mit menschen*—populated with the characters Yiddish was so apt at describing—the *nudnik*, the *nudge*, the *maven*, the *makher*, the *kibitzer*, the *shlepper*, the *shlemiel*, the *shmendrik*, the *shlimazl*, the *shmoozer*, the *schnorrer*, the *shnook*, the *yenta*, the *klutz*, and the *mensch*—the negative characterizations outnumber the positive, but all suggest a certain acceptance into the whole *mishpokhe* (family); each member with his or her own *mishegas* (craziness).

But Marc Kaminsky admonished me for inviting these characters to the table. With the exception of the *mensch* (the evocative Yiddish term for "good and ethical person"), they derive from "the Yiddish folk culture of humor, the sphere of everyday life in which a denigrated people administered homeopathic doses of ridicule to each other." These sarcastic terms passed into American culture via vaudeville and TV sitcoms, reflecting the dominant culture's disdain for the greenhorn Yid and the immigrants' ambivalence about their culture of origin. As a therapist, Marc finds their "raging ghosts" haunting his patients' unconscious.

But musician, friend, and klezmologist Henry Sapoznik just laughed and noted that there was no way to exclude them, because, over time, these *shlimazls* and *shlemiels* have become more humorous than denigrating, part of the way a younger generation relates to Yiddish culture; for better or worse, they are among the enduring contributions of Yiddish culture to contemporary Jewish (and gentile) life, and their presence is expected at any Jewish storytelling gathering.

In *The Big Book of Jewish Humor* Waldoks and Novak suggest that Jewish immigrants from Europe enriched America's language and humor in some of the same ways that blacks enriched American music; while the improvisations of African Americans created musical styles such as jazz, the verbal improvisations of Jewish immigrants contributed Yiddish words and rhythms to American speech. Others have suggested that Jewish humor is kind of verbal equivalent to the blues, a "laughter through tears," a parallel response to persecution—and "a victory gained by the Jewish spirit over centuries of adversity, an exultant defiance of persecution and harassment, an affirmation of the will to survival in the face of an over impending doom." As one storyteller put it, "Jewish people always wanted to laugh at situations even at times when they should have cried."

But writer and humorist Moshe Waldoks devotes an entire lecture to getting beyond this perception, this sense that suffering is what binds Jewish communities together, this investment post-Holocaust Jews seem to have in the notion that laughter and suffering go together and constitute the essence of Jewish culture. He calls his lecture "Beyond Laughter through Tears." Nonetheless, when he is finished, inevitably, an audience member comes up to him to say, "You're right, Moshe, it really is laughter through tears."

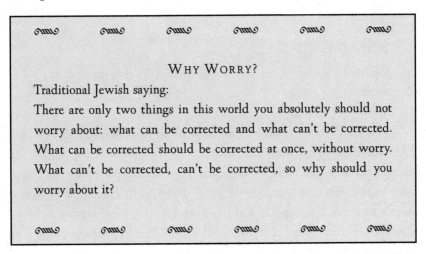

WHY WORRY?
Traditional Jewish saying:
There are only two things in this world you absolutely should not worry about: what can be corrected and what can't be corrected. What can be corrected should be corrected at once, without worry. What can't be corrected, can't be corrected, so why should you worry about it?

TALMUDIC REASONING

Jewish humor often emerges from a peculiar turn of mind, a kind of convoluted logic often dubbed "Talmudic reasoning." Many Jewish writers and storytellers have come up with their favorite quintessential examples. Leo Rosten tells of a letter he received from Groucho Marx. It began:

Dear Junior, excuse me for not answering you sooner, but I have been so busy not answering letters lately that I have not been able to get around to not answering yours in time.

My son told me about a sign he saw in a bookstore, also attributed to Groucho: "Outside of a dog, a book is a man's best friend. Inside of a dog, it's too dark to read."

"It boggles the mind," Rosten says, "to think of these inversions of humor." A soul can experience vertigo trying to bend the mind around this convoluted imagery. To cite another mysteriously profound quip from Groucho Marx (later quoted by Woody Allen)—"I don't want to be part of any club that would have someone like me as a member."

Or the Hasidic definition of a big liar—not only what he said isn't true, but the opposite of what he says isn't true, either!

Or the Jewish definition of a pessimist and an optimist:

Pessimist: Things can't get any worse.
Optimist: Yes, they can get worse, absolutely, they can get much worse.

Perhaps there is no more classic example of this reasoning process than the comedian Jackie Mason's discussion of his visit to a psychiatrist. In today's folklore, the rabbi, or *rebbe*, has often been replaced by contemporary stock figures, among them the psychiatrist. In this piece, Jackie Mason seems to draw upon an old Yiddish saying, *"Az ikh vel zayn vi er, ver vet zayn vi ikh?"* Translated that means "If I should be like someone else, who would be like me?"

I know who I am. That's the trick, the great trick is to know who you are—most people don't know, thank God I know. I didn't always know. I'm not ashamed to admit it, there was a time I didn't know who I was. I went to a psychiatrist, I did. He took a look at me, right away he said, "This is not you." I said, "This is not me, then who is it?" He said, "I don't know either." So I said, "Then what do I need you for?" He said, "To find out who you are. Together," he said, "we're going to look for the real you." I said, "If I don't know who I am, how do I know who to look for? And even if I find me, how will I know if it's me?" . . . . He said, "The search, the search for the real you will have to continue, that will be a hundred dollars, please." I said to myself, If this is not the real me, why should I give him the hundred dollars? I'll look for the real me, let him give me the hundred dollars. I said, "I'll tell you what, I'll charge you fifty dollars, we'll call it even."

Jewish talk often twists around the windy streets of a Talmudic argument. Daniel Bell, a Harvard professor and Jewish writer, talks about another ingredient of Jewish storytelling. He calls it the *"pilpul*, the very thing you learn in Talmud." The term suggests the "why here and not there" that runs through much of Jewish religious learning. Bell recalls how, when a boy at the Jewish elementary school, or *kheyder*, he was asked to start reading the five books of Moses. The rabbi would ask him what is the first letter of the first word: "*Beys.*" Why does God begin the world with the letter *b*? To explain, the rabbi asks why he didn't begin it with the letter *shin*. Well, if God began the world with the letter *shin*, the world would be too compromised, because *shin* also stands for *sheker*, which is a lie. And the rabbi goes through every letter of the alphabet until the only one that's left is *beys*, which stands for *barukh*, which is blessed, and blessed are those who accept the Word of God. This convoluted way of introducing children to religious study, Bell suggests, is the classic Talmudic *pilpul*. He goes on to say:

When we'd go to school later, we'd drive our teachers crazy. The teacher would start a poem: "Into the valley of death rode the six hundred." "Say, teacher, why six hundred? Why not five hundred? Why not seven hundred?" She didn't know. So you would say, "If into the valley of death rode seven hundred, it would be a hundred too many. If into the valley of death rode five hundred, it would be a hundred too few. So into the valley of death rode the six hundred." And I thought of this the other day, because there was a marvelous story in the *Times* that they had found some papers of Tennyson, who'd written the poem, in which it was pointed out to him that actually into the valley of death had ridden seven hundred. But he didn't like seven hundred because metrically it didn't fit in, so he made it six hundred. So actually the logic was absolutely right.

FINAGLING THE RITUALS

This Jewish turn of mind is also apparent in the elaborate layers of ritual established by Orthodox tradition and the elaborate and ingenious ways Jews use to get around them. Some of these ways of finagling rituals with counterrituals are the source of many stories about, for instance, the *Shabbes goy*, the special designation for a gentile paid to perform tasks Jews are forbidden to do on the Sabbath.

Circumventing rituals is the subject of many Jewish stories and suggests the kind of logic that runs through the tales. In Howard Simon's *Jewish Times*, journalist Ari Goldman tells a story about finagling the rituals:

> I remember once sitting in the state legislature in Albany, and I'm very aware of the clock. Being a Sabbath observer, you're very in tune with the seasons: *Shabbes* is early now; *Shabbes* is late. I didn't want to violate the Sabbath, but the legislature was going on into debate, and I was sitting there in the press box, and I was watching the clock and taking notes on the debate. I'd learned when I was in *yeshiva* on *Shabbes* that what you're not allowed to do is write with a pen, because that can't be erased. But if you write with a pencil, that's not as bad a sin because it can be erased. I watched the clock —here I'm a *New York Times* reporter in Albany and I'm worrying about *Shabbes*—and I put away my pen and took out my pencil and I covered the legislature.

This reaches its epitome with Moshe Sacks, the rabbi for beleaguered congregation of elderly Jews in the last Jewish synagogue in a burned-out area of the South Bronx. Each week he struggles to put together a *minyan*

—the minimum ten men required by Jewish law for Sabbath services. "When only nine men show up," Sacks says, "let God come down and see we only have nine. He can count. And when he comes down, we'll count him in." On one occasion, there were only six men. Sacks noted that every person over sixty-five actually gets two deductions each year from the Internal Revenue Service, and if the IRS counts each person twice, certainly God could do the same (on that particular occasion, he was apparently overruled).

COMMENTATOR: STEVE ZEITLIN

Until his death in 1995, Moshe Sacks was the unofficial rabbi of the last Jewish synagogue in the South Bronx, and a classic Talmudic reasoner. (He's also the subject of Jack Kugelmass's wonderful book, *Miracle on Intervale Avenue.*) He told me he was worried that he hadn't been mugged lately. He thought it was a sign that the neighborhood was going downhill. Then, in the doorway of his *shul* he was robbed, pushed down the steps of the synagogue. His skull was fractured slightly, and the doctor told him that it would take ten years for it to fully heal. He told me that he was trying to live until his head healed.

QUESTIONING

In addition to the ingredients of language, the accent, and the *pilpul*, the recipe for these tales includes the use of questions as part of the rhetorical strategy. In fact, many of the greatest Jewish quotations are framed as philosophical questions. The words of Rabbi Hillel:

If I am not for myself, who will be for me? If I am only for myself, what am I? If not now, when?

And Shalom Aleichem's classic question, retold in *Fiddler on the Roof*:

> God, I know we are your chosen people, but couldn't you choose
> somebody else for a change?

And perhaps this explains the legendary deathbed conversation of writer Gertrude Stein. When asked on her deathbed, "So what is the answer, Gertrude?" she purportedly responded, "Ah, what is the question?" What a quintessentially Jewish response!

We see the questions in the jokes as well. Moshe sees a sign up in a tailor shop on the Lower East Side. The sign reads:

> My name is Fink,
> So what do you think—
> I press clothes for nothink.

So Moshe gets his shirts together, brings them in, comes back a few days later, and there, with his shirts, much to his surprise, comes a bill. So he says to the tailor, "What about the sign—it says you press clothes for nothing."

"Oh no," he says, "you're reading it wrong. It says:

> My name is Fink,
> So what do you think?
> I press clothes for nothink?"

In another classic, little Sammy tells his grandfather about the great scientist Albert Einstein and his theory of relativity.

> "Oh, yes?" says the grandfather. "And what does this theory
> have to say?"
>
> "Our teacher says that only a few people in the whole world
> can really understand it," the boy explains. "But then she told us
> what it means. Relativity is like this: If a man sits for an hour with
> a pretty girl, it feels like a minute. But if he sits on a hot stove for a
> minute, it feels like an hour. And that's the theory of relativity."

Grandpa is silent and slowly shakes his head. "Sammy," he says softly, "from this your Einstein makes a living?"

There are so many interesting things about this joke, even apart from its use of a question in the punch line. First, it is notable how Einstein himself is a folk hero in contemporary Jewish folklore. (Philip Roth's fictitious talent agent, M. Lippman, wants to put Einstein on the radio so that the whole world will know that "the genius of all time is a Jew.") Second, it's somehow appropriate that the Jews would reduce the theory of relativity to a tiny morsel of Talmudic wisdom. Third, it's a joke that proves an often cited quality of Jewish humor, that the punch line can work even without the joke. I had special proof of this at the end of one of my lectures on Jewish humor, when a gentleman raised his hand, stood up, shrugged, and asked the audience, "From this he makes a living?"

A Personal Relationship with God

Another ingredient in humorous Jewish stories is the propensity of Jews to address God directly. In his Catskills monologues Rubin Levine tells about Moses going up to the mount. God tells him that He has some commandments for him. Moses asks, "How much are they?" God says, "They're free." Moses says, "I'll take ten!"

Another story set in the 1970s describes Jimmy Carter's negotiations with world leaders to bring peace to the Middle East. At one point he visits the pope in the Vatican.

On his desk, the pope has three telephones. Jimmy Carter grows curious and asks what they are for. "Well," the pope says, "one is for local calls in Rome, one for long distance, and the red phone is to talk with God."

As the negotiations and discussion grow more complicated, Carter asks if he can use the phone to call God. He calls, and when he hangs up, the pope tells him, "I'm sorry, but before you leave, we have to charge you twenty-five dollars for the call."

A few months later, Carter is negotiating with Menachem Begin in Jerusalem. Again, he is surprised to see three phones on Begin's desk. Again, he asks and is told, "One is for local calls in Jerusalem, one for long distance, and one to talk with God."

Well, these negotiations between Egypt and Israel are especially tough, and again, Carter decides to take the matter up with God. Again, he uses the red phone. When he hangs up, Begin tells him, "by the way, we need to charge you twenty-five cents for the call."

"Oh, thanks," Carter says, "I called God from the pope's office, and he charged me twenty-five bucks."

"Ah yes," said Begin, "but from Jerusalem, it's a local call."

It is not just in jokes but in everyday life that Jews perpetuate this personal relationship with God. Richard Rabinowitz recalls that as a boy playing on the streets of Brooklyn, life was completely secular. God never figured into the lives of children as it did in the lives of their parents— except in the "do-overs," when a play was inconveniently interrupted by a passing car or other disturbance. According to Richard, that was the only time in a child's life when God intervened in human affairs. God always made sure that the repeat of the play turned out the way it was originally intended. God personally ensured the fairness of "do-overs."

Ann Katz captures this personal relationship with God in an anecdote she tells about her aunt:

> My aunt was celebrating her ninetieth birthday, and her family made her a lovely party. And her oldest son said, "Mama, I think you should get up now and say something to your guests." And I swear to God, she got up and she said, "I'm very, very lucky. God has been very good to me. He should only live and be well."

BRINGING HEAVEN DOWN TO EARTH

In addition to a philosophical disposition—this personal relationship with God and a cosmic perspective on the everyday—a practical, earthy quality runs through the stories in the same way it has always run through Jewish lives. The string of adverse circumstances in which they found themselves in the *shtetls* of Europe and the low-rent neighborhoods of America required dealing constantly with nitty-gritty issues of survival. Much Jewish humor emerges from two opposing qualities of the Jewish psyche—a philosophical bent and a practical mind—which constantly undercut each other; it is as if Jews have a mind halfway in heaven and feet firmly planted in the real world—a head in the clouds and feet mired in the tar of the Lower East Side. As one critic, writing about the Yiddish theater, put it, "It reaches toward the heavens but has dust on its shoes."

Many of these humorous Jewish stories are engaged in bringing heaven down to earth. They're about "a sudden thrusting downward from the exalted to the workaday, from the tragic to the trivial, from the Hebrew to the Yiddish, from the biblical cadence to the commercial slogan." This dual sensibility can be heard in the most casual conversations. Often the heavenly is brought down to earth, but at times the earthy is carried heavenward as well. At a senior center in Venice, California, anthropologist Barbara Myerhoff recorded this characteristic dialogue:

Manya: It's disgusting to see how some people come around here. The men wear a little G-string, not much better than nothing. Feh! You can see everything.
Sophie: Who told you to look?
Manya: Sophie, I'm only human, like you are.
Shmuel: If nakedness is sinful, why did God send us into the world without any clothing? If nakedness is not in tune with God, why do you think he did not prohibit it himself? Why didn't he put trousers on the animals? ... Now, I will tell you a piece of important wisdom from the commentaries, very wise, little known: even the greatest among us, underneath his clothes, he is naked!

In this dialogue, the response to the scanty, sexy California bathing suits ranges from the practical—"Don't look"—to the philosophical— "Underneath our clothes, we are all naked."

The stories mediate between worlds. As Abe Lass tells it, the following illustrative story took place at Dubrow's cafeteria in Brooklyn, where the over-eighty crowd gathered for breakfast each morning. Harry, Irving, and Moshe were discussing the *summum bonum*, the "greatest good."

Harry said that for him, the "greatest good" was *davening* on Yom Kippur at the synagogue, for that was the time when he truly felt cleansed of his sins. Irving said that, for him, it was coming home on Friday evening to the Sabbath table, seeing the table set, the *challah*, and his wife lighting the candles, knowing that the work week was over and all was at peace.

Then Moshe cracked that for him, the *summum bonum* was a trip he took as a salesman with his secretary to see a furniture showroom in Las Vegas. "When we got to the hotel, we had sex, before we went to sleep we had sex, and then in the morning we had sex again."

"Hold it, hold it, hold it right there," protested Harry and Irving. "That's not fair. We're talking 'good'—you're talking 'very good.' "

The philosophical *summum bonum* and the deeply earthly pleasures of sex are united in one tale. Abe Lass, noting that most aspects of Jewish life are well recorded for posterity, bemoans the disappearance of dirty Yiddish stories that are vanishing without adequate documentation. He took it upon himself to record more than seven hours of dirty jokes in Yiddish from his friends. It is not uncommon to find in Jews the highest spiritual yearnings side by side (some would say counteracted) with a fascination for the earthiest varieties of sexual expression. Despite his contentious politics, no one juxtaposes the spiritual and the mundane more effectively than Jackie Mason:

One person is all you need for human happiness—because through that one person and within that relationship every means of communication and involvement, every significant emotion, every relationship, everything happens that means anything with that one person. That's right, because if you've found that one person, you could spend the rest of your life, the rest of your life with that one person. That's all you need. And you sit in the house, the rest of your life.

And you look at each other, and look and keep looking, and keep waiting, and looking and waiting, and wondering, and here he is, he's going to the toilet, he came back from the toilet, he came back, he sat down, he got up, he's watching television, he's almost watching, he forgot to watch, he'd like to watch, he got the wrong station, the right one, the wrong one, he got it—he wants something, he got it already, he don't need it, he has it—and what do you say, you say, "Thank God I found a *shmuck* like this!"

The different worlds that Jews inhabit are also manifest in two classic Hasidic tales. It is said, for instance, that the Stoliner *rebbe* in Borough Park, Brooklyn, wore two watches, one on each hand—on one he kept the time in Borough Park, on the other, the time in Jerusalem. In another story:

An exhausted Hasid came running to his *rebbe*. "*Rebbe*, help. Take pity. My house is burning."

The *rebbe* calmed the Hasid. Then, fetching his stick from a corner of the room, he said, "Here, take my stick. Run back to your house. Draw circles around it with my stick, each circle some seven handbreadths from the other. At the seventh circle, step back seven handbreadths, then lay my stick down at the east end of the fire. God will help you."

The Hasid grabbed the stick and started off.

"Listen," the *rebbe* called after him, "it wouldn't hurt also to pour water. Yes, in God's name, pour water. As much water as you can."

Even the traditional Jewish responses, "*Oy, vey,*" "*Oy!*" and the gestures that accompany them are not simply curses hurled at the real world —they express not only a gut response to some practical disaster, but a kind of philosophical resignation that a person should endure such aggravation.

Leonard Kurzman tells about four women playing a game of canasta at a bungalow in the Rockaways. The concentration was extreme. After a few moments the silence is broken by the first woman's "*Oy.*" Then, total silence, broken at last by the second woman's *"Oy vei."* Silence again. Then the third woman mutters, *"Oy vei iz mir."* Finally, unable to contain herself, the fourth woman exclaims, "All right, I thought we weren't going to talk about our children." *Oy* is not a word, Leo Rosten notes, it's a vocabulary. "It is uttered in as many ways as the utterer's histrionic ability permits. It is a lament, a protest, a cry of dismay, a reflex of delight.... *Oy* is an expletive, a ejaculation, a threnody, a monologue."

In *Play It Again, Sam*, Woody Allen plays Allan Felix and attempts to pick up a young woman as both stand before a Jackson Pollock painting in the Museum of Modern Art in New York:

Allan: What does it say to you?

Woman: It restates the negativeness of the universe. The hideous lonely emptiness of existence. Nothingness. The predicament of man forced to live in a barren, godless eternity like a tiny flame flickering in an immense void with nothing but waste, horror, and degradation, forming a useless bleak straitjacket in a bleak absurd cosmos.

Allan: What are you doing Saturday night?

Woman: Committing suicide.

Allan: What about Friday night?

VISITOR: MARK SHECHNER
WHY THE JEWISH COMIC CARRIES A VIOLIN

For comedians as diverse as Jack Benny, Henny Youngman, and Morey Amsterdam, the instruments are their credentials. The violins are the remnants of the European high culture that Jews sought to adopt as an avenue of escape from the ghetto. Such aspiration produced in our own day the great Jewish virtuosi of German and Russian music—David Oistrakh, Jascha Heifetz, Yehudi Menuhin, Isaac Stern, Itzhak Perlman, Vladimir Horowitz, Pinchas Zuckerman —and the comedy that alludes to them is the token of how successfully, and with how much guilt, their example has been evaded. In carrying his instrument on stage with him, the comedian carries his past as a sight gag, a mechanical straight man who testifies to the stringencies of the ghetto and the dreams of Jewish parents. The Jewish comedian and his violin are not unlike the ventriloquist and his dummy, though roles are reversed. Whereas the ventriloquist plays straight man to his dummy, it is the comic who plays dummy to his violin, which is also his muse, his past, his superego, his parent, his better half.

Obviously, this strategy of splitting oneself up for comic purposes, when dressed in the colors of particular history and tradition in which such inner divisions are validated by cultural duality, can give rise to a humor in which the tradition itself is interrogated and its own tensions brought clearly into focus. The Jewish comedian is himself a one-man comedy team, an Abbott and Costello, Smith and Dale, Burns and Allen, Bergen and McCarthy, Caesar and Coca, Cheech and Chong, all in one. That is because at heart, and by historical design, he is really two men, equally alive to God or the claims of high culture (our secular substitute for God) and to carpeting or baseball or sex.

Typically, there is a difference between the jokes others tell about Jews and the jokes they tell about themselves. Jokes with anti-Semitic overtones don't evoke the contrast between the philosophical and the practical but highlight one or the other; the most common anti-Semitic jokes are one-dimensional, portraying Jews as greedy and materialistic. They are "Jew jokes" rather than "Jewish humor."

Often, Jews turn the stereotypes on their head. My close friend Solomon Reuben told me a story about two Jews who are walking down a street in Brooklyn when they pass a Catholic church. They are astonished to see a large sign on the gate that reads "Convert to Catholicism, get $5,000." One friend says to the other. "What do you think that means, 'Convert to Catholicism, get $5,000?' It sounds interesting." His friend says, "You can't be serious." The other says, "Five thousand dollars is five thousand dollars, I'm going in." The man goes in, his friend waits. And waits. And waits. When he comes out, his friend asks, "Well, did you get the five thousand dollars?" The man just looks at him and says, "Is that all you people think about is money?" The traditional Jewish stereotype is turned upside-down, and a much more complex picture emerges.

In *Jews without Money*, the writer Michael Gold offers a classic example of the philosophical in Jewish stories:

> Old Barney was one of the odd characters on our street. He was a Jew of seventy who worked as a porter for a basement factory that made brass beds. Winter and summer he was rigged in a fantastic costume, a cloak green with age and stuffed with rags. There must have been fifteen pounds of the rags, but even in the summer heat he shed none of them. . . . There were always curious people watching Barney as he worked, or while he sat resting on the stoop, his long pilgrim's staff in his hand. Some of them whispered that he was a miser and had money concealed in his rags. Others said he was only crazy. . . . The giggling children would gather around and ask:
> "Barney, what are you waiting here for?"
> The mad, solemn eyes turned upon us, and the old man said slowly: "I am waiting for the Messiah, my children."

"And what will the Messiah bring you, Barney?"

"A glass of cream soda," he said.

"We laughed and scampered way," Michael Gold concludes. "The old man was not hurt by our laughter, but sat there waiting. I sometimes asked him other questions, because I believed the Messiah was coming, too. It was the one point in the Jewish religion I could understand clearly. We had no Santa Claus, but we had a Messiah."

But Jews are philosophical even about that: "God has protected us from Pharaoh and Haman," goes one well-known punch line. "He will protect us from the Messiah, too."

Jewish laughter—God's sense of humor.

SECTION SEVEN

MEANINGS AND

REFLECTIONS

A story. There was once a young Hasid who devoted his life to studying the religious texts of our people. One night, without any apparent reason, this pious young man closes his Talmud and runs out of his house into the middle of the town square, crying out, "What is the meaning of life? I cannot go any further, I cannot study one additional verse of Torah without knowing the meaning of life."

Other Hasidim come running to his aid from their homes, from their studies. They try to calm him down, to convince him to return to his Talmud, but to no avail. Finally, the local Hasidim recommend that he take a trip to the residence of the *rebbe*, a few towns away.

The young Hasid leaves immediately for the *rebbe's* home. When he finally gets in to see the *rebbe*, he whispers nervously, "Rebbe—what is the meaning of life? I must know, I cannot go on any longer, I cannot study another page, until I know: What is the meaning of life?"

The *rebbe* rises from his seat, walks over to the young man, looks him over very carefully—and suddenly slaps him.

"Why, Rebbe? Why did you slap me? What have I done? All I did was ask, 'What is the meaning of life?' "

"You fool," answered the *rebbe*. "You have such a good question—why exchange it for an answer? It is the answers which separate us, the questions which unite us."

In this old Hasidic tale, which comes to us from Rabbi Edward Schecter via Elie Wiesel, Jews seem intent on discovering or at least searching after meanings and posing questions about meanings. Telling stories is a way of establishing meaning. Thinking about stories, telling stories about stories, is not just a way of figuring out what any given story means, it's a way of deepening the significance of stories by layering them with meanings.

Stories are also a form of remembrance. "Remembering," Peninnah Schram told me, "is such an important Jewish message. We Jews are a people who talk and remember and who are bound by our memories." Elie Wiesel suggests that wherever we look in our sacred texts, we stumble upon the Jewish injunction against forgetting. Our rituals and our stories are rooted in remembrance.

In *Tell Me a Story: A New Look at Real and Artificial Memory*, Roger C. Schank writes: "We need to tell someone else a story that describes our experiences because the process of creating the story also creates the memory structure that will contain the gist of the story for the rest of our lives. Talking is remembering."

SHELLEY BRENNER

In Flatbush, Brooklyn, her parents owned a store called Bell Glass and Mirror, named after her mother, Annabelle. As a young girl, Shelley Brenner loved to spend the day at the store. She was intrigued by glass and mirrors. She loved to see her reflections echoing into infinity in the rows of mirrors. "I could count twelve of me," she said, "and I was all twelve of the dancing princesses. Cutting the glass into shapes was something like ice sculpture. It was very magical. Once I was so fascinated that I ran my finger along the edge of the glass and cut myself. It bled profusely."

Part of Shelley's interest in storytelling and fairy tales derives from her days in the shop. "It created a different reality," she told me. "It was dazzling, and I was taken with the sparkle and the shine. In those days, my parents seemed like magicians in their competencies. It seemed like magic to be able to do things like that with their hands. The same was true at home. When my mother would iron and sew, I couldn't understand how she could do such complicated things with her hands." Another influence was her sister, who, in a compelling voice, read J. R. R. Tolkien to her as a child, along with True Confessions magazine. "I learned a lot about story structure from True Confessions."

Those magicians and tellers in Shelley's family didn't fare so well in life. When Shelley first heard the story "Ezekiel's Wheel" in her travels, she thought immediately of her family and later spun this parable.

EZEKIEL'S WHEEL

Once, there were four *rabbonim* who were awakened by an angel who carried them off to the Seventh Vault of the Seventh Heaven, where they were able to see the sacred wheel of Ezekiel. Now somewhere in the descent from paradise to earth, the first rabbi, from having seen such splendor, lost his mind and went frothing and foaming through the desert for the rest of his days.

The second rabbi was very cynical about the experience. He said, "Well, I only dreamed that I saw Ezekiel's wheel. Nothing really happened. I imagined it all."

The third rabbi gave sermon after sermon on the intricacies of Ezekiel's wheel. He analyzed how it was built and what it all meant. He was obsessed with the wheel, and in this way, he betrayed his faith.

The fourth rabbi was a poet. He was inspired by the wheel. He took paper and reed, and sat by the window, and wrote song after song in praise of the evening dove, his daughter in her cradle, all the stars in the sky. And he lived his life better than before.

I tell the story because it reminds me of my family and the way each of us chose or was chosen to navigate through the world. In my family's story, "Ezekiel's Wheel and the Seventh Vault of the Seventh Heaven" is a vision of the world as it should be, that perfect world that all of us have somewhere in our minds; a perfect world, with all its chaos and beauty.

And the first rabbi in our family is my sister, who died last year. During her life she was troubled by chronic mental illness. She often said that it was painful to feel joy or excitement because soon it became just an uncomfortable overstimulation. So she shielded herself from the world with medication or excessive sleep or just isolation. Like the first rabbi, she lost her way.

The second rabbi who denied he saw the wheel is my mother, who died in 1993. She too was given to isolation; she denied the world, as though it didn't exist and the events in it didn't really happen. She loved her house and made a fortress of it. Outsiders were not to be trusted. And I remember when I was seven years old, asking my mother if God existed, and she answered very cynically: "We don't know if he does, but we say he does, because if we said he doesn't, and he does, he'd be angry." Like the second rabbi, she denied the world.

The third rabbi who gave sermons about the wheel is my father, whose way of being in the world is often as a giver of instructions, directions, criticisms, corrections. The family story goes that when he and my mother were newlyweds, he taught her how to wash dishes, because he didn't think she did it the right way. And his way of teaching her was to have her rewash every dish that she had already washed, with his supervision. Like the third rabbi, he gave lectures, unable to surrender himself to the poetry of life.

So it was given to me, of the four in my family, to become, like the fourth rabbi, the storyteller: to simply behold the world, and praise it, and to give it away, over and over and over again.

STORIES ABOUT STORIES

A PENCHANT FOR PARABLE

STEVE ZEITLIN

Rabbi Kranz, the *maggid* of Dubno, was asked why he always talked in parables when there were so many truths to be told. He answered with a parable about parables. In a small village, there lived both Truth and Parable. Truth walked around naked, but no one would talk with him, he had no friends. Parable, on the other hand, dressed in all of his finery, was the most popular soul in town. One day, Truth became despondent and came to Parable for advice. Parable answered quite simply, "How can you expect anyone to talk to you when you walk around stark naked?" Parable was kind enough to offer Truth some of his clothing. Suddenly, everyone was willing to talk with Truth again. "So you see," Rabbi Kranz told his congregant, "I don't distort the truth, but merely dress it up—for no one wants the naked truth."

The Jewish disposition to bring the philosophical to bear on the everyday manifests itself in a penchant for parables. A parable is an illustrative story answering a question or pointing out a moral. The elements of a parable run parallel to and illuminate a situation in real life. In this way, parables transport actual situations into the domain of story and bring them back illuminated with fresh insights.

"One of the stories that I start almost every program with is a parable of the Dubner *maggid*," Peninnah Schram told me. "A *maggid* was a traveling storyteller rabbi in Eastern Europe, and the Dubner *maggid* lived in the 1700s and was especially beloved for his parables." Peninnah suggests that Jewish parables have their own particular quality: "There is the *nimshal* and the *mashal*. The story itself is the *mashal*, or parable in Hebrew. But the parable itself is embedded like a jewel in a setting. The end frame, or the *nimshal*, is the situation to which the parable is applied. Once," she begins her programs, "a student was walking with the Dubner *maggid.*"

And as they're walking along, the student turns to the *rebbe*, the teacher, and says, "Tell me, my teacher, how is it you always have the perfect story to fit the subject under discussion?"

And the *maggid* says to his student, "I'll answer that question with a story." And then he continues on to the *mashal* itself, the parable:

A nobleman sent his young son to the military academy one day to learn how to shoot, and after five years the lieutenant was riding home on his horse, his chest covered with medals and a diploma in his pocket. And as he was riding through a little village, he looked up and saw on the side of a barn a hundred circles drawn in chalk, and in the center of each of those circles was a bullet hole. This lieutenant stopped his horse and he yelled out, "Who is this amazing marksman who could shoot a hundred perfect bull's-eyes? I must meet him!"

Just then a child who was walking across the road looked up at the lieutenant on his horse and said, "Oh, that's Narele, he's the town fool."

"I don't care what he is," said the lieutenant. "Anybody who could shoot a hundred perfect bull's-eyes must have won every gold medal in the world. Even I can't do that. I must meet him."

"No, you don't understand," said the child. "Narele doesn't draw the circle first—and then shoot. First he shoots, and *then* he draws the circle."

"And that's the way it is with me," said the Dubner *maggid*. (And now we're into the *nimshal*.) "I don't just happen to have the perfect story to fit the subject under discussion. No! First, I read a lot of stories. I listen to a lot of stories. I keep those stories in my head—and then when I find a story I especially like and need to tell, then I introduce the subject for which I have that perfect story!"

STORYTELLER: PENINNAH SCHRAM

I loved Mama's matzo ball soup as a girl and frequently wondered how my mother could get the egg yoke exactly in the middle of the matzo ball. The parable of the Dubner *maggid* would later resolve the mystery: my mother put the matzo ball around the egg yoke and did not insert the egg yoke into the middle of the matzo ball!

But Peninnah nests the story within another layer of parable, applying it to her own storytelling program. "So then I talk about what the theme of my program will be, and I tell my audiences that I just happen to have a few perfect stories—because, coincidentally, our subject is the Jewish people: love, laughter, lullabies, and legacies."

The Jewish Torah, the first five books of Moses, is replete with parables. From the Second Book of Samuel: "And it came to pass one evening, that David arose from his bed, and walked upon the roof of the king's house: and from the roof he saw a woman bathing; and the woman was very fair to look upon. And David sent and inquired after the woman. And one said, Is not this Bat-sheva, the daughter of Eli'am, the wife of Uriyya the Hittite?" King David lies with her that night and then orders her husband to war, transferring him to the "forefront of the hottest battle," where he is killed. Bat-sheva becomes one of King David's many wives and bears him a child. Then:

The Lord sent Natan to David. And he came to him, and said to him, "There were two men in one city; the one rich, and the other poor. The rich man had very many flocks and herds: but the poor man had nothing, except one little ewe lamb, which he bought and reared: and it grew up together with him, and with his children; it did eat of his own bread, and drank of his own cup, and lay in his bosom, and was like a daughter to him. And there came a traveler to the rich man, and he spared to take of his own flock and of his own herd, to prepare it for the wayfaring man that was come to him; but took the poor man's lamb, and prepared it for the man that was come to him." And David's anger burned greatly against the man; and he said to Natan, "As the Lord lives, the man that has done this is worthy to die; and he shall restore the lamb fourfold, because he did this thing, and because he had no pity."

And Natan said to David, "Thou art the man. . . ."

And David said to Natan, "I have sinned against the Lord."

"In the literary and popular collections," writes Barbara Kirshenblatt-Gimblett, "one is indeed struck by the frequency with which great sages such as the Dubner *maggid* convert ordinary folktales into parables and treat every narrative as a potential analogy." Frequently, international tale types that appear in non-Jewish sources as stories told strictly for entertainment are narrated as didactic metaphors in Jewish collections.

On each Sabbath of the year, observant Jews gather in synagogues to read a passage from the Torah; once a year, Jews celebrate the holiday of *Simchat Torah* when the reading of the Torah is completed and begun again. With the weekly reading of scriptures meticulously proscribed, almost every sermon delivered from the pulpit each week (and every talk given by a Bar or Bat Mitzvah child) draws on the Torah portions as parables to discuss contemporary life. Jewish sermons use parables to explicate, expound, and expand on biblical texts, applying its messages to people's lives. Torah provides the *mashal* for the *nimshal*. There is a sense in which each generation "parable-izes" the experience of the previous generations in Jewish tradition.

Reading Jewish folk stories, I am often struck how not only are the stories told as parables, but the very characters in the tales often use parable and its cousin metaphor to extricate themselves from the dilemmas they face. In one story, for instance, a weaver who worked for King David stopped at an inn, ordered a boiled egg, and forgot to pay the surly innkeeper. A year later he stops to pay for the egg, and the innkeeper tries to charge him not only for the egg, but for the chicken that would have been born and all the chickens that would have been born to that chicken. The weaver refuses to pay, and the matter is brought to King David.

King David's son, Solomon, is a friend of the weaver's. Already showing signs of the wisdom that would make him famous, he hatches a plan to convince King David that the weaver should owe the innkeeper for only a single boiled egg. The next morning, the two friends go out into the garden with a hot plate of boiled beans and begin planting them. When King David sees them carrying out this foolish act, the young Solomon says to him, "If it's possible to hatch a chicken from a boiled egg, then it's possible to plant crops from boiled beans!" Kind David is convinced, and Solomon reveals his wisdom at an early age. Metaphor saves the day.

According to tradition, King Solomon is responsible for the parable in Jewish culture. "The Torah until Solomon's time," commented Rabbi Nachman in the Aggadah, "was comparable to a labyrinth with a bewildering number of rooms. Once one entered there one lost his way and could not find the way out. Then along came Solomon and invented the parable, which has served as a ball of thread."

But the penchant for parable carries through to contemporary Jewish life. Barbara Kirshenblatt-Gimblett writes about her mother, Doris Kirshenblatt, who uses parables to alleviate difficult situations in her family. Confronted with stingy relatives, she has a parable for the occasion: a stingy man discovers that he can reduce his horse's feed each day, teaching the beast to live on less. Finally, he actually succeeds in training the horse to live on nothing but is dismayed when the horse keels over and dies. "Just when I taught him to live without food, he goes ahead and dies." The stinginess of her relatives can be self-defeating!

Some of her parents' stories show how important it is for children to take care of their parents, even in older age. Doris Kirshenblatt, who is well known in her family for her wonderful parables, is fond of saying, "One mother can take care of ten children, but ten children can't take care of one mother." Mayer, her husband, put it in the form of a parable. A father tells his son to tear a blanket in half and bring half of it out to his grandfather, who is now living in a small hut outside of their home. The son does it, but the next day his father sees him tearing his own blanket in two. "Why are you doing that?" he asks his son. "I am getting ready for the day when I ask you to move out of the house," his son replies.

Yes, my mother too used to repeat this expression, in Yiddish, about how "one mother can take care of ten children, but ten children cannot take care of one mother." But I also know that taking care of one's older parents, while a *mitzva* to perform at any age, is only part of the whole tapestry of life. So there is a relationship with another story that I tell, "An Offspring's Answer." The earliest known version of it is actually from the eminent Jewish matriarch Glueckel of Hameln (1646 – 1724), who, after the death of her husband, wrote a memoir addressed to her children. The story goes like this:

> There once was a mother bird who knew it was time to migrate to warmer lands. She began to get ready for the long journey. Knowing that her fledgling was too young yet to fly, especially over such a great distance, she decided to take it on her back. She loved her child and was willing to do anything for her.
>
> And so the little bird got on her mother's back and the mother bird began to fly. At first, the flight was easy enough. But as time went by, the bird began to feel heavier, and, after the first day, then the second, and finally the third day, the mother bird was tired. . . .
>
> The mother bird turned to her fledgling. Speaking in a guarded tone, she asked, "My child, my dear sweet fledgling, tell me the truth. When I get old and will have no strength to fly over such a big sea, will you take me on your back and fly me across?"
>
> Her fledgling answered, "My mother, I can't promise to do that. I may not be able to fly you across a sea because I may be busy flying my own children on my back just as you are doing for me."

In another contemporary situation, a storyteller told me about a friend of hers who became the principal of a Hebrew school, where he became friendly with the rabbi's wife. One thing led to another, and he ended up sleeping with her. When they awoke the next morning, both felt horribly guilty. He decided to tell her a traditional Jewish story that popped into his mind:

Once there was this man named Mr. Horowitz, and Mr. Horowitz went to heaven because he did so many *mitzvas* [good deeds]. And he went to heaven and they said, "Mr. Horowitz, we're sorry, but we can't let you in here."

He says, "What do you mean? I never did anything wrong in my life."

And they said, "That's the point. You have to do something wrong in your life, you have to commit a sin. And after you commit a sin, then we can let you into heaven. We don't admit perfect people. So just go back down and do something wrong, for heaven's sake."

Well, this was hard for Mr. Horowitz because he wasn't used to doing anything wrong. So he looked around, and he saw this nice senior citizen, Mrs. Cohen, and he slept with Mrs. Cohen. After they had made love, Mrs. Cohen looked at him, and she said, "Mr. Horowitz, what a *mitzva* you've done me this night."

With its message that, on the one hand, no one is perfect and, on the other, that pleasurable sex can be a great *mitzva*, this was the perfect story for a Hebrew school principal to tell—apparently, it eased the guilt.

Even during the Holocaust, Jews were sometimes able to apply stories and parables to the horrifying situations in which they found themselves. In a *yizker bikher*, or memorial book published by a *landsmanshaft*, hometown society, to commemorate to the communities lost in the Holocaust, Berl Manperl recalls how he read a Jewish parable to an SS officer:

Saturday, May 1, 1943. Today we returned early from work, because May 1 is a "holiday" for the brown-shirt Hitlerite hordes as well. We are a group of slaves harnessed in hard labor outside the ghetto at the Mezritsh local command post, where several hundred Jews survive by performing various tasks for the German garrison.

A group of twenty of us sit in the home of Berl Vakhtfoygl, lonely and saddened.

I sat on my straw sack, from beneath which I had just pulled out the few books which I had managed to rescue from my library and hidden here from the wild eyes of our torturers. A bad end awaited anyone caught carrying anything printed, especially in Yiddish; for such a crime the sentence was a bullet in the head. . . .

Suddenly there was a banging on the front door, and before we had time to think about who it might be, the local commander, SS Captain Klauck, entered the room.

I sat frozen with my book open; I hadn't had time to shove it under my mattress. He ran up to me, grabbed the book, and said in a grating voice:

"What are you reading, Jew?"

Pale as death I stammered: "Yiddish literature, Commander."

"Is there such a thing?"

"Yes, Commander."

"Read some of it," he ordered me.

A deadly silence reigned in the room; no one dared move a muscle, and everyone, including myself, thought that my life was over and Death had won this bet. But if I had no choice but to read for him, I wanted to choose something that would remind him of our situation. . . . [I read] one of Shtaynberg's *Parables:* "The Needle and the Bayonet." The content, more or less, is this: A soldier returned from the war and placed his rifle, with bayonet attached, against a dresser. A needle was stuck into the cloth on top of the dresser. The needle was terrified by the rifle and the bayonet and, trembling, asked the bayonet what it pierced. When the reply came back, "I pierce people, people," the needle broke out in a fit of helpless laughter and shouted:

"I pierce bolts of linen, I make shirts, I make things. But you pierce people from now until Doomsday, what can you make out of them?"

When I finished reading, the captain flung the book onto the floor and hissed through his teeth: "Shit...pacificism!" With a sharp bang he slammed the door and went out.

This memorial book parable (which appears in Jack Kugelmass and John Boyarin's *From a Ruined Garden*) remained a rhetorical weapon against the Nazi, even when other forms of resistance were untenable.

Parable, along with humor (see pages 249–71), speaks to the historical realities of Jewish culture. Always outsiders, Jews had to juggle multiple realities, and their response was to develop a sense of humor and of parable. Their historical situation created a people with multiple perspectives—sometimes conflicting perspectives—on their own situation. Jokes and parables enabled them to put their complex situations into perspective. As wanderers through the Diaspora, their past was their home country. Parable was the backpack that enabled them to bring biblical situations and episodes in ancient history to bear upon their lives, that rendered their past imminently present and kept their tradition intact.

Recently, as I was debating what kind of Bar Mitzvah to have for my son, I met a doctor, Joel Silverman, at a party. I asked him what he had done for his son on his thirteenth birthday. "We did nothing," he told me. "I'll tell you why. We went to the rabbi and asked about the possibility of doing something less than a full-scale Bar Mitzvah. He answered with a story, which might appropriately be called 'The Poor Man's Latke' ":

There was a poor man who lived in a *shtetl*, and every day, on his way home, he passed a rich man's house. Each Friday before the Sabbath he smelled the aroma of *latkes* wafting through the kitchen window, and he longed to experience the taste. One day, when he arrived home, he asked his wife, "Please, let's cook some *latkes* for the Sabbath."

"Well," she said, "I have the recipe, but we don't have any milk."

"Make it without the milk."

"Okay," she said, "I'll try." But a few minutes later she complained again, "Goodness, we have no butter."

"Oh, make it without the butter."

She tries to make it without the butter, and just at sundown, for the Sabbath meal, she serves her family some small, dark squares of dough. Her husband tastes it, grimaces, and says, "I just don't see what the big deal is about *latkes*."

"The rabbi was telling us this story as a parable," Joel Silverman told me. "If you don't do it right, it will seem like nothing at all." The story belies the poverty of the *latkes* without the traditional ingredients, the paucity of a Bar Mitzvah that is not a Bar Mitzvah.

As he told me that story, I was suddenly struck that Jewish tradition has another well-known parable that is, in some sense, an answer to this. My favorite version is from Barbara Myerhoff. When the great Hasid Baal Shem Tov, the Master of the Good Name, had a problem, she writes, it was his custom to go to a certain part of the forest. There he would light a fire and say a certain prayer, and find wisdom. A generation later, a son of one of his disciples was in the same position. He went to that same place in the forest and lit the fire, but he could not remember the prayer. But he asked for wisdom, and it was sufficient. He found what he needed. A generation after that, his son had a problem like the others. He also went to the forest, but he could not even light the fire. "Lord of the Universe," he prayed, "I cannot remember the prayer and I cannot get the fire started. But I am in the forest. That will have to be sufficient." And it was.

Now, Rabbi Ben Levi sits in his study in Chicago with his head in his hand. "Lord of the Universe," he prays, "look at us now. We have forgotten the prayer. The fire is out. We can't find our way back to the place in the forest. We can only remember the story. That must be sufficient." And it was.

I told Joel Silverman this story. The poor man's *latke* must somehow be sufficient. He laughed and said, "But how could both of those stories be right?"

"Well," I answered, "there's a story about that, too. You've probably heard it. The rabbi is deciding a case between two men having an argument about a horse. He listens to one man's story, and he says, "You're right." Then he hears the other side, and again, he answers, "You're right."

At that point the *rebbitzen*, his wife, looks at him and says, "Wait a minute, how could they both be right?"

He looks at her and says, "You know, you're right, too."

VISITOR: NATHAN AUSUBEL
THE VENEER OF SILVER

A rich but stingy man once came to his rabbi to ask for his blessing. The rabbi suddenly arose, took him by the hand, and led him to the window looking out on the street.

"Tell me—what do you see?" asked the rabbi.

"I see people," answered the puzzled rich man.

Then the rabbi drew him before a mirror. "What do you see now?" he again asked him.

"I see myself," answered the man, bewildered.

"Now, my son, let me explain to you the meaning of my two questions. The window is made of glass—as is also the mirror—only the glass of the mirror has a veneer of silver on it. When you look through plain glass you see people. But no sooner do you cover it with silver than you stop seeing others and see only yourself."

VISITOR: FRANZ KAFKA
ON PARABLES

Many complain that the words of the wise are merely parables and of no use in daily life, which is the only life we have. When the sage says, "Go over," he does not mean that we should cross to some actual place, which we could do anyhow, if the labor were worth it; he means some fabulous yonder, something unknown to us, something too that he cannot designate more precisely, and therefore cannot help us here in the very least. All these parables really set out to say merely that the incomprehensible is incomprehensible, and we know that already. But the cares we have to struggle with every day: that is a different matter.

Concerning this, a man once said: "Why such reluctance? If you only followed the parables, you yourself would become parables and with that be rid of all your daily cares."

Another said: "I bet that is also a parable."

The first said: "You have won."

The second said: "But unfortunately only in parable."

The first said: "No, in reality: in parable, you have lost."

COMMENTATOR: STEVE ZEITLIN

A parable to explain parable. Once, in a classic Jewish tale, a restless, unhappy man from Warsaw wakes up one morning determined to find the legendary town of Paradise. He travels deep into the night until he finds himself on the side of a mountain where he decides to get some rest. To be sure that he remembers which way he is traveling, he points his boots in the direction of Paradise. Then, in the middle of the night, a good (or could it be an evil) demon turns his shoes around. When he awakens, he proceeds in the direction of his shoes to a city that looks so much like Warsaw. He even finds a house that looks just like his, and a woman who looks so much like his wife. Convinced he's now living in Paradise, he moves in—and his life seems so much better!

A parable is like that pair of shoes. It appears to transport us to a higher plane of existence, and though it leaves us in the real world right back where we were, it creates the illusion that we are residing on higher ground.

RABBI TSVI BLANCHARD

When storytellers begin talking about how "stories heal the world," my eyes glaze over. Yes, stories heal the world, but so do love, laughter, poetry, and platitudes of all kinds. Typically, the statement is made without any suggestion of why stories are more effective, say, than love or peace. Yet, hearing Rabbi Tsvi Blanchard address the 1994 Jewish storytelling conference at Stern College, I understood, for the first time, how stories heal, why they heal, how they provide what he calls narrative intelligibility for our lives.

Rabbi Blanchard, who has a doctorate in both clinical psychology and philosophy, admits that stories cannot heal as medicine; we cannot cure the wound through stories; we can only tell a story that includes the wound. "Sometimes you can't cure *the person, but you can heal the situation,"* he told me. *"You give it narrative intelligibility. Arguments convince people, but stories translate arguments into felt reality."*

STORIES ABOUT STORIES

THE HEALING POWER OF JEWISH STORIES

Let me tell you half a story. This is a story that starts when the Jews are at the Red Sea, with the Egyptian army at their back and the sea in front of them. The sea splits. The Jews go through, and what emerges is an enormously powerful praise poem called *"Shirat Ha-Yam: A Song of the Sea."* Later, the rabbis tell the following *midrashic* story about that occasion. It says, "The Angels sought to give forth in song," celebrating their victory. When God heard the angels he turned to them and said, "Quiet. My handiwork is drowning in the sea, and you want to sing a song of praise?"

Now, it's half a story because at the very same time that God is quieting the angels down below, the Jewish people are indeed singing that song; while the angels are quieted from singing, the Jewish people are praising God for their miraculous redemption at the Red Sea. So how come the angels don't get to sing and people do?

I first understood this story many years ago thanks to Rabbi Chaim Tsvi Hollander, who in an offhand comment explained its meaning in the most clear way. He said angels, you see, are the kind of beings that do only one thing, and they do it 100 percent. Whatever their task is, they're 100 percent focused and that's it, whereas human beings are just a little bit more complex. People can entertain at least two and sometimes three or four contradictory and conflicting views and feelings all at once. So for God to allow the angels to recite *"Shirat Ha-Yam,"* to sing his praises while people were drowning, would be to allow unconditional celebration at a time when people were dying. On the other hand, the Jews could at one and the same time rejoice that they were saved and redeemed and also suffer that it cost the lives of those Egyptians. That's why on the Passover *seder*, when we recite the ten plagues, we dip ten times into the cup of wine and take out a drop to say that our joy can never be complete if the price of human redemption is the death of others.

Now the reason I'm interested in that half a story is the fact that human beings are complex, and we keep things that are at odds with each other all floating around within the same human being—we are not angels! This is the center of how stories and rituals are able to heal people. For when we are wounded, parts of ourselves are at odds with other parts of ourselves. Something that belongs in this corner is not connected to something that belongs in another corner. When you are wounded, when you get hurt, when you get separated, you find that the wholeness of yourself is for a moment fragmented and shattered.

And if you start with the notion that human wholeness is our ultimate goal, then it is symbols and stories that enable us to take the various parts of ourselves, and of our society and of our history and of our people and of the wider consciousness of the entire human race, and access, get a hold of them, bring them together, and make them present in ways that find a harmony together, find a wholeness together. And when that process is complete for a moment, there is a kind of healing that takes place.

If you figure that the Jewish people could tell the story of enslavement in Egypt in such a way that, with all the bitterness of that event, it still turns out that 94 percent of the Jewish people run to a *seder* every year to retell that story and to gobble down that bitter herb, and then say, "Wow, that was great!"—then you have to figure that stories create symbolic contexts that make even the most bitter enslavements and pains tolerable. Only a story can make slavery in Egypt into a symbol for redemption. To accomplish that, we have to go back to Abraham, talk about a promise and a prediction of that enslavement, and tell about Moses and Mount Sinai, and then, when we've told the whole story, all of a sudden it doesn't feel like the same pain that it was before.

Some stories tell about wounds and about pain that cannot be cured, that can only be endured. Here's a story from my family. My father-in-law was one of the most successful pediatricians in the New York area. This is a story that's still told about him in the hospital and in the family.

My father-in-law was a pediatric anesthesiologist working with a boy who had continually recurring cancer. The treatments were very painful, but, in this boy's case, my father-in-law could usually alleviate that pain. One day the boy caught a cold, but he had to have the treatment. His name was Brian, eleven-year-old Brian. And my father-in-law can't give him the anesthesia because, with a cold, it can be extremely dangerous.

So my father-in-law sits the boy down and he says, "You know, Brian, I love you very much, and I have to give you this treatment. But I can't give you the anesthetic this time. I can't take the pain away. But every time I apply the treatment, I'm going to hold you, I'm going to hold you through the whole thing. And each time the pain comes, I'm going to be there and hold you, and you'll feel better." And sure enough, it worked.

Now that story is important. It shows what you can do when you can't do anything more to stop the pain. Because, you know, life is like that. Nobody can have all the pain taken away. There are times when there's nothing to do but say to someone—I can hold you when the pain is there, but this time I can't take it away.

But in the family the story plays another important role. It says to all the kids, You have a father who's a pediatrician. There are times when you want him. Do you want to know where he is? He's at Montefiore Hospital holding Brian, that's where he is. The story serves as a symbol of a father's love, which transcends the limits of what human beings can do, not by erasing those limits, but by suggesting a way of transcending them. It's a story that accepts the limitations of human life and the need to endure through compassion and love.

There are those who know what is going on in the world—for instance, the *rebbe*. What a wonderful symbol! A person who knows the meaning of things—even the things you can't grasp. There is a famous story about a hunchback who, because he was a great rabbinic scholar in a Hasidic family, was hooked up to be married to a beautiful woman. But when she took one look at him she was so shocked by his deformity that she refused to marry him. When he heard the news, he told the families, "I'll be happy to cancel the marriage even though we've arranged it, but I just want five minutes to talk with her." So they gave the couple five minutes alone.

When the two of them came out of the room, the families were astonished: suddenly she's happy to marry him, delighted. So a student said to him, "*Rebbe*, what did you say in five minutes that turned her around?"

He said, "Very simple, I made her see the moment at which, forty days before we were both conceived, there was a heavenly announcement that said, 'This man is to marry that woman.' And at the same time there was an equally powerful announcement that said, 'but one of them is to be a hunchback.' And she saw my soul say 'Oh, my God, if one of us is to be a hunchback, I can't let it be her. Let it be me.' So I was the hunchback. And when she saw the way it happened, she said she would marry me."

Now if you have the power to tell a story like that, you have a way of healing things. Having a hunchback is a wound! But in that story, it's not a wound; all of a sudden it's healed, through a story. Through that tale, love actually triumphs over the disfigurations, the wounds, and the scars of life.

How many scars do you have from protecting and caring for other people? If you raise children, you have lots of them. Raising kids is a series of alternations between the agony and the ecstasy, and you know what the agony is like. There are scars and they hurt. Loving another human being is the same way, and committing yourself to a cause is the same way: it leaves real scars. But the scars take on a very different view if the story tells you that they're an expression of love, if the story is that forty days before you were created you were matched with this person or with this cause or matched with this child, and you said if there's to be pain here and disfiguration here, if there's to be a scar here, let it be me. That is a completely different story.

So there are stories that tell about holding people while they cry with the pains of this world, and then there are other stories that show the possibility of really coming full circle, of being transformed. The stories show us what it means to actually be able to touch all parts of ourselves and bring them together, and to access what is available not just in our own memory, but all across the spectrum of our family's memory, of our community's memory, of the human race's memory, and perhaps in spiritual domains we can only begin to understand.

VISITOR: DANIEL TAYLOR

Meaning is different from happiness. Included in meaning is poverty and other unhappy states. . . . Our greatest desire, greater even than the desire for happiness, is that our lives mean something. This desire for meaning is the originating impulse of story. We tell stories because we hope to find or create significant connections between things. Stories link past, present, and future in a way that tells us where we have been (even before we were born), where we are, and where we could be going. Our stories teach us that there is a place for us that we fit, they suggest to us that our lives can have a plot. Stories turn mere chronology, one thing after another, into the purposeful action of plots, and thereby into meaning.

VISITOR: ELIE WIESEL

What remains of a story after it is finished?
Another story.

Grateful acknowledgment is made to the following for permission to reprint previously published material:

Crown Publishers: "The Veneer of Silver," "The Worriers of Chelm," "Rabbi Levi Yitchak of Berditchev," from Nathan Ausubel, A Treasure of Jewish Folklore, © 1975.

Henry Holt & Company, Inc.: "The Most Precious Thing," "Jacob's Sukkah," "Bird in Hand," from Nina Jaffe and Steve Zeitlin, While Standing on One Foot: Puzzle Stories and Wisdom Tales from Jewish Tradition, © 1993.

Jason Aronson Inc.: "A Tale of Reb Nahum Chernobler and a Tikkun," from Peninnah Schram, Chosen Tales, © 1995; "An Offspring's Answer," "The Czar's Army," from Peninnah Schram, Stories One Generation Tells Another, © 1987.

Ms. Shirlee Kresh Hecker: "Ike the Pike," from Maury Leibowitz, Legacies (New York: Harper & Row, 1994).

Houghton Mifflin Company: "What Mr. Blatt Can't Eat," from Howard Simons, Jewish Times, © 1988.

Ms. Barbara Kirshenblatt-Gimblett: Traditional Storytelling in the Toronto Jewish Community: A Study in Performance and Creativity in an Immigrant Culture (Ann Arbor: University Microfilms, 1972).

Marvin Worth Productions: "Djinni in a Bottle," "The One Who Killed Our Lord."

Miriam Altshuler Literary Agency on behalf of Yaffa Eliach: Hasidic Tales of the Holocaust (New York: Oxford University Press, 1982).

Orchard Books: "The Founding Fathers," from Steve Sanfield, The Feather Merchants and Other Tales of the Fools of Chelm, © 1991.

Shengold Publishers: "Saving My Sanity," from Renée Fodor Schwarz, Renée, © 1991.

Sterling Lord Literistic, Inc.: "The Tax Man in the Tailor Shop," from Sam Levenson, In One Era and Out the Other (New York: Simon & Schuster, 1973);

SOURCE NOTES

INTRODUCTION

I first heard the idea that God created people because he loved stories from an inscription in Elie Wiesel's *The Gates of the Forest,* translated from the French by Frances Frenaye (New York: Holt, Rinehart & Winston, 1966). A version of it is credited as a "traditional Hasidic story" in *Storytelling: Process and Practice* by Norma J. Livo and Sandra Rietz (Littleton, Colo.: Libraries Unlimited, 1986), p. 1. Elie Wiesel's inscription, which begins, "My father, an enlightened spirit . . ." comes from *Souls on Fire: Portraits and Legends of Hasidic Masters* (New York: Random House, 1972), p. 1.

A *Table with People* is the title of a volume of poetry by Marc Kaminsky (New York: SUN, 1982). The quote from Esther Schwartzman is drawn from material published in "A Table with People: Storytelling as Life Review and Cultural History," in ed. Jack Kugelmass, *Going Home,* YIVO Annual XXI (New York: Northwestern University Press and YIVO Institute for Jewish Research), pp. 87–132. The quote about Jewish talk is from Michael Gold, *Jews without Money* (1930; rpt, New York: Carroll & Graf Publishers, Inc, 1984), pp. 112–113. Barbara Kirshenblatt-Gimblett's quote about eloquence in Eastern European culture comes from her Ph.D. dissertation, *Traditional Storytelling in the Toronto Jewish Community: A Study in Performance and Creativity in an Immigrant Culture* (Ann Arbor: University Microfilms, 1972), pp. 1, 62. The quote from Marianne Moore is from "Poetry," in *Marianne Moore, Collected Poems* (New York: Macmillan, 1951), p. 40; Arthur Strimling's reworking of it appears in Peninnah Schram, *Chosen Tales* (New York: Jason Aronson, 1995), p. 363. Marc Kaminsky's comment about Ruth Rubin is from a letter written in 1992 to help raise funds to keep Ruth in her apartment. My source for the well-known quote from Lenny Bruce about "Jewish and goyish" is ed. John Cohen, *The Essential Lenny Bruce* (New York: Douglas Books, 1971), p. 31. On page xxxii of her book, *Yiddish Folktales,* translated by Leonard Wolf (New York: Pantheon, 1988), Beatrice Silverman Weinreich suggests that any Yiddish story told by a Eastern European Jew in Yiddish is a Yiddish story, regardless of content. Dov Noy's ideas on the subject can be found in the Foreword, "What Is Jewish about the Jewish Folktale?" in Howard Schwartz *Miriam's Tambourine: Jewish Folktales from around the World* (New York: Oxford University Press, 1988), pp. xi–xix.

SECTION ONE. ANCIENT TIMES IN CONTEMPORARY TALES

"Bread—that is Halacha . . ." is a line attributed to the "sages of old" by Nathan Ausubel in *A Treasury of Jewish Folklore* (1948; rpt. New York: Crown Publishers, 1975), p. xxiii. The quote from Peninnah Schram is from an interview with her on May 16, 1995. "The Most Precious Thing" originally appears, and the quote from it is, in the volume *Midrash Rabbah; The Songs of Songs*, translated by Maurice Simon, M.H., p. 49; Nina Jaffe's version appears in the children's book I coauthored with her, *While Standing on One Foot; Puzzle Stories and Wisdom Tales from Jewish Tradition* (New York: Henry Holt, 1994), pp. 26–32. "Challahs in the Arc" is recorded on Syd Lieberman's cassette *Joseph the Tailor and Other Jewish Tales* (1988). His source is Howard Schwartz, *Gates to the New City: A Treasury of Modern Jewish Tales* (New York: Jason Aronson, 1991), pp. 540–43. I interviewed Syd on October 2, 1994, and communicated with Rabbi Zalman Schacter Shalomi by phone and fax on June 26 and 27, 1995. "Elijah and the Wish" and "Merit of the Sabbath" appear on the cassette that Cherie Karo Schwartz issued as a storyteller, *Worldwide Jewish Folktales of Wishes & Wisdom* (1988). I interviewed Cherie in New York City in April, 1995. "Elijah and the Poor Man's Wish" is Cherie's signature story. It is adapted from a tale in the Israel Folktale Archives, collected and retold by Kamelia Shahar from a Judesmo-speaking woman in Israel who heard it from her grandmother in Izmir. It is translated by Steven Levy in Howard Schwartz's *Gates to the New City*, p. 480. Lenny Bruce's "Djinni in the Bottle" is from *The Best of Lenny Bruce*, Fantasy Records. "Merit of the Sabbath" is originally a folktale from Yemen, recorded in the Israel Folktale Archives, as told to N. B. Gamlieli by J. Gible; it appears in Gamlieli's *The Chambers of Yemen*. It has been retold in English in *Seventy and One Tales for the Jewish Year: Folk Tales for the Festivals* by Barbara Rush and Eliezer Marcus. Ilana Harlow read the manuscript and offered her comments in June and July 1995. I collected the stories and comments of Joe Elias in two interviews on October 19 and November 6, 1995. The episode told by Julius Lucius Echeles, a lawyer from Chicago, appears in Howard Simons, *Jewish Times* (New York: Houghton Mifflin, 1988), pp. 11–12. The comment about Joha by Peninnah Schram is found in her wonderful book, *Chosen Tales*, pp. 279–280. I interviewed Rabbi Schecter on April 24, 1995, at Temple Beth Shalom in Hastings, New York. He was kind enough to share with me his collection of sermons from 1972 to 1991. Bob Dylan's full lyrics to "Highway 61 Revisited" can be found in *The Writings and Drawings of Bob Dylan* (New York: Knopf, 1973), p. 196.

SECTION TWO. THE *SHTETL*

The quote from Maurice Samuel is from *Little Did I Know: Recollections and Reflections* (New York: Alfred Knopf, 1963). The Tevye stories, which first began appearing in 1894, have been reissued in Shalom Aleichem, *Tevye the Dairyman and The Railroad Stories*, translated and with an introduction by Hillel Halkin

(New York: Schocken Books, 1987). Every student of *shtetl* culture should read Barbara Kirshenblatt-Gimblett's new introduction to Mark Zborowski and Elizabeth Herzog, *Life Is with People* (1952; rpt. New York: Schocken Books, 1995), ix–xviii. For classics that established the image of the *shtetl*, see Bella Chagall, *Burning Lights* (New York: Schocken Books, 1946); and Maurice Samuel, *The World of Shalom Aleichem* (New York: Knopf, 1943).

Eve Penner Ilsen's story appears in Peninnah Schram's *Chosen Tales*. "The Teller of Tales" is a story that Rabbi Schecter heard from Elie Wiesel and used in his sermon on Rosh Hashanah morning 1981. "Levi Yitchak Burns the Evidence" is based on the story by Isaac Loeb Peretz as retold in Maurice Samuel, *Prince of the Ghetto* (New York: Alfred A. Knopf, 1963), pp. 183–88. It was delivered as part of a sermon on Rosh Hashanah eve in 1976. The tale from Nathan Ausubel is from his classic, perhaps *the* classic, work on Jewish stories, *A Treasury of Jewish Folklore* (1948; rpt. New York: Crown Publishers, 1975), pp. 160–161. My introduction to "The Tales of Chelm" is adapted from the children's book I coauthored with Nina Jaffe, *While Standing on One Foot*, pp. 62, 65. Steven Sanfield's story is part of *The Feather Merchants and Other Tales of the Fools of Chelm* (New York: Orchard Books, 1991), pp. 2–5. Syd Lieberman's "Chelm Medley" is one of the selections on his cassette *Joseph the Tailor and Other Jewish Tales*. Ausubel's story about the worriers of Chelm appears in his *Treasury*, p. 338. Comments by Ilana Harlow, Peninnah Schram, and Henry Sapoznik were shared with me after they read the manuscript. Michael Wex's tale "The Kugel" appears on his cassette *Shlepping the Exile* and his book by the same title (Oakville, Ontario: Mosaic Press, 1993). Corey Fischer's story "The Golem Haunts the Cemetery in Prague" is a selection on the cassette tape "Stories Make the World," produced by Corey Fischer and Claire Schoen for A Traveling Jewish Theatre. It premiered on American Public Radio in April 1991. A Traveling Jewish Theatre premiered *Coming from a Great Distance* by Corey Fischer, Naomi Newman, and Albert Greenberg, in March 1979 in Los Angeles; *The Last Yiddish Poet*, by the same authors, premiered in June 1980 in New York.

The comments and stories from the marvelous Rita Fecher are edited from taped interviews I conducted with her on January 31 and April 11, 1992, and June 9, 1995. I recorded "The Czarina's Dress" from Peninnah Schram when I ran into her on the train going up to Westchester after a lecture on February 20, 1992. I recorded "The Czar's Army" and other comments at her home in Yorktown Heights on May 16, 1995. A related version of "The Czar's Army" also appears in *Jewish Stories One Generation Tells Another* (New York: Jason Aronson, 1987), p. xxvii. Alan Ludwig's "The Pots" appears in Steven J. Zeitlin, Amy J. Kotkin, and Holly Cutting Baker's *A Celebration of American Family Folklore* (1982; rpt. Cambridge, Mass.: Yellow Moon Press, 1992), p. 200. Henry Sapoznik's "Tants! Tants!" originally appeared in the *Oak Report*, Fall 1980, pp. 19–20. Henry's comments about *klezmer* music are drawn from "Klezmology 101," taught at KlezKamp, the Yiddish Folk Arts Program in the Catskills, December 25–30, 1994. Marc Kaminsky's opening quote appears in ed. Jack Kugelmass, *Going Home*, p. 87. His essay and his grandmother's stories are drawn from material that appears in his aforementioned essay from *Going Home* and in the unpublished manuscript *All That Our Eyes Have Witnessed: Remembering Storytelling and Creativity in Aging*, currently being edited for the University of Virginia Press. Esther Schwartzman's story also appears in *Going Home*, pp. 117, 118.

SECTION THREE. THE IMMIGRANT EXPERIENCE

"The waves were not to part" is a quote from William Humphreys's novel *The Ordways* (New York: Alfred A. Knopf, 1964), p. 58. Roslyn Bresnick-Perry's stories and comments are from personal interviews and the cassette *An American Girl: Stories of Immigration and Acculturation* (New York: Global Village Music, 1994). A version of her story about Zisl and the sled also appears in Peninnah Schram's *Chosen Tales*, pp. 58–65. Marvin Sakolsky's family tale about bananas appears in *A Celebration of American Family Folklore*, p. 82.

Barbara Kirshenblatt-Gimblett's quote about folklore in the immigrant community appears in her doctoral dissertation, *Traditional Storytelling in the Toronto Jewish Community: A Study in Performance and Creativity in an Immigrant Culture*, p. 226; the essay is drawn from pp. 231, 232, 237, 238, 255, 256, 288, 290–294, 301–306. Mildred Trencher told me the story "If I Were Rich as Rockefeller" after one of my Jewish humor lectures in April, 1996. I interviewed Charlene Victor shortly before she died at her home in Brooklyn on March 13, 1990. Ruth Rubin's reminiscence about meeting Grandpa's second wife comes from the William E. Wiener Oral History Library of the American Jewish Committee. She was interviewed in 1976. The material from Rosa Kuinova is from personal interviews taken down by hand in June 1996. Rosa Kuinova is a pseudonym.

SECTION FOUR. THE LOWER EAST SIDE AND BEYOND

For a thorough discussion of Jews on the Lower East Side, see Irving Howe with Kenneth Libo, *World of Our Fathers* (New York: Harcourt Brace Jovanovich, 1976), pp. 67–416. Harry Golden's description of the Lower East Side appears in *Only in America* (Cleveland: World Publishing Company, 1958). Howard Simons's discussion of southern Jews is from *Jewish Times*, p. 219. For a well written and insightful history of Jews in the Catskills see Stefan Kanfer, *A Summer World* (New York: Farrar Straus Giroux, 1989). The quotes about the Yiddish theater are from Irving Howe, *World of Our Fathers*, pp. 473, 481, and 494. Charlene Victor made the offhand remark about Thomashefsky to me during our interview on March 13, 1990. The description and quotes about Jewish summer camps are from ed. Jenna Weissman Joselit with Karen S. Mittleman, *A Worthy Use of Summer: Jewish Summer Camping in America* (Philadelphia: National Museum of Jewish History, 1993), pp. 15–28.

Sam Levenson's family saying can be found in *In One Era and Out the Other* (New York: Simon & Schuster, 1973), p. 11. He talks about "cultivating a folklorists' mind" in the 1976 interview with him for the William E. Wiener Oral History Library of the American Jewish Committee, p. 8. The lines about the clothesline are from *Everything but Money* (New York: Simon & Schuster, 1966), pp. 30–36. The accompanying story by Abe Lass is from my interviews with him on March 20, 1991, and November 14, 1993. "The Tax Man in the Tailor Shop" is from *In One Era and Out the Other*, pp. 57–60. "A Philosophy of *Shmattes*" is from Maurice Samuel, *Little Did I Know* (New York: Alfred A. Knopf, 1963), p. 6. "Crucifiction" is from the 1976 American Jewish Committee interview, p. 27. "Christ Killer" is from a personal interview with Roberta Singer on July 1, 1996. Lenny Bruce's famous monologue "The One Who Killed Our Lord" is from *The Essential Lenny Bruce*, p. 30. "A God Cannot Be Killed" is from an interview conducted with Baruch Lumet on December 12, 1976, in the William E. Wiener Oral History Library, pp. 1–5. I interviewed Gus Tyler for the book on July 20, 1995. "Crotona Park" is a story contributed anonymously for *A Celebration of American Family Folklore*, p. 118. Gerald Siegel is a pseudonym. "The Rent Strike" is from my raucous interview with Charlene Victor, March 13, 1990. The Sam Levenson joke is adapted from *Meet the Folks: A Session of American-Jewish Humor with Sammy Levenson* (New York: The Citadel Press, 1946), p. 71. I collected "Pazamentry" on tape from Jack Tepper on August 31, 1990. Shirlee Kresh Hecker has written up a number of her family stories, and after telling me the story on the phone in June 1996, she sent me a written version. I first heard "Ike the Pike" on a tape recorded by Maria Green for City Lore on July 12, 1989. Later, Shirlee Kresh Hecker sent me a written version of her family story, which won a prize in the Legacies contest. The accompanying poem is from Lila Zeiger, *The Way to Castle Garden* (Pittsford, N.Y.: State Street Press Chapbooks, 1982), p. 7. I thank Professor David Altabe for putting me in touch with Hank Halio, who sent me his piece on Ashkenazi/Sephardic Cultural Differences, originally published in the *Sephardic Home News*. I interviewed his wife, Phyllis, by phone in June 1996.

Solomon Blatt's southern reminiscences appear in Howard Simons's wonderful book *Jewish Times* (New York: Houghton Mifflin, 1988), pp. 229–231, 235, 236. A version of "Zipky" appears in Carolyn Lipson-Walker's doctoral dissertation, "Shalom Y'All: The Folklore and Culture of Southern Jews" (Ann Arbor: University Microfilms, 1986), pp. 244–245. Joey Adams's reminiscences appear in Joey Adams with Henry Tobias, *The Borscht Belt* (New York: Bobbs-Merrill, 1966). David Kotkin's reminiscence "Kesl Gartn" appears in *A Celebration of American Family Folklore*, p. 155. Baruch Lumet was interviewed for the William E. Wiener Oral History Library of the American Jewish Committee on December 12, 1976, by Anita M. Wincelberg. His reminiscence appears on pages 111–121. "Sleep with a Baker" appears in William Novak and Moshe Waldoks, *The Big Book of Jewish Humor* (New York: Harper & Row, 1981), p. 261. I taped an interview with Zypora Spaisman, Jacob Adler, and Elyse Frummer on June 27, 1995, and interviewed them again for the radio with Dave Isay on September 13, 1995. I interviewed Rabbi David Holtz at Temple Beth Abraham in Tarrytown, New York, on September 20, 1995.

SECTION FIVE. THE HOLOCAUST

Marc Kaminsky's ideas on survivor stories are drawn from his unpublished manuscript "The Storyteller's Wor(l)d Destroyed and Re-membered: Narrative Struggles after Auschwitz and Hiroshima." Elie Wiesel's quote is from "Does the Holocaust Lie Beyond the Reach of Art," *The New York Times*, Sunday, April 17, 1983, p. 12. The stories from Rabbi Israel Spira are reprinted from Yaffa Eliach, *Hasidic Tales of the Holocaust* (New York: Oxford University Press, 1982), pp. 155–159, 151–153, 3–4. Yaffa Eliach's quote about recording the stories is from pp. xxiv–xxv of her book. All three stories are based on conversations with Rabbi Israel Spira and Baruch Singer on January 3, 1975. Yaffa Eliach heard the stories at the rabbi's home. "In Your Hands" appears as "A Bird in the Hand" in Nina Jaffe and Steve Zeitlin, *While Standing on One Foot*, pp. 87–90. Sam Levenson's "The Wand" is from his 1976 interview for the William E. Wiener Oral History Library of the American Jewish Committee, pp. 130–131. I taped interviews with Melvin Katz in December 1991 and January 1996. "The Wounded Jester" and "The Face in the Mirror" were sent to me by Toby Blum-Dobkin and are from interviews she conducted with her father, Boris Blum, in Yiddish and translated into English. Renée Fodor Schwarz's reminiscence is from Renée Fodor Schwarz, *Renée* (New York: Shengold Publishers, 1991), pp. 107. I taped an interview with Lisa Lipkin on July 5, 1995. As a storyteller, she performs "What My Mother Never Told Me" for both Jewish and non-Jewish audiences across the country. Barbara Myerhoff talked about becoming a "little old Jewish lady" in *Number Our Days* (New York: E. P. Dutton, 1979), p. 19. Her quote about experiencing the self as stable through time is on p. 222. See also her collection of posthumously published essays, *Remembered Lives: The Work of Ritual, Storytelling and Growing Older*, edited by and with an introduction by Marc Kaminsky (Ann Arbor: The University of Michigan Press, 1992). "The Shoebox" is from "Stories as Equipment for Living," a lecture given numerous times and in numerous versions by Barbara Myerhoff. It appears in print as part of "Story of the Shoebox: The Meaning and Practice of Transmitting Stories," in ed. Thomas R. Cole, David D. Van Tassel, and Robert Kasenbaum, *Handbook of the Humanities and Aging* (New York: Springer Publishing, 1992). "Going Home to Nowhere" is a story Roslyn Bresnick-Perry told me and that I asked her to write up for this book in June 1996.

SECTION SIX. HUMOR IN CONTEMPORARY JEWISH LIFE

Barbara Kirshenblatt-Gimblett's ingenious questions appear in her dissertation, *Traditional Storytelling in the Toronto Jewish Community: A Study in Performance and Creativity in an Immigrant Culture*, p. 87. In *The Big Book of Jewish Humor*, Waldoks and Novak draw primarily on well-known humorous writers. Other important resources for anyone looking at Jewish humor are Rabbi Joseph Telushkin, *Jewish Humor: What the Best Jewish Jokes Say about the Jews* (New York: William Morrow,

1992); Eliot Oring, *The Jokes of Sigmund Freud: A Study in Humor and Jewish Identity* (Philadelphia: University of Pennsylvania Press, 1984); Dan Ben Amos "The 'Myth' of Jewish Humor," *Western Folklore* 32 #2 (1973) p. 112–131. and ed. Sarah Blacher Cohen *Jewish Wry: Essays on Jewish Humor* (Bloomington, Ind.: Indiana University Press, 1987). "The Health Club" is transcribed from a tape Moshe Waldoks made of one of his lectures.

The joke about the Russian peasant combines versions found in Irving Howe's essay "The Nature of Jewish Laughter," in *Jewish Wry*, p. 16, and in Ausubel, *A Treasury of Jewish Folklore*. Marc Kaminsky's quote about stock Yiddish characters appears in "Discourse and Self Formation: The Concept of Mentsh in Modern Yiddish Culture," *The American Journal of Psychoanalysis* 54, no. 4, December 1994, 293–316. The insightful comparison with Jewish humor and African American music appears in Waldoks and Novak, p. xviii. The quote about "a victory gained by the Jewish spirit" is from I. Kristol, "Is Jewish Humor Dead? The Rise and Fall of the Jewish Joke," *Commentary* 12 (1951), 432; quoted in Barbara Kirshenblatt-Gimblett, *Traditional Storytelling in the Toronto Jewish Community*, p. 89. Jackie Mason's psychiatrist routine is from his Broadway show *The World According to Me*, produced by Brooks Arthur for Warner Brother Records in 1987. Daniel Bell's ingenious application of the *pilpul* to Tennyson's "Charge of the Light Brigade" is from Howard Simons, *Jewish Times*, pp. 58–60. Ari Goldman's reminiscence is also from *Jewish Times*, pp. 161–162. Anyone interested in Moishe Sacks should read Jack Kugelmass's wonderful book *The Miracle on Intervale Avenue* (1986; rpt. New York: Columbia University Press, 1996). The joke about Einstein is from Waldoks and Novak, *The Big Book of Jewish Humor*, p. 36. For Philip Roth's "Letters to Einstein," see Waldoks and Novak, p. 34. The quote about the Yiddish theater is from Alexander Mukdoyni, *Teyater*, 1927, p. 135; quoted in Irving Howe, *World of Our Fathers*, p. 488. The "sudden thrusting downward" is from Gerald Mast, "The Neurotic Jew as American Clown," *Jewish Wry*, pp. 125–140. The comments Barbara Myerhoff recorded at the Israel Levin Center in Venice, California, appear in *Number Our Days*, p. 62. Abe Lass's story about the *summum bonum* are from my interview with him on November 14, 1993. A copy of his seven hours of dirty Yiddish stories are archived at City Lore in New York. The excerpt from Jackie Mason is also from the Warner Brothers recording of his Broadway show *The World According to Me*. The Hasidic story about pouring water can be found in the inscription to Stefan Kanfer's, *A Summer World*. His source is Beatrice Silverman Weinreich, *Yiddish Folktales*. Leo Rosten's quote about *oy* is from *The Joys of Yiddish* (New York: McGraw-Hill Book Co., 1968), p. 273. The Michael Gold description of Old Barney is from *Jews without Money*, pp. 183–184. The line about God protecting us from the Messiah is cited in Waldoks and Novak, *The Big Book of Jewish Humor*, p xiv. "Why the Jewish Comic Carries a Violin" is a passage from Mark Schechner's essay "Dear Mr. Einstein: Jewish Comedy and the Contradictions of Culture," in *Jewish Wry*, pp. 141–157. A printed version of the Woody Allen scene can be found in *Play It Again, Sam: A Play in Three Acts* (New York: Random House, 1969), p. 48.

SECTION SEVEN. MEANINGS AND REFLECTIONS

Rabbi Edward Schecter told the story "The Meaning of Life" at his Temple's Kol Nidre service in 1974. Peninnah Schram gave me her quotation in comments she made on the manuscript. She also gave me the quote from Roger C. Schank, *Tell Me a Story: A New Look at Real and Artificial Memory* (New York: Scribner's, 1990). The quotes from Shelley Brenner are from a personal interview in 1996. "Ezekiel's Wheel" is one of the stories she tells in her storytelling programs and was taken down from a tape she made of her stories.

I recorded Peninnah's Schram's version of the Dubner *maggid* story in my interview with her on May 16, 1995. The story also appears in her *Jewish Stories One Generation Tells Another* (New York: Jason Aronson, 1987), pp. 2–5. The parable about King David, brought to my attention by Ilana Harlow, is from the *Second Book of Samuel*, chapter 11, verses 1–18, and chapter 12, verses 1–9. Barbara Kirshenblatt-Gimblett's observations about parable are from *Traditional Storytelling in the Toronto Jewish Community*, p. 84. "The Case of the Boiled Egg" appears in numerous Jewish folktale collections, including the children's book I coauthored with Nina Jaffe, *While Standing on One Foot*, pp. 18–22. The reference to King Solomon and the origin of parable is from Nathan Ausubel, *A Treasury of Jewish Folklore*, p. 56. The parables of Doris Kirshenblatt are from *Traditional Storytelling in the Toronto Jewish Community*, pp. 444, 445. Mayer Kirshenblatt's parable was recorded for the documentary film I co-produced with Paul Wagner and Marjorie Hunt, *The Grand Generation*, Filmmakers Library 1994. Berl Manperl reading a parable to a Nazi officer appears in Jack Kugelmass and Jonathan Boyarin, *From a Ruined Garden: The Memorial Books of Polish Jewry* (New York: Schocken Books, 1983), pp. 168, 169. Barbara Myerhoff's version of the frequently told parable about the Baal Shem Tov appears in *Number Our Days*, pp. 111–12. "The Veneer of Silver" appears in Nathan Ausubel, *A Treasury of Jewish Folklore*, p. 60. Franz Kafka's parable about parables appears in *Parables and Paradoxes* (New York: Schocken Books, 1983), p. 11. I heard the story about the unhappy man from Warsaw who goes off to seek paradise from storyteller Laura Simms. Peninnah Schram's stories are from comments she made about the manuscript as one of my readers. The story about the "mother bird" appears as "The Offspring's Answer" in *Stories One Generation Tells Another*, pp. 454, 455. Rabbi Tsvi Blanchard's talk was delivered as the keynote address for the storytelling conference held at Stern College for Women of Yeshiva University in New York City, April 24, 1994. Daniel Taylor's quote is from *The Healing Power of Stories* (New York: Doubleday, 1996), p. 1. The final quote from Elie Wiesel is from *Sages and Dreamers: Biblical, Talmudic and Hasidic Portraits and Legends* (New York: Summit Books, 1991), p. 79.